The Idea of Landscape and
the Sense of Place
1730–1840

The Idea of Landscape and the Sense of Place
1730–1840

An Approach to the Poetry of John Clare

JOHN BARRELL

CAMBRIDGE
At the University Press
1972

Published by the Syndics of the Cambridge University Press
Bentley House, 200 Euston Road, London NW1 2DB
American Branch: 32 East 57th Street, New York, N.Y.10022

© Cambridge University Press 1972

Library of Congress Catalogue Card Number: 77-160092

ISBN: 0 521 08254 4

Printed in Great Britain by
W & J Mackay Ltd, Chatham

Contents

v

Illustrations

TO DONALD DAVIE

Acknowledgements

I would like to thank Tim Clark, Gabriel Pearson, and Donald Wesling, who read parts of the book and made detailed and valuable suggestions. Mr P. I. King of the Northamptonshire Record Office, and Mr Daniel Crowson, Parish Clerk of Helpston, helped me to collect the local historical material the book includes. Miss Mary Bonner and Mrs Marjorie McGlashan, of the Department of Literature at the University of Essex, typed the manuscript; and Professor Philip Edwards allowed me a very generous share of the department's Research Endowment Fund, to enable me to complete my research. My wife drew the maps, and the book owes much to her criticism and advice. This book is dedicated to Donald Davie, because while writing it I discovered how much my approach to poetry owes to his own.

JOHN BARRELL

University of Essex
December 1970

Introductory Note

The first two chapters of this book are intended to introduce the third, so that there is, I imagine, no need for another, formal introduction to the book as a whole. The material of the three chapters, however, may seem rather disparate, at least as far as it can be guessed at from a casual inspection of the list of contents; and so I should perhaps explain that my main intention has been (as my title suggests) to offer an approach to the poetry of John Clare, and in particular to his earlier poems, in the context of the enclosure of his parish, Helpston; and also to describe what seems to me to be Clare's notion of the 'identity' of Helpston – what I mean by that phrase becomes clear, I hope, in the third chapter. The first two chapters consider two sets of attitudes which it seems to me that Clare understood as threatening his idea of Helpston's identity. The first is a set of attitudes to landscape, which were found fairly generally among the sophisticated reading public in the second half of the eighteenth century in England, and which Clare encountered chiefly in his reading of the poetry of that period. The second set of attitudes are more specifically the property of what I tentatively describe as the 'rural professional class'; the attitudes that, for Clare, found concrete expression in the enclosure of Helpston.

1. The idea of landscape in the eighteenth century

There is no word in English which denotes a tract of land, of whatever extent, which is apprehended *visually* but not, necessarily, *pictorially*. The nearest is probably 'terrain', but in practice the uses to which this word can be put are very limited: it would be awkward, for example, to speak of the 'terrain' of a county, and we generally apply the word to areas of land which can be seen, if not at a glance, at least without travelling too far in any direction. The word we do use, of course, is 'landscape': we can speak of the 'landscape' of a county, but in doing so we introduce, whether we want to or not, notions of value and form which relate, not just to seeing the land, but to seeing it in a certain way – pictorially.

And in the first place the word 'landscape' is, obviously enough, a painter's word: it was introduced from the Dutch in the sixteenth century to describe a pictorial representation of countryside, either as the subject itself of a picture, or as the by-work in a portrait, the background of scenery behind the main subject. Later the word came to include within its meaning both this sense, of countryside represented in a picture, and another, more loose, of a piece of countryside considered as a visual phenomenon: the first example, given in the *Oxford English Dictionary*, of the second sense, is taken from Milton's 'L'Allegro', of 1632.[1] Both these senses of the word 'landscape' had this in common, that they referred to a tract of land, or its representation in painting, which lay in prospect – that is to say, which could be seen all at one glance, from a fixed point of view; and in this respect both senses referred to particular locations, whether the locations themselves were real or imaginary. But later still, a more general meaning attached itself to the word, so that one could now talk of '*the* landscape' of a place, as I did in the first paragraph; and this sense of the word had clearly outstepped the limitations of space which the sense of *a* landscape, as a prospect, had imposed on the word. To this new sense of 'landscape' the definition given in the *O.E.D.* for 'terrain' might well be applied: 'a tract of country considered with regard to its natural features, configuration, etc.'.

When this general sense of the word came into use, apparently in the mid-eighteenth century, it was not at first easily separated from the earlier and more particular senses. The confusion can be clearly enough seen in this definition Johnson gives for 'landscape': 'a region; the prospect of a country'; which appears to refer to the general sense of the word, while Johnson's examples all refer to *a* landscape, not, simply, to landscape. The *O.E.D.* comes nearer to sorting out the meanings: it offers, as one definition, 'a view or prospect of natural scenery, such as can be taken in at a glance from one point of view: a piece of country scenery'. That is, precisely, *a* landscape, a *piece* of scenery. It gives also: 'in generalised sense, inland natural scenery, or its representation in painting'; that is, land seen, but not seen, necessarily, at one glance. And so we can trace these stages of the word 'landscape': from first denoting only a picture of rural scenery, it comes to denote also a piece of scenery apprehended, as it would be in a picture, in prospect, and finally, it denotes as well land 'considered with regard to its natural configuration'.

This extension of the second meaning into the third is, clearly, a most important one. It implies a change in attitude to land something like this: in the first place, a particular piece of land, under the eye, is considered pictorially; in the second place, the whole of natural scenery is considered as having, somehow, a pictorial character, whether or not a piece of it is actively being considered as if it were a picture. This is a slight exaggeration of the case, for in the new meaning some of the consciously pictorial sense of 'landscape' has been lost; but, because this new meaning (as Johnson's definition suggests) was not quickly or easily established, a person of much education in the eighteenth century would have found it very hard, not merely to describe land, but also to see it, and even to *think* of it as a visual phenomenon, except as mediated through particular notions of form. The words 'landscape', 'scene', and, to a lesser extent, 'prospect' (which, as our definition from Johnson shows, could be used in a general, non-local sense) demanded, in short, that the land be thought of as itself composed into the formal patterns which previously a landscape-painter would have been thought of as himself imposing on it. A good example of this way of thinking is this statement, by the Scottish critic Lord Kames, that 'natural objects readily form themselves into groups'.[2]

II

A history of the increasing interest, in eighteenth-century England, in landscapes and in landscape-art has often been attempted,[3] and there is not the space nor, especially, the need for another account in this book. It is sufficient to recall here that it was, of course, during the eighteenth century that the contemplation of landscape – in nature, or as represented in literature and the visual arts – became an important interest of the cultivated; the evidence for this is widespread and immediately apparent to anyone at all familiar with the period. The source of this interest was primarily Italian: it was an interest which, it is usual to say, was brought back from Italy by young men who went on the Grand Tour, and came back *virtuosi*. Actually, the degree to which the trip over the Alps, and the confrontation, in Italy, with the Roman Campagna and with the painters who had represented it, impressed the young gentlemen with an ineradicable taste for landscape, has probably been exaggerated. Boswell seems to have been more struck by the lack of interest shown by his compatriots in the galleries of Florence, and tells of two gentlemen who preferred to hop to the end of the Uffizi and back, for a bet, than make a respectful examination of the pictures.[4] This rings rather truer than the impression some historians give, of some sort of mass conversion taking place in Switzerland or Italy. Certainly the effect of the tour on some tourists was sudden and remarkable: in his *Remarks on Several Parts of Italy*,[5] for example, we can watch Addison taking an increasing interest in landscape the further he travels south, an interest which he did not leave behind in Rome. But for the most part the tourists seem either to have made the tour anxious to be converted, and so half-converted already, or else to have survived the experience without any particular interest in natural beauty

3

growing within them; though that is not to say that, on their return from Italy, they did not feel obliged to give evidence of a taste which, for reasons I have hardly space to examine, was becoming part of the fashionable equipment of the age.

Though the influence of the tour, then, was probably a good deal less immediate than it is often presented as having been, it is nevertheless true that by the middle of the eighteenth century the predominant influence on English taste in landscape was Italian. It was at this time that the collecting of landscape-paintings became a fashionable activity, and the value – and numbers – of works ascribed to the Poussins, to Salvator Rosa, and to Claude increased so rapidly. Landscape very quickly became the most popular genre of painting, and in the private collections of the very rich it was the newly-acquired Claudes and Salvators that were most admired. By 1747 one collector, Jonathan Richardson, owned at least eighty of Claude's drawings,[6] and by 1750 thirty-five of the paintings illustrated by Claude in his *Liber Veritatis* are known to have been in England.[7] But however many pictures of landscape in the Italian manner were imported, the demand still far exceeded the sources of legitimate supply, and the trade in imitations, copies, and forgeries was considerable. A number of English artists – George Lambert, John Wootton, and the Smiths of Chichester among others – were able, or were thought to be able, to imitate so precisely the manner of one or other of the Roman painters that they came to be regarded as important and valuable artists in their own right. The demand for landscape-art was met also by the engravers:[8] many of the works of Claude and others were available as prints, which, though not especially cheap, were sufficiently so to be bought in quite large numbers by the cultivated but less well-off portion of the aristocracy and gentry; and 'looking over prints' became a recognised way of getting through the afternoon. The interest in landscape expressed itself also, of course, in gardening, in poetry which dealt with rural subjects, and in the study of aesthetics, which, though previously it had taken its examples mainly from rhetoric, now concerned itself with aesthetic values chiefly as they were revealed in the contemplation of landscape.

But, over and above the expression of this interest in the direct practice of the arts, there is a sense in which, in late eighteenth-century England, one can say that the simple contemplation of landscape, quite apart from its expression in painting, writing or whatever, came to be regarded as an important pursuit for the cultivated and almost in itself the practice of an art. To display a correct taste in landscape was a valuable social accomplishment quite as much as to sing well, or to compose a polite letter. The heroines of a number of late eighteenth-century novels are made to display this taste with an almost ostentatious virtuosity,[9] and not only the simple fact of having a taste for landscape or not, but also variations of taste within the general one, are regarded by some novelists as legitimate indications of differences in character. The contemplation of landscape was an activity with its own proper procedure, which involved recognising the stretch of land under your eye not, simply, as that – as an area of ground filled with various objects, trees, hills, fields – but as a complex of associations and meanings, and, more important, as a composition, in which each object bore a specific and analysable relationship to the others. This recognition of the formal structure of a landscape was not a purely passive activity – a considerable amount of jockeying for position, of screwing up the eyes, of moving back and forth, of rearranging objects in the imagination, had to be gone through before a view came right: this is William Gilpin describing how he looked at a landscape: 'The whole view was pleasing from various stands: but to make it particularly picturesque by gaining a good foreground, we were obliged to change our station backward & forward, till we had obtained a good one. Two large plane trees, which we met with, were of great assistance to us.'[10]

If Gilpin's tone is ironic here, it is defensively so: he appears amused at the performance he went through, in case we are, but we are not encouraged to believe that he did *not* usually go through this sort of procedure. And to go through it, to encourage the landscape to reveal itself at its most correctly composed, and to have sufficient taste to recognise when it was so, was indeed an artistic practice in everything except that no especial need was felt to represent in an artistic medium the composition which emerged. But then in eighteenth-century theory, especially with regard to the visual arts, the representation of one's conception, the actual execution of it according to the rules of a craft, was of fairly minor importance, and by the patrons of art at least was thought to connect the Sublime and the Picturesque unnecessarily with the skills of the artisan. 'When I speak of a painter,' writes Uvedale

Price, 'I do not mean merely a professor, but any man (artist or not) of a liberal mind, with a strong feeling for nature as well as art, who has been in the habit of comparing both together.'[11] What did matter was the ability to conceive a landscape as a pictorial composition, and that this was so is further suggested by the enthusiasm with which collectors tolerated the numerous bad imitations of Claude, bad copies, and even bad forgeries; no doubt many connoisseurs included forgeries in their collections in bad faith, but for others, what they valued in paintings was essentially the way the subject was conceived, the way that conception fulfilled the procedural requirements of the art, and not much at all the simple imitation of the conception. Similarly Arthur Young, the agricultural writer and 'picturesque traveller', in his remarks on the galleries of the country houses he visits, is not very concerned with the precise authorship of the paintings he describes. For him, 'a Claude', 'a Rosa', seem to mean paintings professedly in the style of those two.[12] It isn't so much that he does not question the authorship of copies and forgeries, but that he does not consider it important: the names are trade marks for him, which guarantee a style of conception but not a quality of realisation.

III

The contemplation of landscape was not, then, a passive activity: it involved reconstructing the landscape in the imagination, according to principles of composition that had to be learned, and were indeed learned so thoroughly that in the later eighteenth century it became impossible for anyone with an aesthetic interest in landscape to look at the countryside without applying them, whether he knew he was doing so or not. These principles were derived from the Roman landscape-painters of the seventeenth century, Nicolas and Gaspard Poussin, Salvator Rosa, and Claude Lorrain. And it is particularly the influence of Claude, and, to a lesser extent, of Nicolas Poussin, that is relevant to this study. The painting of Salvator, for example, led to a dramatic and rhetorical appreciation of landscape, and not to a primarily formal one: in his work, the objects and figures invite interpretation, and it was this rhetoric perhaps more than the formal elements of his pictures which excited attention; although, as we shall see, at the end of the century the distinctive roughness of his technique came to be much admired by theorists of the Picturesque. It is generally true, then, of Salvator's pictures in the eighteenth century, that the effort of comprehension the viewer made was towards an understanding more of what ideas and emotions they suggested, than of how they were constructed. I do not want to undervalue the importance of these extra-formal aspects of the eighteenth-century appreciation of landscape, and I do not want to suggest that Claude's pictures did not invite interpretation and evoke associations, as Salvator's did: Deborah Howard has remarked that enthusiasm for Claude in England was 'an aspect of Classical taste', and his pictures were admired (in the early eighteenth century) more on account of their close reference to, for example, the particular passages of the *Aeneid* they illustrated than for their evocation of 'the beauty of the Italian landscape'.[13] But the paintings of Claude, Poussin, and their imitators did invite also a specifically formal appreciation, and it was chiefly in response to the work of these men that the English connoisseur of the eighteenth century developed his characteristic way of looking at landscape. This expressed itself in a specialised vocabulary, and a grammar, as it were, of landscape patterns and structures, established so thoroughly in his language and imagination that he became less and less able to separate any one landscape from any other, because he applied the same visual and linguistic procedures to them all. *A* landscape was fitted into *the* established set of landscape patterns, and so became part of the *universal* landscape, which included any tract of land the connoisseur chose to examine.

There developed, then, the habit of seeing landscape as arranged into the sort of compositional patterns employed by Claude and his followers. These patterns do vary considerably, of course, from one landscape by Claude to another, and I don't want to appear in what follows to be unaware of the inventiveness of Claude's compositions; but it has perhaps become fashionable recently to emphasise the variations that Claude achieves at the expense of any explicit statement of the theme, so to speak, that they are variations on; so that it is worth reasserting here that most of Claude's paintings of whatever period do start from one basic, and very rigid, structure. A landscape by Claude employs, in the first place, a fairly high viewpoint – high enough, that is, for a distant horizon to appear above any rising ground between it and the viewpoint: and the first impression which everyone must receive, I imagine, on seeing a Claude landscape, is one of tremendous depth: 'you may walk in Claude's pictures', said Richard Wilson, 'and count the miles'.[14] The eye, attracted by an area of light usually set just below the horizon, travels immediately towards it over a long and often steeply contoured stretch of intervening land (it will be helpful to keep glancing at the painting reproduced here as Plate 1 while reading the paragraphs that follow; which are not, however, to be taken as a description of that particular painting). The initial movement in all Claude's landscapes is this one, from the foreground straight to the far distance; and it must I think be understood as a rapid movement, an immediate response to the way the picture is organised. In this I disagree with Michael Kitson when he writes of the space in Claude's paintings in terms of 'a circuitous path taking the eye by easy and varied stages to a luminous distance. The distance', he goes on, 'is the goal of the imaginary traveller in Claude's landscapes',[15] and this is certainly true, but the metaphor (which Kitson may have adapted from the remark of Wilson's quoted above) is not a helpful one, at least in so far as Kitson seems to suggest that the traveller is conscious only of what he sees along his path, and never looks up into the distance. But presumably the traveller decides on his goal in the first place by looking straight at it, into the distance and across the fore- and middle-grounds; and only then does he begin to work out how he can get there. We look at the horizon before we become aware of the painting as 'a world designed for the imagination to enter and wander about it';[16] and the discovery we make then, that the objects are deliberately arranged to lead the eye from foreground to horizon, is the discovery of *how* the eye was immediately attracted to the horizon, of how an effect already experienced was achieved.

And it is certainly true, as Kitson says it is, that the objects in the landscape are all of them arranged in the first place to encourage a movement of some sort or another to the horizon. The foreground itself is usually in the shade of the *coulisse* – a group of trees, or a building, to right or left of the picture, and framing the landscape behind. There is, therefore, a band of fairly dark colour at the bottom of the picture; and, dropping below the level of the land in the foreground, and deeper into the picture, is a

Plate 1. Claude: *Landscape with David at the Cave of Adullam* (1658)

Plate 2. Claude: *The Arrival of Aeneas at Pallanteum* (1675)

second plane, of ground more exposed to the sunlight. A third plane beyond this will be darker again, overshadowed by trees or by a cloud which is understood to have come between this patch of land and the sun. The next plane will be the one that first attracts the eye, and is usually suffused with a clear yellow evening light; and the last will often be blue, and connects the landscape with the colour of the sky. This pattern may be reversed, in that the foreground may be light, the next plane in shadow, and so on, but in that case the number of these planes will be increased (as it may be anyway), to allow the penultimate one to be in sunlight. This technique, of alternating bands of light and dark, makes a contrast between different areas of colour in the picture, but makes sure, at the same time, that whatever attention we pay to these contrasts is directed vertically, up and into the picture. Although we are also asked to recognise the balance of light and tone *across* the canvas, by opposing a dark area, say, on one side with a similar area on the other, the effect of this balance, too, is to lead us further *into* the picture, for it always works by asking us to compare, say, a group of trees in the left foreground with another group set further back, on the right, and so on.

The most serious problem which this classical organisation of the landscape, into a series of planes parallel with the picture surface, presents, is concerned with the relation of the objects, within the several planes, to each other. Within each the objects are represented according to a fixed scale, so that Poussin, in his *Summer* (see Plate 3), where he wishes to present a number of horses one behind the other in the same plane, adopts a *bas-relief* technique to do this, and the group comes to look like one from the Parthenon frieze. The difference in size, however, between a tree, say, in one plane and another tree in the next will be very considerable, and the effect of perspective achieved is one, not of a gradual diminution of the scale of objects within the landscape, but of a series of leaps down from one scale to another through the several planes of the picture. Claude is able to turn these abrupt leaps down in scale to advantage, and indeed exaggerates them; for by them we are able to measure how far and how rapidly we are travelling through his landscapes. Finally, to lead our eye from plane to plane more smoothly, Claude makes an apparent concession to a more gradual perspective, and links one to the next by a road, say, or a bridge, or the slope of a hill, which runs diagonally

9

across the picture. In this way we are reconciled to the rapid diminution in the size of things – and at the same time as it is clear to us that to cross one of Claude's bridges is to step into something like Lilliput.

It is by means such as these that Claude elicits that initial movement of our eye to the horizon, and it is the discovery of these means that Kitson seems to me to have confused with the movement they are intended to elicit. In fact, such a discovery is possible only after this and another contrary movement of the eye have been made. The initial movement is so instantaneous a reaction to Claude's composition that, as Kitson has remarked in what seems to me an altogether better account of Claude's method – he is speaking here of the horizon in *The Arrival of Aeneas at Pallanteum* (see Plate 2), 'this area of the painting is not only the climax of the composition; it is also its starting-point. The light spreads forwards and outwards from here, filling the whole landscape with its radiance and linking foreground and background in a continuous spatial unity.'[17] I do not quite understand the last phrase here, or perhaps I should say that I myself never receive an illusion of continuous space in Claude's landscapes, but if I understand Kitson's main point correctly, that the horizon is at once the climax and the starting-point of the composition, it seems to me a very good one. Thus we look straight at the horizon when we look at the picture, and no sooner do we do so than our eye is brought circling back to a portion of the landscape, focused, framed, set-off (in tone, and often by physical barriers) from the rest, in the foreground of the painting. 'This dual movement', writes Tim Clark,

is what prevents the picture registering merely as a 'space-box' or 'window' – it is the to-fro movement of the eye from prospect to foreground, from distance to detail, from one end of the tonal range to another, which, in the end, confirms and establishes the medium: informs us of the conditions of illusion in a way quite intrinsic, I think, to the strength of this kind of landscape-painting.[18]

Our eye, then, is led straight to the horizon, and is brought circling back to the foreground, which it can now apprehend as detail, and not as something to be looked over or through as we look towards the distance. It is this 'to–fro movement' which enables us to become aware of the composition, but our awareness of the composition changes our experience of it, and the planes and the objects within them, which were arranged in the first place to

10

attract the eye immediately to the horizon, are now apprehended as 'easy and varied stages to a luminous distance'.

I have gone into some detail, and been perhaps over-explicit, in describing the arrangement of landscape as Claude conceived it, because, as we shall see, this arrangement became, even in its minute particulars, a standard one in English painting, and in English poetry too; and, because it became so important, I would like to examine a few of the presuppositions, about the way we examine landscape, on which this arrangement rests. It is clear, in the first place, that however instinctive and habitual it became to see a view in terms of a series of horizontal bands, nevertheless to think of perspective in terms of a series of abrupt leaps into the distance, and not as a gradual diminution in the size of things, did represent a definite modification of the sort of notions of perspective which had been developed in the Renaissance. And it was a change which meant that a certain composition of the landscape within those bands became obligatory. There had to be objects, or convenient contours, in the landscape, which would smooth the transition from band to band. The painter's viewpoint had to be on rising ground. The trees and buildings in each band had to be disposed in such a way that the shadows they made would differentiate a particular band from those above and below it in terms of colour and tone: Kenneth Clark says of the drawings of trees in Claude's notebook that they were not 'ends in themselves'; he goes on: 'his mind was always looking forward to their use as part of a whole composition, and parallel with these studies from observation he made sketches of ideas which could be used as the basis for pictures'.[19] It would be true to say, then, that at a very early stage in the making of a landscape in this tradition the development of the painting was almost completely determined: particular features, particular lights, were demanded by the composition, and were supplied. There was no question of the painting representing a place, a particular valley, for example, except in the most general way; for a painter painting from nature, or a poet describing a view he had seen, would inevitably rearrange what he saw to a very high degree, to satisfy the compositional demands of the structure. This is William Gilpin again: an artist, he says,

has no right, we allow, to add a magnificent castle – an impending rock – or a river, to adorn his fore-ground. These are *new features*. But he may certainly break an ill-formed hillock; and shovel the earth about him as he pleases, without offence. He may pull up a piece of awkward paling – he may throw down a cottage – he may even turn the course of a road, or a river, a few yards on this side, or that. These trivial alterations may greatly add to the beauty of his composition.[20]

Gilpin is writing late in the century, when the main demand for landscape-art was for topographical painting, more or less 'faithful' delineations of real places, and especially of country seats and parks. But Gilpin's notion of fidelity is not very much more cavalier than that of those English followers of the Roman painters, who applied the structure of Claude and Poussin to their own 'faithful' painting from nature. The Roman painters, of course, made no pretence that their work represented particular places: the painting of landscape was, for them, the creation of ideal landscapes, of models, as the critic Thomas Twining explained, 'of improved and selected nature';[21] and the rules of improvement and selection they established were found very hard to break by topographical painters who were hired on the guarantee of producing proper likenesses of the places they painted.

IV

I have said that the technique of composition used by Claude and Poussin was taken over by virtually everyone in mid-eighteenth-century England who looked at landscape for the aesthetic pleasure it offered, and I am especially concerned in this chapter with how this technique was adapted by poets who introduced passages of landscape-description into their work. The two poets in whom the influence of Claude is usually first located are James Thomson and John Dyer. Now Thomson's *Seasons* first appeared complete in 1730,[22] and I should say now there is apparently no evidence that Thomson had encountered any paintings by Claude at this time – though, for that matter, there is no evidence that he had not. In later life, however, he was certainly something of an expert on landscape-painting, and owned a collection of prints which he bequeathed to Thomas Gray. The evidence concerning Dyer is as inconclusive, but he was a painter before he was a poet, and no doubt had some knowledge of how to compose a classical landscape by 1726, when 'Grongar Hill' first appeared[23] – not that he seems to me to have made use of that knowledge in the poem. I cannot, anyway, state categorically that Thomson learned his technique of landscape-description directly from the study of Claude's work, but I hope to make it clear enough in what follows that his own technique is remarkably like Claude's, so like indeed that if he did not derive it directly from Claude, he must have done so from an acquaintance with the work of his imitators and disciples; and there is not much question that the knowledge of how to compose a landscape in the classical Italian manner was available in England in the late 1720s. This is so, even though, as Deborah Howard has pointed out, 'few English landscape painters visited Italy before the middle of the eighteenth century'.[24] They did not need to; the Claudes came to England instead, and the trade in imitations was well established by 1730. I might add here, however, that the passage from Thomson I shall be mainly concerned with – the description of the view from Hagley Park, in 'Spring' – first appeared in the 1744 edition of *The Seasons*.[25]

It has been said often enough that Thomson's landscapes are like Claude's but to say so is clearly to beg questions about how a description in words can be *like* a pictorial representation, and Ralph Cohen, in his enormous work on the history of criticism of Thomson, *The Art of Discrimination*,[26] is certainly right when he says that critics who have suggested this similarity have quite failed to notice the questions of aesthetics which it involves. As I understand it, the direct connection between Claude's way of looking at landscape and Thomson's was fairly generally assumed in the eighteenth century, and precisely because no other way of looking except Claude's could easily be imagined. Uvedale Price speaks of 'a fine evening in nature, or (what is almost the same thing)...a picture of Claude',[27] and Thomas Twining explains that the ancients 'had no Thomsons because they had no Claudes';[28] that is, Claude had shown us nature as she really is, and Thomson had simply copied the nature which appeared in landscape-painting. The notion of art as the imitation of nature answered most of the questions raised by analogies across the arts, and the same critical vocabulary could be applied both to the painting and to the poetry of natural scenery. A passage of Dyer's *Fleece*,[29] for example, was commended by a contemporary reviewer in *The Critical* just as if it were a picture: 'In this agreeable landscape we perceive that the objects are properly placed, the figures well grouped, and the ordonnance of the piece just and natural. The colours are excellent, the strokes masterly, and the whole picture highly finished.'[30] The two arts are too deliberately confounded in this passage for it to be typical: but throughout the latter half of the century, it was a common practice to look for counterparts for the Roman painters among the English poets of landscape, comparing one with 'gentle Poussin', another with 'savage Rosa'.

Much of Cohen's book, however, is an attempt to dismantle the connection which Price and Twining accepted, and perhaps the best way I could try to answer his objections would be to present, briefly, the account he gives of the history of criticism of one passage, the description I referred to earlier of the view from Hagley Park, and then offer my own analysis of the passage. In the lines immediately preceding those we shall be considering, Lord Lyttelton has been described as walking with his wife through Hagley Park, towards a hill from which a view extends as far as the Welsh mountains:

> Meantime you gain the height, from whose fair brow
> The bursting prospect spreads immense around;
> And, snatched o'er hill and dale, and wood and lawn,
> And verdant field, and darkening heath between,
> And villages embosomed soft in trees,
> And spiry towns by surging columns marked
> Of household smoke, your eye excursive roams –
> Wide-stretching from the Hall in whose kind haunt
> The hospitable Genius lingers still,
> To where the broken landscape, by degrees
> Ascending, roughens into rigid hills
> O'er which the Cambrian mountains, like far clouds
> That skirt the blue horizon, dusky rise.
>
> (*The Seasons*, 'Spring', lines 950–62)[31]

The first critic whom Cohen cites as having 'destroyed the fiction of the painting analogy of Hagley Park'[32] is an American geologist, Hugh Miller, who visited Hagley Hall and published his reflections on it in his *First Impressions of England and Its People*, which came out (in London) in 1845. What disturbed Miller in Thomson's description was what appeared to him to be a mere list of the features in the landscape: hill, dale, wood, lawn, and so on: 'he rather enumerates than describes. His pictures are often mere catalogues in which single words stand for classes of objects.'[33]

But when Miller saw the view which Thomson had described, he seemed to find a justification for this 'enumerative style': 'All is amazing overpowering multiplicity – a multiplicity which neither the pen nor the pencil can adequately express; and so description, in even the hands of a master, sinks into mere enumeration.'[34] Though Cohen accepts this account only with reservations – he sees the list as more than simply that, and suggests rather briefly (and not, I think, convincingly) that the various nouns are juxtaposed in such a way as to oppose the natural features of the landscape with those introduced by civilisation – he does seem to approve of Miller's statement that 'the single words stand for classes of objects' (as they certainly do, for example, in 'L'Allegro'[35]). It is worth pointing out here that Miller attaches no significance to the order of the nouns in the list, and that, if we accept Cohen's account of its significance, we must agree that the list is not very competently arranged to bring out the opposition he sees: the first noun we can certainly associate with 'man' and not with 'nature' is the fifth, 'field'. I do believe that *The Seasons* presents what Thomson sees as a dialectical relationship between civilisation and nature, and I shall return to this idea later; but it does not seem that the case can be argued simply from the position of the nouns in this passage.

Cohen certainly appears to endorse another of Miller's beliefs, that an inspection of the actual landscape, the subject of this description, will explain the technique used to describe it: and he uses Miller's observations to argue against Elizabeth Manwaring, who also discusses this passage, in her book *Italian Landscape in Eighteenth-Century England*. Miss Manwaring makes her case for the importance of the Roman painters in the history of eighteenth-century interest in landscape very well; but it must be admitted that her parallels between Thomson and Claude are rather shakily drawn, and depend too much on a study of the *content* of Thomson's descriptive passages, without showing any great interest in the problem of how a visual arrangement can be translated into a structure of words. She does not usually look in Thomson for much more than a particularly Claudian effect of light; and writing of this passage, too, she is rather vague: it is, she says, 'the most elaborately composed of all his landscapes, with real Claudian distances'.[36] This seems to me to be true, but not, as far as it goes, very helpful; Cohen, however, does not think it is even true, because, he says, Hugh Miller found it to be 'a careful replica of the scene – instead of an artificial composition – and there is reason to believe that many of Thomson's landscapes are described as he saw them'.[37] And he quotes a third critic of this passage, C. V. Deane,[38] who says it is 'not a formal composition at all. It is what Thomson names it, a "prospect"'.[39] 'Probably', adds Cohen, 'written from an exact impression.'[40] The difficulty here is that, so far has Cohen come from equating Claude and nature, that he offers us what is to me, at least, an unimaginable antithesis between the two. On the one hand we have 'artificial compositions', on the other, 'landscapes as we really see them'. Against this antithesis I can only argue that if, for Uvedale Price, Claude and nature were the same thing, it was *because* Price was so saturated in Claude's way of seeing and composing landscape, that he could see it himself in no other way: what he *really* was able to see was landscape artificially composed. So that, when I say Thomson describes landscape composed as it would be in a painting by Claude, I do not see that this involved a deliberate distortion of what he really saw into what he really did not see. An eighteenth-century landscape-painter, though he would have seen, no less than would Price or Thomson, a landscape as if it were already composed into the accepted structure, would have been aware that for that structure to be best revealed, the features in the landscape might have to be manipulated and distorted quite considerably. But the process of selection and improvement a poet performs is a good deal less apparent, perhaps even to him, and he can feel less restricted by the notion of fidelity of description; if only because he does not expect the description of a landscape he produces to be so capable of being visualised that it can be compared with the *actual* landscape, the original he works from. 'It is', wrote Thomas Warton, 'the peculiar privilege of poetry...to place material objects in the most suitable attitudes.'[41]

Nevertheless Cohen is certainly right when he concludes of Miss Manwaring's work, and of the work of other critics who offer evidence of some direct translation by Thomson from Claude, that similarities of content in a passage by Thomson and a painting by Claude, though taken along with other points of similarity they may be significant, are not, in themselves, especially so, because they tell us nothing about any similarity in the way Thomson and Claude *saw* their subjects; and Cohen is right, too, when he says

16

that critics who have tried to go further than this, and talk in terms of 'composition', assume too readily that 'verbal and visual organisation are interchangeable'.[42] He does not say so, but I imagine the mistake Cohen feels these critics make is something like this: that, though to look at a landscape in the way I have been describing was, as I have said, an active process, which involved the manipulation of objects and the creation of new relationships between them, the composition which is the result of this process, and which can be represented in a picture, is inevitably a static image – however true it may be that to respond to this image is, once again, an active experience. But a descriptive poem does not simply present us with an image, but, through the energy and disposition of its verbs especially, it can imitate the *way* in which the poet has perceived relationships between the objects he describes, and between those objects and himself. A poem, therefore, which describes a landscape as a composition, does so particularly by imitating – through syntax, grammar, and the order of words – the process of composition which the poet performs. To abstract a static image from this – a group of cattle, say, drinking at a pool, in the shade of trees – and to say that, because we can imagine these objects composed as they would be in a picture by Claude, they are composed pictorially in the poem, is certainly to confuse the different sorts of organisation possible in painting and in poetry.

But, however different these sorts of organisation are, I do not think, as Cohen seems to, that no analogies can be drawn between them, and it does seem to me possible to draw a useful analogy between the way a classical Italian landscape is organised, and the way Thomson organises this description of the view from Hagley. This analogy will have to be, in the first instance, between the composition of a landscape, and the verbal structure – the syntax, particularly – of the passage: and if the examination of the verbal structure is fruitful, we will then be entitled to go on and look for other similarities.

V

The first thing to be said about this passage, then, is that its structure is quite unusually complex: it contains thirteen lines all organised as one sentence, but, within that sentence, there are only seven clauses, five of them in the last eleven lines. The first two clauses, contained within the first two lines, could be a sentence in themselves; but instead there follows another main clause, constructed in parataxis with the first, and connected to it directly by 'and'; and the rest of the sentence – eleven lines – is all part of, or dependent on, this second main clause.

But after those first two lines we are kept waiting a long time for the second main verb, and even for the subject of that verb: we know it will agree with 'snatched', but have to wait five lines to discover what it is that is thus snatched over the landscape: it is, we eventually discover, 'your eye'. John Scott, a later poet of the eighteenth century, though he constructed his own descriptions of landscape in a way similar to Thomson's, was very puzzled, in his capacity as a critic, by this unnecessary (as it seemed to him) delay:

'*Snatch'd*'…is placed at such a distance from the verb '*roams*', with which it must connect, in order to save the period from being nonsense; that the reader at first does not perceive the connexion. The adjective '*excursive*', and the compound, '*wide-stretching*', are also supernumeraries. The sentence placed in its natural order, will read thus: 'Your eye, *snatch'd* over hill and dale, &c. *roams excursive, wide-stretching* from, &c.' Blank verse, where such violent transpositions and unnecessary epithets are used, surely is not unjustly accused of obscurity.[43]

This delay in reaching the subject seems to me, however, quite intentional, and its effect is to create a tension and a sense of expectation in us, so that we read the intervening lines between 'snatched' and 'your eye' at great speed, to discover what the verb is, and, particularly, what the subject is, and so to make sense of the 'period'. It is worth noticing that even Scott, who is in his criticism very Johnsonian and much opposed to mimetic distortions of syntax, does not suggest that the main verb should, with the subject, be placed at the beginning of the clause, although it was the position of the verb he appeared to object to; and so, even in his pale revision, some of the tension and pace Thomson intended are preserved.

After the subject and the main verb have been located, the pace of the sentence slackens: but what follows is perhaps not much more lucidly constructed, by Scott's standards. 'Your eye' remains the subject, and the last six lines are all attached to it in a participial relationship, by the phrase 'wide-stretching'. After that first phrase, 'wide-stretching from the Hall', we have two subordinate clauses, one adjectival and one a noun clause, which describe the landscape in much more detail than had previously been possible; and to the word 'hills' in the second of these clauses is attached a further adjectival clause, which itself contains yet a further adjectival clause. It is clear that for some reason Thomson feels he has, at this stage of the sentence, much more time to be expansive, discursive, than he had allowed himself earlier.

When I was discussing, in the third section of this chapter, how a landscape by Claude or Poussin was composed, I said that the objects in the picture, and the system of planes across it, were so arranged as to encourage the direct flight of the eye over the landscape and towards the area of light invariably located a little below the level of the horizon. In this journey from foreground to horizon, the eye passes over the objects and the areas of ground intervening, registering about them at most only their tonal value, and a rapid diminution in their size. Only after this initial journey has been made, I said, does the eye return to examine, at leisure, the objects it has passed on its way.

It is evident, I think, that the structure of the passage from Thomson invites us to respond to the landscape it describes very much according to the same procedure. The eye is drawn immediately to the horizon, and registers the objects in the landscape only briefly and in passing. I take it that the objects mentioned at the beginning of the list – hill, dale, wood, lawn – are singular not because, as Miller suggested, they are standing for classes of objects, but for a different reason: one hill, one wood, as against, later, the plural nouns: villages, trees, towns. The device of using singular nouns which give way to plural nouns is used, I take it, to suggest that the eye is registering, in its motion, the diminishing size of the objects it passes.[44] No adjectives attach themselves to the objects in the first line of the list, because the eye has no time to register anything about them: but in the second line, adjectives which suggest the tonal value of the different areas of ground are admitted; so that we can assume the landscape is being thought of as arranged into lateral bands like Claude's, and the objects named are representing those bands, which follow each other in sequence up the landscape: hill and dale first, then wood and lawn, presumably lighter than the dark heath which comes next, then the verdant field. As the eye reaches the area just below the horizon – as Thomson is conscious of coming nearer to revealing the subject of this clause, and its verb – it has time to notice in more detail the features of the landscape; and whereas before the only adjectives admitted were those necessary to distinguish, as briefly as possible, one band of the composition from the next, we now have adjectival phrases, which give us descriptive information for its own sake, not simply as a help to grasping the structure of the composition.

After we have reached the subject and main verb, the pace can afford, as I have said, to slacken further, and the eye is able – as it is after its initial journey to the horizon in a painting by Claude – to move back and to examine in rather more detail the objects in the landscape. The verb we do reach, however, 'roams', is semantically very different from 'snatched', and immediately changes the nature of the movement we are making. The eye, snatched to the horizon, roams: we are reminded – I am not suggesting that Thomson could ever have articulated his response to a Claude landscape as well as a twentieth-century art historian, but we are reminded of that notion Kitson offers of the horizon as at once the climax and the starting-point of the composition of *The Arrival of Aeneas at Pallanteum* (Plate 2). Our eye is drawn to the horizon instantaneously; but the first movement it is aware of itself as actively making is that roaming reassessment of the scene which I suggested occurred after the eye has been led to the horizon first, and then back – back here to the hall, which has to be understood (which in fact is, in the view from Hagley which was Thomson's original for this passage) as placed in the foreground. The eye now becomes more aware of detail: of the personified genius of hospitality, for example, beside the hall like a figure in the foreground of a Claude painting, and then moves off again, apparently both *across* the landscape – 'wide-stretching' – and also, without hurry now, over and into it, towards the horizon once more. In the last six lines, not only adjectival phrases but long clauses may be introduced, to describe the objects in the view; and Thomson has time even to introduce the strange simile – 'like far clouds that skirt the blue horizon' – the effect of which is to make the imaginary clouds, which are introduced to be compared with the Cambrian mountains, themselves now somehow part of the landscape, and skirting the actual horizon.[45]

VI

I hope that this no doubt too thorough analysis has been justified, and that it has established the possibility of some sort of analogy between the techniques of organisation used by Claude and Thomson. I want to examine, very much more briefly, some other passages of Thomson and of later eighteenth-century poets, in which it seems to me the same technique is used or something like it; but before I do so I would like to discuss one or two other aspects of Thomson's way of looking at the view from Hagley, which it seems to me can also be related to the procedures of classical landscape-painting. And in the first place, like a classical landscape, this passage presents a view seen from a height: Lord Lyttelton and his wife have been, in the preceding lines, walking up the hill, but Thomson makes no comment on the views they must have seen as they were climbing, and only when they reach the summit is the prospect permitted to burst upon their sight. This is a common procedure in eighteenth-century topographical poems: all those poems about hills – 'Grongar Hill', for example, and *Edge-hill*[46] – are not in fact about the hills themselves, but about what can be seen from the top of them; and from the *top*, not from half-way or three-quarters of the way up. So Richard Jago, climbing Edgehill, keeps his back scrupulously turned to the landscape below him, and his mind on the difficulty of the ascent, until 'the summit's gained!'[47] and he allows himself to spin round and be overwhelmed by the vastness and the beauty of the prospect under his eye.

The main point of this insistence on a high viewpoint is that it creates a space between the landscape and the observer, similar in its effect to the space between a picture and whoever is looking at it. So, in this passage, Thomson is able to see the landscape, not as something in which he is involved, and which is all round him, but as something detached from him, *over there*: his eye may wander over the view, but his own position is fixed, and from his viewpoint he can organise the landscape into the system of parallel bands and flat perspectives by which only can he comprehend what he sees.

The eye is, then, actively exploring the prospect; but that it can do so depends very much on Thomson's being able to regard the prospect as an object separated from him by an actual, measurable, distance. We can recall at this point that in the eighteenth century one did not look *at* a print, one looked *over* it, and that phrase indicates how little – either in looking at pictures, or in the exploration of an actual view – the eye could be engaged by its object. It indicates how much the impression made upon the eye was a general one: an impression of the order of its own progress over the objects in the landscape, rather than of those objects themselves. And it is in this respect, as I have said earlier, that this exploration the eye makes is *active*: it is able to move at such speed over the landscape, only because it can organise so efficiently the objects in its path into a preconceived structure, which allows them an identity only as landmarks on the journey the eye makes to the horizon.

This habit of perception gives the objects in the passage a very limited status, at least in the first lines, when the eye is being snatched over them towards the horizon. In the first place, of course, they have to be enumerated in the same order as they appear to the poet's eye as it moves – though the line 'And verdant field, and darkening heath between' is an awkward exception to this, which reverses briefly the movement of our attention, and in doing so enables us to differentiate all the more successfully the several planes of the landscape. The features of the landscape are, certainly, active themselves – they can snatch the eye towards them – but at the very same time they are being so thoroughly controlled by the poet's eye that they cannot impose themselves on him or demand any more of his attention than he is prepared to concede. And the sense in which they are *subjected* to the poet is reflected, as we should expect, in the grammar of the passage especially. They draw the eye into the landscape, but are in turn governed by the preposition 'o'er', as the eye is snatched over them. In other passages of Thomson, or of other landscape-poets after him, the features of a landscape will often all be placed as objects of a single verb: 'survey', for example, or 'view'. They are made to be passive under the eye, if they are not always felt to be so, and they suffer the action of the verb.

Now it is clear, I think, that if the landscape and the features within it are to be successfully subjected to the poet, and to be organised by him, until they become as far as possible the landmarks on his eye's journey, elements in a general composition which does its best to prevent the particular things within it from asserting themselves at all, the poet must have the space between the landscape and himself which a high viewpoint affords. Only as it looks from rising ground can the eye separate the immediate, disorganised foreground from the malleable area beyond it. The importance of this separation of the poet from the landscape he describes is reflected in the poetic vocabulary of the eighteenth century, and particularly in those words which were more or less interchangeable with the word 'landscape' itself – 'view', 'prospect', 'scene' – all of which make the land something out there, something to be looked at from a distance, and in one direction only. 'Prospect' carries this sense from its Latin root, *pro-spicere*, to look forward, or out into the distance: before anything else a prospect is what is in front of you – the phrase *en face* perhaps expresses it best – and some distance away. And though in the eighteenth century this sense of direction became gradually more submerged, it did keep a limiting influence over the sense that could be made of the word. Thus, when Thomson writes in this passage that the 'prospect' spreads immense 'around', there is certainly a tension between the sense of 'prospect', something in a fixed and opposite position to the observer, and 'around', which suggests a wide arc of landscape stretching out beyond the arc of the poet's vision. This tension relates very closely to the process of organisation both Claude and Thomson were engaged in: that of organising what was in fact an arc – the 'circling landscape' as it was often called by eighteenth-century poets – on to a flat surface, that of the canvas or an imaginary one. It was partly to make this feat of organisation easier for the connoisseur of landscape that the Claude-glass was invented: a plano-convex mirror which 'gathers every scene reflected in it into a tiny picture'.[48]

The word 'scene', applied to a landscape, assumed also that what was being described lay opposite the observer, *en face*: and this sense came with it from its theatrical origin – the flat and square-shaped σκηνή behind the orchestra in a Greek theatre, and the square frame of the proscenium arch which the English theatre had adopted since the Restoration. A 'scene', then, in the description of landscape, is something opposite you and enclosed by the limits of your vision in very much the same way as a painting is enclosed within its frame, or, within the painting, the area beyond the foreground is marked off by the *coulisse* – the word can mean the wings of a stage. A 'scene' directs attention to itself as a self-contained and separate entity, apart from the rest of the country-side, and apart from the observer. The word 'scenery' does not appear to have been used of landscape until Cowper used it in *The Task*,[49] in 1784. This is an almost predictable development, perhaps, to anyone familiar with Cowper's passages of landscape-description: the word keeps the landscape remote, insofar as it accepts the analogy with the stage – it is still something *over there* – but it directs attention less to the scene as a general entity than to the particular components of it. This is a balance of emphasis which, as we shall see, is characteristic of Cowper's attitude to landscape.

It is clear, I think, that the attitude to landscape Claude and Thomson share – that, for example, it must keep its distance, and the features within it be kept in subjection to our sense of the general composition – is part of a very different attitude to nature from, say, Ruskin's, who, a century later, advised whoever wanted to look at or to paint a landscape to lie down and start with the blades of grass in front of his face.[50] I said earlier that *The Seasons* seems to me to express a dialectical relationship between nature and civilisation, in which the effort of civilisation to control nature is resisted by nature, which in turn threatens the progress of civilisation and threatens to control it. Thomson is by no means sure of his own position within this dialectic, and when he describes the tropics, for example, the luxuriance and superabundance of the vegetation fill him with a sensuous enthusiasm which looks forward to the writing of his admirer, Chateaubriand.[51] But, generally speaking, he cannot give himself up to the control of nature as Ruskin more easily could, for Thomson's idea of nature is neither as of a complaisant and plastic mass, to be moulded into ideal forms – the notion at times apparently held by Pope, notably in his 'Epistle to Burlington'[52] – nor is it as of a spirit to be held in religious veneration, a spirit which can be trusted, as it often is for Ruskin. Thomson instead feels he must control nature in order not to be controlled by it, and it is in this respect that the, so to speak, moral significance of his insistence on describing landscape from a high viewpoint is best understood. The crucial phrase here is perhaps a 'commanding height', a phrase borrowed of course from the language of military tactics, and by no means used, by eighteenth-century poets, without a sense of embattled hostility to what is being commanded, the landscape below. The idea is a commonplace in the descriptive poetry of the eighteenth century: the example that occurs to me at present is from 'The Landscape',[53] by John Cunningham –

> Stretch'd upon these banks of broom,
> We *command* the Landscape round
>
> ('The Landscape', lines 3–4)

– and more explicit in its sense of control, is this military image from Cowper –

> Now roves the eye;
> And, *posted* on this *speculative* height,
> *Exults in its command.*
>
> (*The Task*, book i, lines 288–90)

(The italics in this quotation and the one above are, of course, my own.) It is, I think, in the context of Thomson's anxiety to control nature – an anxiety which became common, as we often say, among writers two and three generations after Newton – that Thomson's way of proceeding, in his passages of description, is best understood, and also his way of organising the things he sees in a landscape into a very rigid and complex syntactical pattern. And even in the passage we are examining, the description of a landscape very much in the grip of civilisation, this anxiety is everywhere finding expression, in the words Thomson uses no less than in the syntax imposed on those words. The tension in the second line – between 'prospect', on the one hand, and, on the other, 'bursting', 'spreads', 'immense', 'around' – I have already noted. In the next line the eye is 'snatched' – presumably by the objects in the landscape demanding its attention – but, even as it gives way to the attraction they exert, it is organising, defining, placing them as it passes on. Later in the passage the 'hospitable Genius' is contrasted with 'the broken landscape', the 'rigid hills', but these give way to and are mitigated by the soft blue light at the end of the prospect.

The dialectic, then, between civilisation and nature is evident in this passage in the sort of objects Thomson chooses to describe, and the epithets he applies to them – 'soft', 'broken', 'rigid', 'dusky' – and, more especially, in his application of the very rigid structure I have gone to some length to describe; for the devices he borrows from the Roman painters, and finds expression for in his syntax, he borrows as a means of organising and so of controlling the landscape he sees. But if we are to understand this dialectic we must remember that, after all, one description of a 'prospect' in Thomson is not exactly like every other: there are differences between them which the rigid structure cannot suppress. So that the dialectic can perhaps best be expressed like this: that Thomson begins with an 'idea' of landscape, a design conceived of in terms of planes and the eye's movement across them, but still, if we like, an 'idea-in-itself', not yet applied to any particular landscape. For the idea to have any concrete existence, it has to be applied to, or discovered in, a tract of land, but this tract of land is to be understood as hostile to the notion of being thus organised. The synthesis Thomson arrives at is one in which the objects retain to some extent their individuality – each landscape is different from any other – and yet appear to be organised within a formal pattern; and one on the other hand in which the formal pattern is clearly apparent, and yet which does not manage wholly to suppress the sense that the view from Hagley is a different one from, say, the view from Shene (which we shall examine in the next section). The form of this synthesis is, precisely, the form of the syntax in each passage: as we shall see, Thomson tries to impose the same syntactical forms on other descriptive passages as he used in the one we have been looking at, and if these forms differ it is largely because the objects in each view – the only material in which the idea can find existence – have resisted the organising tendency of the syntax. And finally, the form of the syntax of each description is also, of course, an analogue of the form of each landscape as Thomson apprehends it.

I want to leave this passage now, and look briefly at two or three other pieces by Thomson, but first I would like to emphasise how completely this landscape is apprehended in *visual* terms; or, since the word 'landscape' applies itself only to visual descriptions anyway, perhaps I had better say, how completely the area between Hagley Park and the Welsh mountains is apprehended as a landscape. By this I do not mean, simply, that the place is not at all experienced by Thomson, as it might be by Wordsworth or Cowper, in terms of sounds and textures as well, but also that Thomson allows himself to introduce into his description very little of the knowledge that he might well have had about the area – which counties it forms part of, who owns it, what the names are of the

26

towns and villages. I am not arguing that the sense of the area as a particular place is thus completely suppressed – as I suggested in the previous paragraph, the final form of the description is one in which the individuality of the landscape is made, in some way, to exist in the design imposed upon it; but nevertheless an 'idea' of landscape has been imposed, and this place has now become a landscape which we can compare with others, without being disturbed by too many intrusive details that might make us aware of it as a particular locality, and not as an ideal landscape. I shall have more to say about this later in the chapter.

VII

The technique of description I have been examining in relation to Thomson's account of the view from Hagley Park is one he attempts to use in almost every description of extended landscape in *The Seasons*; and the composition, the syntactical structure it produced, occurs, with variations, quite often in the poem. It was a structure invented to imitate the response of the *eye* to the landscape it looks over: it is, as I have suggested, only the visual impression of landscape which Thomson is normally concerned to describe. In this next passage, however, which reproduces very exactly the structure of the passage we have already looked at, this technique of imitation is in some conflict with Thomson's desire to say a good deal more about the landscape than it will normally allow, for Thomson is indulging a favourite habit of eighteenth-century travellers, that is, enumerating the various lords' and gentlemen's seats the view contains, and attributing them, with an elegant compliment, to their several owners. The view from Shene, which is described here, was particularly well supplied with expensive houses, so that this was, I imagine, a lucrative passage to have written. But most interesting is to see how Thomson's characteristic structure, which was invented, as I say, to imitate a visual process of organisation, can be adapted to accommodate information whose source is not primarily visual at all.

> Here let us sweep
> The boundless landscape; now the raptured eye,
> Exulting swift, to huge Augusta send,

> Now to the sister hills that skirt her plain,
> To lofty Harrow now, and now to where
> Majestic Windsor lifts his princely brow.
> In lovely contrast to this glorious view,
> Calmly magnificent, then will we turn
> To where the silver Thames first rural grows.
> There let the feasted eye unwearied stray;
> Luxurious, there, rove through the pendent woods
> That nodding hang o'er Harrington's retreat;
> And, stooping thence to Ham's embowering walks,
> Beneath whose shades, in spotless peace retired,
> With her the pleasing partner of his heart,
> The worthy Queensbury yet laments his Gay,
> And polished Cornbury woos the willing muse,
> Slow let us trace the matchless vale of Thames;
> Fair-winding up to where the muses haunt
> In Twit'nam's bowers, and for their Pope implore
> The healing god; to royal Hampton's pile,
> To Clermont's terraced height, and Esher's groves,
> Where in the sweetest solitude, embraced
> By the soft windings of the silent Mole,
> From courts and senates Pelham finds repose.
>
> (*The Seasons*, 'Summer', lines 1408–32)

In the first sentence the eye, though it is said to be 'sweeping' the landscape, presumably from one side to the other, is in fact being sent out from the viewpoint in a series of separate journeys, to Augusta (London), to Harrow, and to Windsor. Thomson, who first describes the landscape as 'boundless', is so quick to reassure himself, to set 'bounds' to it, and to take his bearings by the landmarks on the horizon, that he has no time to say even briefly what his eye moves over as it moves to London and then to the two hills. But it is the third sentence, beginning 'There let the feasted eye', that is especially interesting, because, though it contains much more information than Thomson found room for in his account of the view from Hagley, it uses a very similar syntactical structure indeed, and very much for the same purpose. The eye is 'unwearied', and must move: it does not choose to rest on the individual objects in the landscape; and so, when a place is to be described in some detail, and not just in terms of the visual impression it makes, but with information about who lives there, and what his qualities are, Thomson encloses the details within subordinate adjectival clauses – 'and polished Cornbury woos the willing muse', for example – which, though they temporarily arrest the movement of the sentence, cannot do so without creating in us an anxiety to get back into the main stream. The same anxiety is created by the use of the participle 'stooping', which, like the participle 'snatched' in the previous passage, demands a subject and a verb to make sense of the period, but has to wait a very long time for them. Neither, in fact, appears for five lines: and the information in the intervening subordinate clauses is accepted only in anticipation of what is to follow: 'yes', the syntax forces us to say, 'but where is this taking us?' The question is partly answered when the subject – which is no longer, as it turns out, the eye, but us – and the verb finally appear; but the sentence is still unwilling to end.

It is continued, in fact, by precisely the same device as Thomson used at this point in the Hagley passage: instead of 'wide-stretching', we have 'fair-winding', and everything else in this sentence is dependent, as it was in the other piece, on this one participle. The groups of words which follow, all of them beginning 'to', and all attached to 'winding', continue to demand our motion forward yet arrest it, the preposition itself reaching further out each time, the clauses that follow it trying to persuade us to stop and take notice of the information they contain, of the details, the places, they describe. Only after four lines of this does Thomson allow one of these clauses to gather enough weight to drag the sentence to a halt, artfully, at 'repose'.

Thomson is, then, trying to give us a good deal more information about this landscape than he normally does, but still has to enclose it within his usual rigid structure. He first moves into the landscape at some speed, unwilling to rest his eye on the objects he encounters, and prevented from doing so by the syntax; and although, after he has made this initial journey, he can begin to inspect the view at more leisure, he must still do so without his eye being ever quite allowed to stop. It is not just that Thomson's way of looking at landscape is imitated by his syntax; it is imitated apparently by a fixed pattern of syntax, which suggests that his way of looking, too, is as far as possible fixed and invariable, and whatever sense he wants to communicate, about the individual content of the place he is describing, is not to be allowed to impose itself more than is consistent with its revealing the design of the landscape. That isn't to say the individuality of the place has been suppressed; it is apparent everywhere, as the organising eye tries to move on, and is continually arrested by facts and details; but because the place cannot be described at all by Thomson except in terms of an *a priori* idea of its design, arrived at elsewhere and not in response to the particulars of this view, its individuality can emerge only as a particular existence of that general idea.

We can get some idea of how habitual this way of looking at landscape was for Thomson – and a further idea, too, of its moral significance for him – from another passage from *The Seasons*, in which he finds himself unable to use the proper Claudian procedures; and if his way of looking is more flexible here, it is because, as he makes clear himself, the eye cannot correctly compose the landscape in this passage. This comes from the magnificent description of summer in the 'torrid zone', in the second book of the poem; it follows immediately after an account of the fruits that grow in the tropics, which shows Thomson at his most amiable towards nature, and indeed infatuated by her.

> From these the prospect varies. Plains immense
> Lie stretched below, interminable meads
> And vast savannas, where the wandering eye,
> Unfixt, is in a verdant ocean lost.
> Another Flora there, of bolder hues
> And richer sweets beyond our garden's pride,
> Plays o'er the fields, and showers with sudden hand
> Exuberant spring – for oft these valleys shift
> Their green-embroidered robe to fiery brown,
> And swift to green again, as scorching suns
> Or streaming dews and torrent rains prevail.
> Along these lonely regions, where, retired
> From little scenes of art, great Nature dwells
> In awful solitude, and naught is seen
> But the wild herds that own no master's stall,
> Prodigious rivers roll their fattening seas;
> On whose luxuriant herbage, half-concealed,
> Like a fallen cedar, far diffused his train,
> Cased in green scales, the crocodile extends.
>
> (*The Seasons*, 'Summer', lines 690–708)

It is the first four lines that most concern us; but to have given those alone would have left us in doubt as to what attitude Thomson was taking up to the experience he describes.

At the beginning of this passage, then, Thomson is imagining himself looking down, from a high viewpoint, on a vast expanse of grassland; and he finds himself quite unable to organise this view, as he can organise others, into a composed landscape. When he was looking out of Hagley Park towards the Welsh mountains, his eye was 'snatched' to the horizon, but, as it gave itself up to this attraction which nature exerted, it was able to measure the distance of its flight, and thus to feel, somehow, in control, by organising the objects it passed into the planes of a composition, the landmarks on its journey. In these savannas the eye is encouraged to wander as it did at Hagley, or as, in another passage from 'Spring', the 'hurried' eye 'distracted wanders',[54] through a landscape-garden. In those properly English and civilised landscapes it encountered enough objects – hills, trees, fields – to act as landmarks; even in the 'boundless' view from Shene Thomson was able to find objects prominent enough by which to take his bearings. But the savannas are 'vast', the meads 'interminable': there is nothing to organise in them, the eye is 'unfixt', without points of reference, and lost in a green ocean of grass.

The first, and most important thing, it seems, that Thomson has to say about the tropical savannas, is that they cannot be looked at properly, and so cannot be described in the normal way. That he should have been able to imagine himself thus disorientated, in this imaginary landscape, is remarkable; but his reaction to the experience is even more so, and shows that Thomson is not a mere spectator on the dialectic in *The Seasons*, which works through the poem because it works in him. He does not give up the task of description, and instead of being disturbed by his inability to use his normal Claudian procedures, he turns his description into something like an attack on the climate and civilisation which produced them. A figure from classical pagan mythology is allowed into the passage, but it is 'another' Flora, with flowers more brightly coloured and more richly scented than those of England, or Europe. The climate is hot and wet; the rivers more than rivers – 'fattening seas' to feed the wild herds and the luxuriant herbage. It is impossible to mistake Thomson's tone here, which is enthusiastic, excited, and quite beyond looking for the sort of imaginative control which the visual procedures he is normally able to use can supply; and this becomes explicit in the contrast between the 'little scenes of art', which Thomson's usual procedures create and enjoy, and 'great Nature' of the tropics.

There is a poem I shall return to discuss elsewhere in this book,

'Inclosure of Open Fields in Northamptonshire', written in Latin in 1823 by the Reverend James Tyley,[55] in which the same sort of experience of disorientation in a landscape is described: I mention it now to contrast Tyley's reaction with Thomson's. The poem is a justification of enclosure, and begins with an invocation to Terminus, 'whose care is the ancient stone and the lawful boundary'.[56] It is soon clear, though, that Tyley's interest in enclosure is not simply that of a farmer trying to make a few farms more productive, though it is that too: Tyley seems genuinely offended – indeed, he seems to feel threatened, in some way – by wide tracts of land unmarked by hedges, and so more or less empty of the sort of natural features that might serve as boundaries or landmarks. This discomfort is, before anything else, a visual discomfort. The land of the Britons, he says (I do not have a copy of the Latin original), had for long been sterile ground, 'distinguished for no beauty, a wide expanse of English soil; roughened by sluggish frost and strident winds the wide fields extended, and *unbroken tracts strained and tortured the sight*...I have seen neighbouring districts stretching out their fields successively for twenty miles with no division' (my italics).[57] It seems to me arguable, from this passage and from others I shall look at in the next chapter, that because of their dependence on the sort of techniques of organising and composing landscape that I have been discussing, the cultivated classes in England felt much more at ease, in the eighteenth and early nineteenth centuries, in landscape which had been enclosed. Another poet writing at the beginning of the nineteenth century, Thomas Batchelor, praised the enclosure movement for having, among other things, 'chang'd the *formless aspect* of the land' (my italics).[58] On the other hand, I have never come across any writers in this period, who had not learned to look at landscape in this particular way – Cobbett, for example – being caused this sort of visual discomfort by the prospect of open fields, though they often thought them ugly, and were uneasy about them for economic reasons.

It is not often, anyway, that Thomson cannot use the techniques he has developed from the structure of classical Italian landscape-painting. A variety of it occurs even in his relatively short passages of description:

> Heavens! what a goodly prospect spreads around,
> Of hills, and dales, and woods, and lawns, and spires,

> And glittering towns, and gilded streams, till all
> The stretching landskip into smoke decays!
>
> (*The Seasons*, 'Summer', lines 1438–41)

There is no need I imagine to analyse this at any length: it is perhaps sufficient to point out that it is the syntactical structure, and particularly that temporal construction identified by the word 'till', which saves these lines from being a mere list: to make sense of the construction, we have to assume that the hills, dales, and towns, are successive planes across the landscape, which recede into the distance until the landscape is lost in haze. In this way we can understand, too, the proper significance of those adjectives in the third line: the towns are said to glitter, the streams to be gilded, because they are imagined to be in that area of light which first attracts our eye; and we can see, too, that in the line before there are no adjectives because the eye has no time to register anything about the objects in it, except what they are.

But I would like, finally in this section, to give one example from a number of passages in *The Seasons* which can perhaps be understood to use the *merely* enumerative style of description that earlier poets, Milton for example, had used, and which thus may not appear to be *landscapes* at all. This passage comes at the beginning of the first book, immediately after the opening invocations:

> And see where surly Winter passes off
> Far to the north, and calls his ruffian blasts:
> His blasts obey, and quit the howling hill,
> The shattered forest, and the ravaged vale;
> While softer gales succeed, at whose kind touch,
> Dissolving snows in livid torrents lost,
> The mountains lift their green heads to the sky.
>
> (*The Seasons*, 'Spring', lines 11–17)

No one here – neither the poet himself, nor anyone else – is presented as looking out over an identifiable piece of ground, and describing what he sees there; and it goes without saying that this is not imagined as a description – a very idealised one, it would have to be – of an actual place. It might seem, therefore, that 'the howling hill' and 'the shattered forest' are indeed standing, in this passage, for 'classes of objects', and are not intended to be understood as separate features in the same landscape, but, instead, as representative features of the general topography of the countryside. And certainly a poet of another period would have described the departure of winter and the advent of spring in terms of *representative* images: the trees do this, the birds do that.

It is true, I think, that Thomson has wanted to suggest by those phrases – 'the howling hill', 'the ravaged vale' – a general image of the whole countryside recovering from the effects of winter; and hill, forest, valley and mountain do that very adequately. But it does seem to me also that the organising technique Thomson has developed is able to give these representative objects, so to speak, a local identity, so that they can be visualised as *one* landscape which contains the elements of *all* similar landscapes. The 'blasts' of winter quit, successively, the hill, the forest, and the vale, and these become the separate planes of a Claudian composition, arranged into place by the movement of the verb 'quit', which has very much the same organising effect as, before, the phrase 'snatched o'er' had in the Hagley passage. It is in following this movement of the 'ruffian blasts' that our eye moves over the landscape, to where the 'softer gales' of spring melt the snow on the mountains, which meet the sky and thus close the view at the horizon. And so the movement of the blasts is marked out into stages, and they are in some way obeying the poet as they obey Winter; which suggests again that the rigid procedures of the Claudian school had an important moral, and civilising, value for Thomson.

VIII

The other poet who is usually given credit for having introduced, along with Thomson, the ideal landscape of Claude into eighteenth-century English poetry is John Dyer. The presence of Claude in Dyer's poetry is located by, among others, Christopher Hussey, in his book *The Picturesque*, where he reproduces a long passage of 'Grongar Hill', and apologises for its length by saying, 'it is difficult to limit quotation in a passage so correctly "composed" into a "unity"'.[59] The lines quoted (37–83, with omissions) do certainly contain a number of images, of castles and mountains, for example, which are not so precisely described that they cannot be visualised as, more or less, the sort of things Claude put into his landscapes; but they are brought into the poem very much at random, and I find no sense of composition or unity. William Gilpin criticised the poem because Dyer had not properly contrasted the foreground and the distance;[60] and John Scott was not at all sure that it was even Dyer's intention to produce 'completed landscapes'.[61] We do not find any very convincing sense of design, either, in Dyer's later descriptions of landscape; in *The Ruins of Rome*,[62] or even (despite the passage in approbation of it I have quoted from *The Critical* – see p. 13) in *The Fleece*.

Dyer's work is relevant to this chapter in another way, however, in that he reintroduced into the tradition of English poetry the topographical poem, which describes and is named after a particular locality. Rather more than the passages from James Thomson we have been considering, the topographical poem might seem to represent a deliberate attempt to give a sense of the individuality of the place being described, and 'Grongar Hill' the more so, in that it does not use a version of the Claudian procedure, and imports no other *a priori* idea of design into the view it describes. I do not find, however, that any of the topographical poets were much concerned to communicate any particular sense of Grongar, Edgehill, Wensleydale, or wherever, and had they wanted to they would have been prevented from doing so, not only by their use (when they do use it) of the procedure we have been examining, but also by what Coleridge called their 'perpetual trick of *moralizing* every thing'[63] in nature. The trick is well described by Earl Wasserman in his article, 'The English Romantics: the grounds of knowledge':

the eighteenth-century poet is forever interrupting his scene-painting to find its moral or emotional analogue. A description of flickering sunlight must be paired with a note on the analogous emotion of gaiety; if the poet observes that 'Those thorns protect the forest's hopes;/That tree the slender ivy props,' he must add, 'Thus rise the mighty on the mean!/Thus on the strong the feeble lean!' (F. N. C. Munday, *Needwood Forest*, 1776.)[64]

In this poetry the landscape becomes a theatre where the poet's own moral reflections are acted out; where the objects do not so much give rise to the reflections, as the ready-made and waiting reflections justify the inclusion of this or that object in the poem. The effect, far from suggesting any sense of locality, instead serves to show that one locality – especially if it has cliffs, and a castle – can be treated in much the same way as another, in that it can be persuaded to illustrate the same rhetorical commonplaces. I do not think, therefore, that we should see the topographical poem as part of a conscious attempt to localise landscape, to represent, not *landscape*, but *a landscape*. The poems read more like incidents on the sort of picturesque tour made (for example) by William Gilpin, except that, whereas Gilpin stopped, or did not stop, to examine a landscape, according to whether it fulfilled or not his 'picturesque rules',[65] the topographical poet chose his subject by its ability to furnish him with apt images to 'moralize'.

And, of course, for the most part, the descriptive poets of the eighteenth century, whether they claimed to be describing actual or ideal landscapes, did attempt to reproduce in their work the landscapes of Claude, as mediated through Thomson; this is true at least of almost every properly *descriptive* – as opposed to merely 'topographical' – poet writing after about 1744, when the revised version of *The Seasons* appeared, and until about 1800. Very few of them, however, could reproduce, with any success, Thomson's technique of composition. The passages of landscape-description in *The Seasons* became enormously influential, but for the wrong reasons: the typical content of a landscape by Claude, and its arrangement into planes, was recognised in Thomson, but not the way he had converted the pictorial image of ideal landscape into one which demanded a distinctively poetic response. And so later poets, following Thomson as they thought, took over from his technique a few of its characteristics only: the order of description, for example, from foreground to horizon, and the habit of containing the entire view within a single sentence – although the particular structure of that sentence as Thomson had used it, and its importance for him, eluded them. The technique became simply a convenience, a way of beginning at the beginning and going on to the end; and though the verse of these poets certainly imitated, as Thomson's had done, the response they made to landscape, the imitation served only to reveal that response as a mechanical and automatic thing.

But perhaps the failure of Thomson's imitators to create a poetry as taut as his should be seen as the result not of any failure on their part to recognise or understand what Thomson was doing, but of a difference in attitudes to nature. The crux of Thomson's method was, as we have seen, the energy of his syntax, arising as it does from the sense he communicates to us, that the landscapes he is trying to organise can challenge and to some extent resist his desire to organise them. It is possible to argue that in expressing this idea of nature, that it is hostile to man and must be subdued, Thomson was using the pastoral to express a radically different attitude to nature from that which it had previously expressed. In earlier pastoral poetry, nature was, of course, understood to be in harmony with man: it brought forth 'of its own kind, all foison, all abundance';[66] and its abundance appeared so immodest to Marvell, in 'The Garden' – Marvell of course an intruder in that aristocratic precinct – that 'ensnar'd with flowers', he fell on grass.[67] To Pope, the objects in his ideal landscape appeared as ever-attentive servants, anticipating and ministering to man's needs:

> Where-e're you walk, cool Gales shall fan the Glade,
> Trees, where you sit, shall crowd into a Shade.
>
> (*Pastorals* 'Summer', lines 73–4).[68]

One of the last great poets, perhaps, to espouse this aristocratic and pastoral idea of nature was Newton, whose cosmology became poetry at the point at which mathematics seemed to become, to his disciples if not to him, a branch of the study of harmony, and not harmony a branch of mathematics. The Whig, and mercantile, ideology in eighteenth-century England saw nature as something to be conquered, and forced to give up her riches – I shall say more about this later, in the context of the Agricultural Revolution. Like Marvell, Thomson was capable of finding even the luxuriance of nature as much a threat as a promise; and *The Seasons* may be read as an attempt to rewrite the pastoral as an expression of man's need to control nature at least as much – Thomson is not always stronger than his allegiance to the pastoral tradition he has inherited – as a celebration of nature's harmony with man.

A good deal of the ambivalence in Thomson's attitude to nature was shared, of course, by later poets in the eighteenth century, but they did not usually regard the description of ideal landscape in the manner of Claude as a suitable vehicle for its expression; and anyway the malevolence of nature for them – I am thinking especially of the 'picturesque' school – was something in turn opposed to the ideology of Thomson, the refusal of nature to be cowed and intimidated by the arts of man. It was for these poets in scenes and objects that were not obviously beautiful, but could be seen as picturesque, or sublime, that nature seemed threatening, and therefore admirable, and the Picturesque came eventually to be thought of as in opposition to the Claudian style of composition, and to the whole notion that landscape should have a structure: it had to do, instead, with the accidents of nature, not with her imaginary ideal form; and these accidents were usually discovered in individual objects – a ruined oak, a scarred cliff – or in small groups of them together, and not in wide areas of land. The attempt by the picturesque poets to break out of the structures of Claude and Thomson was not attended, however, by immediate success, and for a long time the history of picturesque taste, in painting as well as in poetry, can be understood as the history of its successive attempts to emancipate itself from those structures, which lingered on beyond the end of the century. The procedure Thomson had used – or a version of it – was still for most poets in 1790 the habitual one by which a rural landscape was described: it had become progressively looser, but was still a formality at least, to be gone through before the real business of description was begun, and at odds with the spirit of the poem.

But between Thomson on the one hand and the picturesque poets on the other there were still poets who, as I said, tried to use the structures of Claude in some sense as Thomson had used them, but whether because inept, or because they were anxious to keep their descriptions within a tradition of pastoral expressive of the harmony of nature, they were not able, as I said, to reproduce Thomson's tension and urgency. The landscapes they described were untroubled by any tendency to resist being organised in the proper way; they submitted quite passively to the poet. And because a landscape thus described is not experienced as at all active itself, the image of it invites no active response from us. These passive and conventional scenes are everywhere in the poetry of the mid-century, and are often found later. Here is one from Lyttelton, the same man as Thomson imagined exploring the view from Hagley:

> The vale beneath a pleasing prospect yields
> Of verdant meads and cultivated fields;
> Through these a river rolls its winding flood,
> Adorn'd with various tufts of rising wood;
> Here, half conceal'd in trees, a cottage stands,
> A castle there the opening plain commands;
> Beyond, a town with glittering spires is crown'd,
> And distant hills the wide horizon bound.
>
> (*The Progress of Love*, iii, lines 17–24)[69]

This landscape, clearly enough, gave Lyttelton no great trouble, in his attempts to organise it; and that he chose to use heroic couplets for this description, and not the blank verse of Thomson, suggests to us immediately that he expected to be able to arrange the landscape as neatly and as efficiently as in fact he does. The basic procedure is still Thomson's, but as *The Progress of Love* appeared as early as 1732, Lyttelton may not have learned the technique from *The Seasons*. The view is seen from above; it contains, more or less in the foreground, green fields and meadows, through which a river winds, connecting them no doubt with the next band of ground, where there is, on one side, a plain, and, on the other, a castle commanding it. Below the horizon, and just exactly where it should be to attract our eye, a town is picked out by the sunlight, its spires glittering; and lastly there is the horizon itself, with distant hills. The structure is preserved in all its externals: the spatial relationships, for example, between the different areas and objects are meticulously worked out – 'beneath', 'through these', 'here', 'there', 'beyond'; what is missing is the sense that the structure has any particular purpose, or is the result of any effort Lyttelton had to make, to understand and control his response to the landscape. For in an important way he does not respond to the landscape at all, because it can demand no response of him. And this *lack* of response is mimed by the movement of the verse, as Thomson's active attempt to arrange a landscape is: the eye, for example, in this passage, is not presented as snatched towards the glittering spires: it must wait to reach them in good time, and the landscape becomes, as Claude's was for Kitson (see p. 8 above), an arrangement of 'easy and varied stages to a luminous distance'. But now the whole point of placing that luminous area, where it *is* placed, is lost: it can exert no control over the way we look at the view, because it is imprisoned within a syntax and a verse-form that allow only a measured, and even, movement: one clause, one line, for one plane of the composition. Thomson's vocabulary, too, has been taken over to a degree, with his structure: the verbs 'command', 'bound', suggest a tight control, but out of all proportion to the need for it. In the first passage from Thomson the landscape retaliated, so to speak, with an active vocabulary of its own: 'bursting', 'spreads immense', 'snatch'. Lyttelton's vale simply 'yields' a prospect, as the land might yield her fruits to the landlord without any effort on his part, or – we might imagine – on the part of his labourer. Lyttelton was of course a Whig peer, or perhaps I should say, a Whig, but a peer, and his loyalties in aesthetic matters – despite his semi-patronage of Thomson – were clearly more aristocratic than mercantile.

This piece from Lyttelton is by no means an exceptionally bad example of what happened to the structure and energy of Thomson's way of describing landscape; indeed, writing which adopts such an unruffled tone and such a neat, careful procedure cannot, perhaps, be exceptional in any way. This next passage, from one of the half-dozen poems by Gilbert White attached to his *Natural History of Selborne*,[70] is of more or less the same quality, neither good nor bad, as are most other examples of the description of extended landscapes after Thomson:

> Romantic spot! from whence in prospect lies
> Whate'er of landscape charms our feasting eyes;
> The pointed spire, the hall, the pasture-plain,
> The russet fallow, or the golden grain,
> The breezy lake that sheds a gleaming light,
> Till all the fading picture fail the sight.
>
> ('Invitation to Selborne', lines 27–32)[71]

I think we can take it that this does attempt to preserve, again, at least the externals of Thomson's structure, indeed it was probably conceived as an imitation of the very short passage from 'Summer' we looked at in the last section: the word 'till' here, too, assures us that the features of the landscape are arranged in order towards the horizon, and the lake, the last area of the landscape before we reach the horizon, is gleaming, as Thomson's 'gilded streams' were, in the proper way to attract the eye. But, like Lyttelton, White does not respond to the landscape as his use of Thomson's structure suggests he should: we have to wait, again, to reach the gleaming lake, after a leisurely and over-observant progress through the intervening ground. The word 'breezy', too, suggests how meaningless the structure has become for White: he is not clear whether he is over *here*, seeing the lake gleam in the distance, or over *there*, feeling the breeze blow, or watching it make ripples on the lake's surface. Some expectation that White's relationship with the view will be a less formal one than Lyttelton's is aroused by his phrase 'our feasting eyes', which suggests not only an activity on the poet's part, but also that the landscape

40

will be in some way rich and inviting; this expectation is not fulfilled, however, and White no doubt took this phrase over from Thomson as unthinkingly as he took over his structure.

The poet who perhaps best understood the nature of Thomson's descriptive technique was, surprisingly enough, John Scott, whom as a critic I have referred to already, on one occasion when he was criticising Thomson's description of the view from Hagley for precisely that feature of it – the arrangement of the words – which seems to me its main virtue. In his heroic couplets, Scott is as capable of the same flat efficiency of description as Lyttelton or White. But in his poem *Amwell*[72] in blank verse, he comes rather nearer to suggesting at least some of the activity, the motion, of Thomson:

> When melancholy thus has changed to grief,
> That grief in soft forgetfulness to lose,
> I have left gloom for gayer scenes, and sought,
> Through winding paths of venerable shade,
> The airy brow where that tall spreading beech
> O'ertops surrounding groves, up rocky steeps
> Tree over tree disposed; or stretching far
> Their shadowy coverts down the' indented side
> Of fair corn fields; or pierced with sunny glades,
> That yield the casual glimpse of flowery meads
> And shining silver rills; on these the eye
> Then wont to' expatiate pleased; or more remote
> Survey'd yon vale of Lea, in verdant length
> Of level lawn spread out to Kent's blue hills,
> And the proud range of glittering spires that rise
> In misty air on Thames's crowded shores.
>
> (*Amwell*, lines 231–46)

There are a number of other passages in this poem which might have been quoted instead of this not especially remarkable piece of writing. It is, it must be admitted, very difficult to work out quite what is happening in these lines: the poet seems to be walking along woodland paths towards a hill crowned with a beech tree; but then the woodland scenes he describes appear to be seen from somewhere else, and not from the hill at all. The syntax of this is impossibly confused; but the sense conveyed, by those clauses all beginning 'or', is of the eye moving restlessly towards one part of the landscape and then towards another. The cost of this effect, in syntactical clarity, is very high, but it has been incurred because Scott does wish not to present just a ready-made image of landscape, but an impression of his own active response to it. The more or less straightforward piece of Claudian landscape at the end of the passage is far better, too, than Lyttelton's attempt in the same genre, and for just this reason, that it depends for its unity not on a few adverbs and prepositions alone, but on our sense that Scott is actively organising the landscape as he writes: he is 'surveying' it.

Perhaps in the context of this passage I might say something more about the vocabulary which the poets we are examining habitually used: I shall be brief, because what I have to say has been said often enough before, most notably and most fully by John Arthos in his *Language of Natural Description in Eighteenth-Century Poetry*.[73] We have seen that the attitudes to landscape these poets shared produced a vocabulary by which was conveyed the *remoteness* of landscape, the sense of its being over there, under control; the words we particularly examined were 'prospect' and 'scene'. I would like to recall, here, however, that these poets did also have a specialised vocabulary which conveyed the original attitudes to *nature* that underlay their attitudes to landscape. An example from this passage by John Scott is the word 'grove', which is in the first place the name for a group of trees thought to have been deliberately planted, and arranged in a definite pattern. The poets we are considering, however, often used the word of groups of trees occurring in natural landscape, and not deliberately planted at all. I take it that Scott is using it here in this latter sense, and the use does show to what degree the objects in a landscape were seen, in the eighteenth century, as disposed into a composition even before the poet or painter had been to work on them. A 'grove' in natural landscape was, no doubt, thought of as having in fact been designed and planted by God; but more to the point in this chapter is that the language of natural description in eighteenth-century poetry was well supplied with words – another example, from this passage by Scott, is 'lawn' – whose tendency, like that of 'grove', was to present a landscape as an orderly arrangement of objects – a *design*; and the words which did tend, in this way, to reveal a design in nature, were preferred by most writers to those which did not.

IX

I said at the beginning of this chapter that it would have been very hard, in the second half of the eighteenth century, for anyone with an aesthetic interest in nature to describe a landscape without applying to it the structure I have been describing; and the vocabulary he used, too, would have made the task, as we have seen, still harder. To apply this structure became for the poets after Thomson an automatic procedure, and then – among picturesque poets, whom I shall discuss briefly in the next section – an unwanted but somehow necessary formality. The influence of Thomson and his disciples on those who only *looked* at landscape was such that the poets' way of looking very soon became their way, too. There is a remarkable example of what this meant – of what the landscape of Thomson came to mean for the literate public – in a novel by Susanna Harvey Keir, *The History of Miss Greville*: the heroine, out walking, comes to 'a height commanding one of the grandest prospects' she had ever beheld, and immediately takes out her pocket volume of Thomson – who would go for a walk without one? – and finds in it 'a lively description of the whole surrounding scenery'.[74]

Now it is clear that the structure used by Thomson was for him a very different thing, and necessary in a very different way, from the dilution of it used by his successors and disciples, whether poets or not. To say that for Thomson to organise a landscape into that structure was a deliberate, and an intricate, activity, whereas for those that came after him it was an altogether more habitual and automatic procedure, gives some sense of what that difference was. It becomes less important, however, when we turn to that aspect of the description of landscape that especially concerns me in this essay – its use to convey our sense of being in a particular place, and of the place's individuality. However recalcitrant a particular landscape seemed for Thomson, and however submissive to White, the procedure of both these poets in describing the landscapes they saw was to impose on them a very abstract structure, the same for all places. When Thomson imposes this structure, he certainly gives us more the sense of the individuality of the landscape than does White, and this is because the energy by which Thomson attempts to subdue a landscape comes in the first place from the landscape itself: the landscape 'snatches' the eye across it, but the energy by which it does so is immediately transferred to the eye which, even as it is pulled towards the horizon, is organising and controlling what it sees. And so Thomson manages to incorporate the recalcitrant energy of nature into the structure he uses to subdue her: the particular objects which make up the place are certainly allowed to bring with them into the description more of their particularity than White or Lyttelton would allow them, but only as an element in synthesis with an *a priori* idea of their design. There is much more of a sense of place in Thomson's poems than in Lyttelton's; but there is not much in either.

We can hardly say, of Claude and Poussin, that they *imposed* a structure on the landscapes they painted – although, elsewhere in this chapter, I may have used rather loosely that form of words. The landscapes of Claude were not intended and not understood as anything but imaginary creations, very freely based on the general topography of the Roman Campagna. The composition of a painting by him, and the objects it contained, can thus be said to have grown up together: there was no question of the objects in any *actual* landscape being rearranged to conform with the *ideal* structure. The same is true of Gainsborough, for example, who painted ideal landscapes from models set up in his studio, and made of lumps of coal, pieces of broccoli, and bits of broken mirror;[75] and it is true, too, of the passage by Lyttelton, which describes no actual place, and which is handled so effortlessly because the objects in the landscape have no existence except as items in an ideal landscape, chosen to reveal the design in its purest and most abstract form. The other passages we have considered, however – the views from Hagley and Shene, the landscapes of Selborne and Amwell – did certainly claim to refer to particular places, as did a great deal of topographical poetry and painting in England in the eighteenth century which used a Claudian style of composition. And in the delineation of actual places, there was indeed a process of selection, of rearrangement; if it was thought by William Gilpin to be illegitimate to add especially dominating features in what was offered as the description of an actual view (see p. 11), it was not thought to be so to describe only such views as did happen to be bounded, at the horizon, by mountains; as could be seen from a high viewpoint; and as fulfilled every other condition of the Claudian ideal. The weather, most important of all, had to be exactly right: the cloud and the clear sky in precise proportion, and the clouds so arranged that the roofs and spires just below the horizon could glitter above a green plain in shadow, and below a range of bluish mountains. It is in this way that each individual landscape in the eighteenth century came to be seen as a version of ideal landscape, so that Miss Greville could find a view Thomson had certainly never seen nevertheless described by him, in *The Seasons*, quite accurately enough for her taste; and it is this sort of development which is reflected so clearly in the new eighteenth-century sense of the word 'landscape', which I discussed at the start of this chapter. I am not trying to argue here the same case which earlier I argued against, when Ralph Cohen made it (see p. 16), that we can *either* shape a landscape into an 'artificial composition', *or* we can describe it as we 'really' see it. I am sure it is true to say that Thomson and the others did describe nature as she 'really' appeared to them, more or less; and it is true, too, of course, that the notion of a place's 'individuality' is quite as subjective as Thomson's way of looking at landscape. But it is also obviously meaningful to say that one poet describes better than another what it is like to be in the particular place he is describing, and that some poets – notably those in the eighteenth century – are less anxious to convey this particularity than others.

The activity which shows us the ideal conception of landscape at its most synthetic, and which, in doing so, has a very direct bearing on the sense of place, is the landscaping of parks and gardens, which I want to consider now, as briefly as I can. It goes without saying that gardens have always been thought of as the expression of one or other ideal of nature – as the expression of an attempt, that is, to refashion her rough productions into a notion of ideal form. The painting of nature in early medieval Europe is largely the painting of gardens, in which trees and flowers are represented by standardised and perfect shapes. In the seventeenth century the ideal aimed at by gardeners was an architectural one, by which an irregular curve was seen as a deformity, and the land-scape was reorganised into a pattern of straight lines and circles. This doctrine – that nature is striving to realise herself in regular forms – is originally, of course, Aristotelian.[76]

In eighteenth-century England, however, the ideal notion of the garden was thought to have become very radically different from any previous one; in this, especially, that the garden was no longer thought of as rigidly separated from the rest of nature. There is a famous passage from Horace Walpole in which, speaking of the introduction of the ha-ha – a sunken fence which divided the garden, but imperceptibly, from the park beyond it – he says: 'At the moment of its creation appeared Kent, painter enough to taste the charms of landscape, bold and opinionative enough to dare and to dictate, and born with a genius to strike out a great system from the twilight of imperfect essays. He leaped the fence, and saw all nature was a garden.'[77] Most historians of landscape-gardening, coming to the work of William Kent with frank relief after that of Le Nôtre and Bridgeman, infer from this passage that because Kent saw no distinction between the gardens he improved and the natural landscape outside, his style of improving was therefore 'more natural' than his predecessors'. This was a view widely held in the eighteenth century, of English achievements in landscape-gardening generally. 'The only taste we can call our own,' wrote Gray, 'the only proof of our original talent in matter of pleasure [is] our skill in gardening, and laying out grounds. that the Chinese have this beautiful Art in high perfection, seems very probable from...Chambers's little discourse[78] publish'd some few years ago, but it is very certain, we copied nothing from them, nor had any thing but nature for our model.'[79]

Unlike the gardeners of Holland and Versailles, then, the English had nature for their model. We have come across something like this idea before, in Uvedale Price's identification of 'an evening in nature' with 'a picture by Claude' (see above, p. 13); Thomas Ruggles, an agriculturalist we shall meet again in the next chapter, spoke of 'Claud Lorrain's...exact imitations of the beautiful scenes of nature';[80] and the descriptive passages of Thomson and other poets were frequently judged by how faithful they were as 'copies of nature'.

But there can be, of course, more than one reason for seeing no distinction between an actual landscape and Thomson's description of it; and, similarly, the point of Walpole's remark is not that Kent created his gardens to be faithful copies of natural landscape, but that he looked on natural landscape as striving to realise the ideal he created in the gardens he improved. Walpole goes on to say that Kent 'remarked how loose groves crowned an easy eminence with happy ornament, and while they called in the distant view between their graceful stems, removed and extended the perspective by delusive comparison'.[81] These groves – and the use of that word underlines the point – are seen by Kent to be working very deliberately to create in nature the effects that Claude achieved in landscape-painting, and Kent himself in gardening. The activity of the gardener, in manipulating and improving the landscape, was thus given a sanction from nature. I have said before that Claude, because he was understood to be creating ideal landscapes, could not be said to be *imposing* the structure he used on any actual landscape; and we can see how, in the same way, a gardener like Kent would not have thought of himself, either, as imposing an order which, because for him all nature was already an ideal landscape, he must have thought was already inherent in it. He was able to think of himself as copying nature, but only because he saw nature as a copy of his own ideal.

And to a large extent Kent's ideal, like Thomson's, was thought to be derived from Italian landscape-painting. 'He realised the compositions of the greatest masters in painting',[82] said Walpole; and elsewhere, writing of the Earl of Halifax's place at Stanstead, which Kent laid out, he wrote: 'the very extensive lawns at that seat . . . particularly when you stand in the portico of the temple and survey the landskip that wastes itself in rivers of broken sea, recall such exact pictures of Claude Lorrain that it is difficult to conceive that he did not paint them from this very spot'.[83] 'All gardening is landscape-painting', said Pope; 'just like a landscape hung up';[84] and certainly after William Shenstone had designed his garden, at the Leasowes, to be seen as a series of distinct landscape-compositions, there began to develop something of a fashion for composing garden views in a style reminiscent of paintings by Claude or Poussin. The best, and best preserved, example of this fashion is the garden laid out by Henry Hoare, for himself, at Stourhead in Wiltshire, which is thought to be partly based on Claude's *Coast View of Delos with Aeneas*.[85] This method of landscaping inevitably demanded that the pictures thus created be seen from ordained and fixed points of view, connected with each other by walks thickly wooded enough to prevent the pictures being glimpsed from anywhere except the right place: we are reminded of how deliberately the topographical poet, labouring up to his viewpoint, kept his back turned to the landscape beneath him until he reached the summit: for him, as for the landscape-gardener, all nature was a garden, but only when seen from one particular 'station', or point of view. The method also encouraged the careful disposition of contrasted tones in the landscape, by the use of differently coloured vegetation, which created also the illusion of depth in a restricted area; and this practice shows how able the eighteenth-century connoisseur was to separate the impressions he received of a landscape from the reality he knew to exist. Perhaps in no other of the eighteenth-century landscape arts was the landscape kept so carefully remote from the observer, or did it depend so much on his willingness, his anxiety even, to see ideal structures in what he saw.

The movement towards 'nature', towards the illusion of a more natural style of landscape-gardening, was thought to have been further advanced by 'Capability' Brown, whose adopted Christian name – 'I see your park has *great capabilities*', he would say to a prospective customer – suggests that his own attitude to the landscapes he created was much the same as Kent's to his – that he was helping them to realise the order latent in them. Though Joseph Warton decided that he could call him, 'without exaggeration or affectation',[86] a great painter, Brown did not usually create such consciously pictorial landscapes as some of his rivals did, and it became more common to think of him as a great poet, who turned Miss Elizabeth Montagu's garden, for example, at Sandleford, into 'sweet pastorals and gentle elegiacs'.[87] And that he himself thought of his art in terms of some such analogy with writing is shown by Hannah More, who in her memoirs recalls a conversation she had with Brown towards the end of his life:

He illustrates every thing he says about gardening with some literary or grammatical allusion. He told me he compared his art to literary composition. Now there, he said, pointing his finger, I make a comma, and there, pointing to another part (where an interruption is desirable to break the view) a parenthesis – now a full stop, and then I begin another subject.[88]

This passage is very frequently quoted, because it illustrates most remarkably how synthetic was the order which the landscape-gardener imposed upon the ground he improved; and also how the imagery by which he described this order prevented him from seeing how synthetic it was. Some historians of landscape-gardening have seen Brown as applying, even more than other gardeners, a 'cut and dried'[89] system in his work, which the particular nature of each park was not allowed to modify; but this was not the eighteenth-century view of him: 'so closely did he copy nature', said the anonymous writer of an obituary notice of Brown, 'that his work will be mistaken'.[90] We may take it, then, that the analogy by which he appears, from this passage of Hannah More, to have thought of his improvements, would not have been seen as an over-formalistic attitude to nature: he must have been copying, that is, a form, an order, somehow already *there*.

It goes without saying, I take it, that the pauses in a sentence, if they are not completely dictated by the nature of its content, are dictated by it far more than is the content by those pauses. And so Brown, by using the analogy he does, is apparently suggesting that the grammatical order in his landscapes is *not* a synthetic creation, but governed by (something analogous to) the content of a sentence, which is inherent in the landscape and so which he did not put there: the order is not an imposition on the landscape, but arises naturally out of it. Two difficulties appear in this way of looking at landscape-gardening. In the first place, the only thing which can be thought of as analogous to the content of a sentence is, in a landscape-garden, the contours and the objects it *contains*; which Brown somehow organises into a pattern marked out in punctuation. But it is, after all, Brown who is responsible for those contours and objects being admitted into the landscape at all – he himself has refashioned and rearranged them, or at best *allowed* them to remain as they were – and so we must conclude that the content is organised to fit the grammatical order, and that the order does not arise out of the content. Furthermore, if it is, somehow, the *content* of a landscape, something pre-existent in it, which creates the order, we would expect it to be in some sense independent of our own ideas of order – of our habit, particularly, of reading a sentence from left to right across the page. But clearly the grammatical order Brown is describing has to be understood by our looking over the objects in the view in one way only: we do not, after all, understand a sentence properly by reading it backwards.

The art of the landscape-gardener was called by Brown 'place-making',[91] which suggests more unequivocally how synthetic his creations were, that he did not think of his landscapes as places altered or improved, but new-made. It is as if they were somehow not there before his arrival, and the phrase makes it finally clear that his art was not, any more than Lyttelton's and less than

Thomson's, conceived as a response to the particular place he was improving, for all Pope's injunction that he should 'consult the Genius of the place'.[92] As much as Thomson, the gardener took his structure with him into the landscape, whether that structure was, as in the case of Henry Hoare, the traditional Claudian one, or, as with Brown, less directly pictorial, and based on abstract aesthetic notions such as the beauty of the serpentine line. The method of the landscape-gardeners differed from Thomson's only in that, in the first place, nature resisted their desire to improve her, not only by an appeal to the imagination, but also in proportion to the amount of money a landowner was prepared to set aside for the levelling of hills and the diverting of rivers; and that, in the second place, obviously enough, the improvements the gardeners made were not made in the imagination only, but in the actual look and function of the places they took over and made ideal.

x

I want to discuss, as soon as possible, the social and political implications of the attitudes I have been describing in this chapter, but I will need first to say something of the theory of the Picturesque, because it represents, in some ways at least, a very different attitude to landscape, which we will have to take into account. It is arguable that, whereas the attitude to landscape I have so far been concerned with made the individual features of a landscape subordinate to the general composition, the 'picturesque' artist was more concerned with the individual features than with creating a general structure to contain them. He might seem, therefore, to be making more of an attempt to register the particular character of a place, because he was not especially anxious to apply one structure to every scene he painted.

It is true, I think, that at the end of the eighteenth century the picturesque movement did concentrate more on the problem, what makes an *object* picturesque, than on how to create a unified picturesque landscape. The painter most admired by the theorists of the movement was Salvator Rosa, and the virtues they found in him – a roughness of execution, and a preference for irregular and imperfect forms – they noticed especially as they occurred in particular things: a blasted tree, or a decaying bridge. Rosa did not usually paint extended prospects like Claude, but small, enclosed scenes – which were painted, too, by certain seventeenth-century Dutch landscape-painters, whom the picturesque critics also admired. In these enclosed scenes the attention is engaged more – or was, in the eighteenth century – by the texture of individual objects, and by the effect of light upon them, than by the presence of any structure by which every scene could be made into more or less the same unified composition.

William Gilpin, however, who was perhaps the first theorist of the Picturesque, did not seem especially preoccupied with fidelity to the landscape he painted, or to the individual objects within it, in the passage by him already quoted in this chapter (see above, p. 11). He did simplify the structure of Claude: he usually adopted a three-plane technique in his own sketches, and said 'few views, at least few good views, consist of more than a foreground, & 2 distances'.[93] But if we look at his sketches, we will see that in them, even more than in a painting by Claude or by any of his English imitators, the objects in the landscape are represented by very general forms indeed, and that Gilpin's main interest seems to have been, simply, to compose the landscape into planes differentiated by different tonal values. 'It is a breach of the most express picturesque canon', he wrote, 'if the *parts* engage more than the *whole*';[94] and we have already noticed his willingness to manipulate the parts, or to expel them entirely from his composition. He squared this willingness with a reverence for nature in a way not unlike, say, William Kent's: he argued that we are unable to grasp how perfect is nature's order, because we see it only in small parcels at a time.[95] He believed also that 'all objects are best as nature made them. Art cannot mend them'.[96] But nature's best was not always good enough, and Gilpin cheerfully omitted her less perfect objects from the landscapes he chose to sketch.

Perhaps the best example of Gilpin's cavalier treatment of the particular places he sketched is the set of illustrations he made to accompany his *Observations on the River Wye*, which did not at all satisfy his subscribers, because no individual view was recognisable among them.[97] 'I did all I could', explained Gilpin to William Mason, 'to make people believe they were *general ideas*, or *illustrations*, or any thing, but, what they would have them to be, exact portraits.'[98] Because of the omissions and improvements Gilpin

51

made in his sketches, he came to seem a little ridiculous to some critics of the generation after his, as the Picturesque developed into a more naturalistic Romanticism. *The First Tour of Dr Syntax in Search of the Picturesque,*[99] by William Combe, published in 1809, with illustrations by Thomas Rowlandson, was intended as a satire of Gilpin's cavalier practice; and although it soon loses sight of this intention, and develops a narrative not always much to do with the Picturesque, it does include, for example, these pointed lines:

> – and now I'm thinking
> That self-same pond where Grizzle's drinking
> If hither brought 'twould better seem,
> And faith I'll turn it to a stream:
> I'll make this flat a shaggy ridge,
> And o'er the water throw a bridge:
> I'll do as other sketchers do –
> Put any thing into the view;
> And any object recollect,
> To add a grace, and give effect.
> Thus, though from truth I haply err,
> *The scene preserves its character.*
>
> (Canto ii, lines 122–33; original italics)

But among connoisseurs of his own generation it was probably Gilpin's explicitness about the operation he performed on landscape (which he seems to be satirising himself in a passage quoted above, p. 5), and not the simple fact of his performing it at all, which attracted criticism; and it would be a mistake, I think, to conclude from the disappointment with Gilpin's Wye sketches – or from the general demand for 'accurate' topographical painting – that there existed in the late eighteenth century a public which, in asking for 'exact portraits' of views, did really object to seeing the objects in a landscape juggled around, and the 'genius' of the place ignored. Gilpin's customers, and Gainsborough's for example, did not, no doubt, object to the way earlier painters would re-arrange and restructure a landscape; and this was because their way of altering it had become so habitual that it was no longer even noticed. Gilpin and Gainsborough, on the other hand, not only rearranged the landscape in a different way, according, in Gilpin's case, to a modified version of Claude's principles, or, in Gainsborough's, to quite different principles of composition; but in doing so they were quite open about the effect this had on the landscape: Gilpin offered only 'general ideas', and Gainsborough finally refused to do any topographical work at all, but only subjects 'of his own Brain'.[100]

Nevertheless, Gilpin, as I have said, did still hold on to an idea of the importance of composition, however simplified Claude's procedures became in his own sketches; and so too did many of his contemporaries, poets and painters whose work can be described as 'picturesque', and among whom the compositional structures we have been examining lingered on, long after they had ceased to fulfil the strict organisational function they had for Claude, or even for Lyttelton. Picturesque landscape-painting often reveals most interestingly the tension between the old structure and the new taste, and we might take as examples Gainsborough's *Landscape with a Woodcutter Courting a Milkmaid*, and Paul Sandby's *An Ancient Beech Tree* (see Plates 4 and 5). The design of these two paintings is not dissimilar: both use, for the area beyond the foreground, a more or less recognisable version of Claude's structure, including that area of light below the horizon which, in a painting by Claude, ensures that we look in that direction first, across the ground intervening; it must be said that in Gainsborough's picture this light is perhaps intentionally murky. But working against this distant focal point, and right up against us in the immediate foreground, there is in both pictures a gnarled and twisted tree, which dominates the picture and demands our immediate attention. The presence of this tree is not an altogether new feature in the old structure: it has been moved into the centre of the picture from the *coulisse*, the group of trees to left or right of the foreground in a painting by Claude, which served to frame the landscape behind it. The trees in Gainsborough's and Sandby's pictures, however, do not have any function so subservient as, simply, to frame the rest of the landscape: they dominate the landscape, as I have said, and only after we have examined *them* do we move on to look at the more conventionally disposed landscape behind. And, of course, the composition of the distances does become *merely* conventional: we do not look at it at all in the same way, because we cannot look at it in the usual order: the individual features in the landscapes have certainly become more important than the general composition of the landscape.

Generally speaking, the number of poems is small which can be put alongside the (large) number of paintings using this particular development out of the structures of Claude and Thomson; this may be because the poets of the late eighteenth century were discovering other images by which to express fundamentally the same relationship between man and nature as that felt by the picturesque painters. For Gainsborough and for Sandby, the natural landscape seems to have been potentially *more* hostile than it had been for Thomson. In 'Spring', in 'Summer', there is a sense in which we feel the landscape is *allowed* to become more threatening, in proportion as Thomson feels an increase in his own power to control it; the more the objects in the landscape come to demand individual attention, to upset the structure Thomson uses to control them, the more sophisticated and assured Thomson becomes in his handling of the structure. But for Gainsborough, the objects in his landscapes – or the dominant ones, in the foreground – are dominating because they are simply too imposing, too importunate, to be controlled; they demand, as we have seen, immediate, and respectful, attention. Now for Thomson, the landscape was a thing separate from man, in opposition to him; for the picturesque painter, such an image as the foreground tree, in the picture by Gainsborough we discussed, is separate, insofar as he regards it as an image of a natural universe hostile to himself; but it can be felt as in some sense an indirectly 'human' image, too. As well as being grotesque, frightening, it is highly individual in its form; its surface is disfigured by the elements it has had to withstand; it is alone in a landscape it is nevertheless *part* of; and seen in this light the tree is not, or not simply, an image of hostile nature, but of man, individual, isolated *in* nature. And for an analogue in the poetry of the period to these aspects of the image's content, we must look not only to poems of landscape-description, and to, say, Cowper's 'Yardley Oak', but also to the figure of the bard, high on a rock over Conway's flood, in Gray's ode, or to the narrator of his 'Elegy', alone, meditative, melancholy, in the gathering darkness. If the poets could more often represent by a human image what painters usually represented by an image from nature, this was at least partly because it was even harder to make a living in the late eighteenth century as a good poet than as a good painter; and the poet, released from the attempt to live by his work, became by that release both more aware of his isolation, and more free to examine it in forms and images less traditional and less saleable.

Plate 3. Poussin: *Summer* (1661–4)

Plate 4. Gainsborough: *Landscape with a Woodcutter Courting a Milkmaid* (c. 1755)

We do find, however, a treatment of landscape similar to that in those pictures by Gainsborough and Sandby, in a number of picturesque poems in the late eighteenth century; in the sequence of poems by Thomas Gisborne, for example, *Walks in a Forest*,[101] first published in 1794. The poems must be among the worst of their genre, although for a few years after publication they were quite popular, and went through several editions. Gisborne is the subject of an excellent portrait by Joseph Wright of Derby, in the Mellon collection, which shows him sitting on a bench in his woodland parish, holding a folio no doubt of his own picturesque sketches. And his approach to the description of landscape is completely pictorial: more than once in this sequence he describes a scene by explaining how it should be painted. This passage, which I cannot help admiring, is addressed to the 'sons of imitative art':

> Here deign to learn from nature: here, though late,
> Learn the peculiar majesty which crowns
> The forest, when the slowly passing clouds
> Triple preponderance of shadow spread,
> And separate the broad collected lights
> With corresponding gloom; whether, beneath
> These oaks, that o'er the darken'd foreground hang,
> The illumined valley shines, the pasturing deer;
> Or yon recess admits the fronting ray
> Between its dusky barriers; or a gleam,
> Stretch'd o'er the tufted surface of the woods,
> Deepens the blackness of contiguous shade.
>
> (*Walks in a Forest*, 'Autumn', lines 154–65)

This does not require any very full analysis: it is clear enough, I think, that insofar as Gisborne does appear to have a particular scene in view, it is organised very much as say Sandby organised his *Ancient Beech Tree*. The oaks, for example, which still have some of the function of the *coulisse*, and darken the foreground, are now so central to the composition that the landscape appears, not to right or left of them, but beneath their branches. For the most part, however, the attention is on one particular aspect of pictorial organisation, the contrast of lights and surfaces: the only features in the landscape that are described are such as particularly offer that sort of contrast, and the spatial relationships between these various features are not considered. And it may be that they are not even being thought of as part of the same landscape – at least as it appears at one particular time, and so as it can appear in the static image a painter would make of it. Whereas, in the passage we looked at by John Scott, the different clauses beginning *or* were suggesting alternative routes the eye could take through the landscape, in these lines the same construction is apparently referring to the alternative *possible* effects of light, as they might appear in the forest, at one time or another.

William Cowper was not especially involved in the sort of movements we have been looking at in this chapter, and most of his work cannot be usefully discussed in an account of the Picturesque. But his own modification of Thomson's and Claude's structure is not very different from Gisborne's, or, in painting, Gainsborough's, and in this respect at least he can be considered along with them. The first lines of this passage I have already quoted:

> Now roves the eye;
> And, posted on this speculative height,
> Exults in its command. The sheep-fold here
> Pours out its fleecy tenants o'er the glebe.
> At first, progressive as a stream, they seek
> The middle field; but, scatter'd by degrees,
> Each to his choice, soon whiten all the land.
> There from the sun-burnt hay-field, homeward creeps
> The loaded wain; while, lighten'd of its charge,
> The wain that meets it passes swiftly by;
> The boorish driver leaning o'er his team
> Vocif'rous, and impatient of delay . . .
>
> (The Task, book I, lines 288–99)

This is a successful piece of writing, but it does not derive any of its success from the slight borrowings it makes from the procedures of Thomson. It does nothing for the passage to give such a military air to the act of observation, especially as the high viewpoint does not help Cowper to control, or to maintain a unified focus on, what he sees. He is anxious to describe the view more particularly than his remote station will allow, and after a few lines has quite descended, so to speak, into the landscape, to describe a very typically picturesque 'incident' – the driver of one wain shouting at the driver of another to give way. In the next lines, after the passage quoted, Cowper goes on to describe an area of woodland, also part of the landscape, but he gives us no idea of where this woodland is, in relation to the glebe, for example, or the road, and his way of describing the wood is to give, in brief, the characteristics of the different trees he knows it contains, very minutely observed. Then, finally, the valley is said to appear as a map; which once again demands that we imagine ourselves on the high viewpoint we previously seemed to have abandoned. The confusion between a generalising structure, which unifies the landscape, and an interest in the picturesque details of its individual features, is as marked in this passage as in any of Gisborne's descriptions.

Edmund Burke, in his essay on the *Sublime and Beautiful*,[102] had attempted to establish that our aesthetic experience has an objective origin in the properties of things we see, thus, as sublime or beautiful. The characteristics of the Beautiful were, he decided, smoothness, gradual variation, etc., and those of the Sublime, obscurity, vastness, and so on – the theory has been summarised often enough elsewhere. William Gilpin, next, attempted to establish the Picturesque as a third category,[103] of properties which were not, according to Burke's principles, either sublime or beautiful, but which were, nevertheless, more satisfying than some objects in those categories to contemplate in pictures. The attributes of the Picturesque included roughness, irregularity, and so on. It was this aspect of Gilpin's writing that most interested the picturesque theorists of the 1790s, Uvedale Price, especially, and Richard Payne Knight. Price, in his *Essays on the Picturesque* (1794–6), took over the distinction Gilpin had made between the beautiful and the Picturesque, and tried, like Gilpin, to locate the origin of the Picturesque in the visual properties of objects themselves, and not in our subjective experience of them. Knight, on the other hand, did regard the Picturesque as partly a subjective notion: a way of looking at objects, and not a property of the objects themselves. The only visual property an object could be said to have, he thought, was its colour, and the idea of the Picturesque was partly a description of our response to colours variously arranged. But Knight was interested also in the association of ideas the word 'picturesque' itself invited us to make: that a *picturesque* object is one we can relate to others we have seen in *pictures*. The origin of the Picturesque, then, for Knight, was objective insofar as it had to do with the pleasure we derive from colour and light, and subjective insofar as it depended on an association made between actual objects and those represented in pictures. It is not much to the point here to argue the merits of these two theories, though Knight's is clearly the more defensible; but it is worth pointing out that Price's theory, for all its apparent objectivity, in fact depends, as Knight understood,[104] on a theory of association. Roughness, which Price claimed to *see* in things, is in fact an idea acquired from our sense of *touch*; and in *seeing* roughness, Price was in fact associating the idea of roughness with the things he saw.

The style of painting which emerged alongside the development of these theories did away with the 'harmony and continuity',[105] as Hazlitt described it, of Claude's painting, in favour of 'surprise', and 'startling contrast'.[106] A landscape-painting was no longer arranged into a single, over-all structure, but into a number of separate focal points. This did free the objects in it from the patterns that had previously absorbed their identity, and did allow them to be considered individually, for their picturesque qualities. To convey an experience of the particular place he was painting, however, did not now become, any more than before, an important concern of the painter. And for writers, especially, on the Picturesque, the old structure had been chafed away, only to be replaced by a new, and more complex one, of ideas. The ideas were not such as were associated with a particular object – a tree, for example – because they were derived from our previous experience of that tree: they were quite separable from it, they antedated our experience of it, and were anyway the same for all trees. A tree, now, was not seen as conforming to the demands of a pre-existent structure, but as fulfilling a set of 'picturesque rules'.

XI

The attitudes I have been examining in this chapter are characterised, first of all, by a desire to impose an order on landscape, by laying a structure upon it, or by applying to it abstract, general rules; and, secondly, by a willingness to manipulate a view so that it fits the order being imposed upon it. Now, it is important to emphasise again, that these attitudes produced, in those who held them and most notably in Thomson, for example, a remarkable refinement in the way they looked, and saw; but that this was achieved at the expense, somehow, of the objects they were looking at: and this is true even of Thomson, who, as I have suggested, *allowed* the objects to impose themselves on him in the same degree as he felt confident of his ability to impose order on them. It could be said that they saw landscape more purely than it had ever been seen before, in that they learned to separate the abstract vision they had of objects from the intellectual, emotional, historical associations evoked by them – and this is true even of Richard Payne Knight, who, though he was always anxious to make associations between what he saw in nature and what he had seen in pictures, was always very conscious that he was doing this, and of what picture a particular object reminded him. But this way of looking became so refined, and so important to those who employed it, that it became almost their only way of *knowing* the landscapes, if they were actual ones, that they were contemplating. The poets were influenced, in the descriptions they made of places, very little by the accidental knowledge they might happen to have about them, and in particular they had very little sense of what can perhaps be called the 'content' of a landscape–I mean, they gave little evidence of caring that the topography of a landscape was a representation of the needs of the people who had created it. Those who held this attitude to landscape, in short, were able to do so because they were not involved in the landscapes they met with: their eye 'looked over' them, and manipulated the objects in them, simply according to the rules and structures sanctioned by a pure and abstract vision, and without any reference to what the function of those objects might be, what their use might be to the people who lived among them. 'The painter may turn the course of a road, or a river, a few yards on this side, or that . . . he may throw down a cottage' (see above, p. 12): the attitude which approved these imaginary manipulations is precisely that of the improving landowner of Goldsmith's *Deserted Village*, whose new seat 'indignant spurns the cottage from the green';[107] or of Walpole, who wrote that 'an open country' – he is thinking of the country of open fields – 'is but a canvas upon which a landscape might be designed'.[108] Uvedale Price is more willing than most picturesque theorists to take a landscape as he finds it, and speaks of his 'passion for village scenery'; and although he writes at length of how 'a variety of forms and embellishments may be introduced' into a village, at small expense, he hopes that after reading his essay 'those, whom all the affecting images and pathetic touches of Goldsmith would not have restrained from destroying a village, may even be induced to build one'. But Price's passion for villages is in fact inseparable for a desire to improve them; and to improve them is seen exclusively as an opportunity for landed amateurs of the Picturesque 'to show their taste in decoration', and to find in their creations 'sources of amusement and interest'.[109]

As a result of these attitudes, over every actual place and landscape was laid a 'made' place, a synthetic landscape: a good example of what this meant occurs in Richard Graves's satirical novel, *Columella*,[110] which is largely concerned with fashions in landscape-gardening. Columella is showing two friends round his park, when a servant approaches to say that some heifers have got into a new plantation at the bottom of *Aaron's Well*. ' "Aaron's Well! you blockhead," says Columella, "Arno's Vale, you mean." "Nay, nay," quoth Peter, "I know the right name of it is Tadpole Bottom." '[111] It is true, on the other hand, that we often find in the literature of landscape-gardening an injunction to 'consult the Genius of the place': but that very personification suggests the degree to which an alien structure, of aesthetic form, of classical association, is imposed on a place even before its individuality is consulted. And, in Pope's poem, the 'genius' of the place is curiously malleable, and willing to realise its own nature by altering it: first by seeing a hill as, conveniently enough, 'ambitious', and then by helping it to scale the heaven.[112] The agriculturalist William Marshall, in his writings on 'rural ornament', is emphatic in defence of 'the nature of the place', which is, he says, 'sacred':[113] 'do not sacrifice its native beauties to the arbitrary laws of landscape painting'.[114] But then, and apparently to add weight to this injunction, he quotes these lines by Mason –

> Great Nature scorns controul; she will not bear
> One beauty foreign to the spot or soil
> She gives thee to adorn: 'Tis thine alone
> To mend, not change her features.[115]

– where the attitudes to nature, and to place, are ambiguous in everything but the assurance that the features of 'Great Nature' are in need of repair.

The desire to manipulate land and improve nature revealed itself not only in the arts, but also of course in the conduct of agriculture, and in that process of improvement sometimes called the 'Agricultural Revolution' – which, as economic historians of the period now generally recognise, was only marginally the creation of seed-drills and of threshing-machines, and far more the result of improvements in the use and management of land. And I think it is possible to make a connection between the attitudes to land I have so far been describing, and the attitudes to it which emerge as part of the Agricultural Revolution. Now it is true that, at the beginning of the century, many writers and especially many poets were either themselves members of the aristocracy, or were the protégés of aristocratic patrons. As the century progressed, however, and patronage made itself increasingly less available, landscape-poetry, insofar as it had a public outside the literary élite of London and the universities, was probably as much read by what I hope to establish in my next chapter as the 'rural professional class' – of surveyors, for example, and of literate tenant-farmers, among whom the majority of agricultural improvers were to be found – as by the aristocracy and gentry. The agricultural literature of the period is full of references to rural poetry: Thomas Ruggles, a contributor to the *Annals of Agriculture*, can quote Pope, Gray, Thomson, Mason, and Shenstone, and Arthur Young can refer to Shenstone and Thomson, as well as to a number of rural poems whose authors he does not name. This public, however much it wanted to see in landscape-art an image of the Golden Age, understood well enough that this was not the image of nature unimproved; that in art, just as much as in agriculture, the landscapes of Paradise and the Campagna were the product of an ability to control and to manipulate nature, to make its energies benefit mankind, or at least repay investment. There was an almost universal tendency among landscape-poets – until the growth of the picturesque school – to evaluate the beauty of a landscape partly in terms of the expectation it aroused of a good harvest: the description of the view from Shene, for example, is concluded by Thomson with these lines –

> O vale of bliss! O softly-swelling hills!
> On which the power of cultivation lies,
> And joys to see the wonders of his toil...
> (*The Seasons*, 'Summer', lines 1435–7)

– in which 'cultivation' can clearly be taken to refer both to the air of refinement given to the view by the presence of so many large houses, and to the excellent agricultural condition of the landscape. Beyond question the habit of identifying beauty with 'utility' must have been one the poets shared with the majority of their readers.

The theorists of the Picturesque and of the Sublime, of course, explicitly refuse any connection between their own attitudes to landscape and those of the agricultural 'improvers': the movement of interest away from the landscape of the Campagna, and towards a more barren, and a wilder landscape, of heath, forest, and mountain, is a movement from that which appears to invite cultivation, to that which resists it. But the connection persists here, too, in some sense, in spite of the picturesque theorists, and of those agriculturalists as well who discovered a taste for the Picturesque, and who, as we shall see in the next chapter, found it impossible to reconcile with their agricultural interests. What is uncultivated is uncivilised – that is its attraction – and thus also mysterious; but just as a progressive farmer can enclose a tract of heath or moorland, and cultivate it, so the picturesque traveller can appropriate and thus destroy in the places he visits precisely what attracts him to them, the sense that they are mysterious and unknowable: and he does this not only by putting the places he visits on the map, whether literally or in some other sense, but also because the only way he can know a landscape as picturesque is by applying to it a set of 'picturesque rules', as it were categories of perception without which any knowledge of the landscape would be impossible for him. Thus William Mason, in the lines quoted a page or so back, can say at once that 'Great Nature scorns controul', and that her features need mending. For the amateur of the Picturesque and of the Sublime, all horrors become congenial: although he purports to wish for an image of landscape as mysterious, he does so in such a way as to demand that it give up its mystery to him; and his taste finally reveals as Thomson's does a prior need, and a stronger one, to know the landscape by manipulating it into a more or less arbitrary structure by which it can be known.

XII

I want, in the next chapter, to look at the attitudes to land and landscape of the rural professional class, referred to above, whose interest in the land was not primarily aesthetic; but by way of a preparation for that discussion, and as an epilogue to this one, I would like to make one final point about the attitudes we have been examining so far. It is, that these attitudes were the property of a very few social groups, in fact of those classes whose members had this among other things in common, that they were able to move about the country, from place to place, if only over distances of twenty or thirty miles. This mobility is an essential condition of the attitude we have been examining: it meant that the aristocracy and gentry were not, unlike the majority of the rural population, irrevocably involved, so to speak, bound up in, any particular locality which they had no time, no money, and no reason ever to leave. It meant also that they had experience of more landscapes than one, in more geographical regions than one; and even if they did not travel much, they were accustomed, by their culture, to the *notion* of mobility, and could easily imagine other landscapes. In his *Natural History of Northamptonshire*, published in 1712, John Morton writes (p. 19): 'to have an agreeable *Landschape* I wou'd wish...' – and that simple possibility of choice, let alone the inclination to exercise it, was beyond the reach, in the eighteenth century, of all but a relatively small number of people. The emphasis on movement, from place to place, as a condition for the nurture of this attitude, is there for example in the sort of 'picturesque tour' made by William Gilpin, 'to criticise the face of a country correctly'.[116] Of the landscape of the Wye Valley Gilpin wrote, that he did not *prefer* it to the lakes, but it was 'more ornamented, and more finished; and more correct'.[117] The very idea of comparing one landscape – one place – with another, quite apart from the knowledge of the principles by which the comparison might be made, was the property only of the aristocracy, the gentry, and some members of the professions. And the habit, of thus comparing landscapes, with each other and with the 'ideal', was certainly, as Wordsworth argued in a passage of *The Prelude* which we shall examine in a later chapter, a way of obscuring 'the spirit of the place';[118] though whether what Wordsworth called the 'spirit' of a place was a very different thing from its 'genius', we shall, as I say, examine later.

2. The landscape of agricultural improvement

I

I want to discuss in this chapter some of the attitudes to land which it seems to me were fairly generally shared, in the last few decades of the eighteenth century, and the first one or two of the nineteenth, by those most interested in agricultural improvement – by the writers among them, in the first place, but also by what I have provisionally called the 'rural professional class'. To use the words 'class', 'group', and the rest of nomenclature of social classification, is now beyond the competence of the uninitiated, and so perhaps I should say at the outset that it is no part of my intention to argue that the members of the rural professions – among whom I include a certain type of tenant-farmer, as well as surveyors, for example, and land-agents – composed an identifiable group with anything more in common than that they were all members of those professions; and that, for the most part, they shared with each other, as I hope to establish, a progressive attitude to agriculture, and a particular set of attitudes to land which they probably did not share to the same extent with most of the rest of English society at the time.

A great deal of the material of this chapter, by which I hope to identify the attitudes to land which I think were generally shared by members of the different rural professions, will be taken from the two series of reports, *General Views*,[1] on the agriculture of the various counties of England and Wales, submitted to the Board of Agriculture, a semi-official body founded by Sir John Sinclair in 1793. Now it is often argued by economic historians that the *General Views*, which often themselves proceed from widely different assumptions, and put forward widely different ideas, are the productions of men so ignorant in rural affairs, that they are precisely *not* representative of any large group or class beyond the

64

reporters themselves; and whether or not this is so, it is obvious that a body of literature, however much it might be said to represent the 'consciousness' of a particular group, is bound in certain ways to be unrepresentative of it – it is not, after all, any part of the ordinary duty of a surveyor or tenant-farmer to write articles for agricultural periodicals. With regard to these reports, Rosalind Mitchison remarks that 'Sinclair's hope that "intelligent farmers" would be found to do the work was on the whole optimistic. Intelligent and successful farmers would, in most cases, prefer to get on with their farming.'[2] I want to suggest, however, that the attitudes I am concerned with, and which reveal themselves in these reports, can be said to be representative in some way or another of the attitudes to land of the 'rural professional class', and that these attitudes realise themselves in what was, finally, a creation of that class, the landscape of parliamentary enclosure, in the same way as the aesthetic notions of the aristocracy were realised in their ornamental parks and gardens.

There is a myth about the Agricultural Revolution of the second half of the eighteenth century, that its leaders were enthusiastic dukes and earls, and that it was they who sowed the experimental acres of swede and sainfoin, weighed and compared the crops, and wrote up their findings. To some extent this myth is the result of the improvers' own desire to establish themselves around aristocratic figureheads: of the thirty-one founder-members of the Board of Agriculture, for example, fourteen were titled, but this high representation of the peerage, which certainly gave the Board a very respectable appearance, was also perhaps one reason why it became so ineffectual. Arthur Young, the first secretary of the Board, had no high opinion of the practical farming knowledge of these fourteen members in particular, or of that of the aristocracy in general.[3] It is true that there were peers interested in the practical side of agriculture, peers for whom improvement did not just mean an increase in the rentable value of the land they owned. There were such men, Townshend for example, and the Duke of Bedford, but the peerage as a whole was not thought of at the time as making any especially significant contribution to the progress of agriculture. Young, William Marshall and others all complained of the indifference of the aristocracy to agriculture; and in particular Young, though he was anxious at all times to record the improvements of forward-looking landowners, did not often find a peer to praise. The main concern of the great land-owners was, as I have suggested, with the revenue they derived from their estates: with ways to increase rents and to save costs in more efficient management; and precisely how these aims were achieved was of secondary importance.[4]

The vast majority of experimentalists in agriculture would be members not of the metropolitan Board, but only of local agricultural societies, and they were to be found among the bigger tenant-farmers and the more substantial owner-occupiers. This was the opinion of most late eighteenth-century writers on agriculture: Adam Smith thought that the great proprietors were 'seldom great improvers';[5] 'the best of all improvers' were men accustomed to handling money, the new bourgeoisie of the countryside. William Marshall found such men mostly concentrated in the Midlands,[6] and noted about them their willingness to go out and look for new ideas, to go out and meet, so to speak, the new techniques as they spread across the country, and not to await their arrival.[7] It was from among this new order of professional farmers, and from among the rural professional class as a whole, that the writers emerged who were responsible for virtually all the agricultural literature produced between about 1750 and 1820, including the *General Views* of the Board. It was chiefly through its publications that the Board made itself known; and so, insofar as the reporters were qualified for the tasks they undertook, the Board did come to represent the various opinions and interests of those who, though properly progressive in their attitudes to agriculture, were not represented among its members.

I do want, however, to avoid giving the impression that the agricultural writers were generally in agreement in the ideas they put forward. They all do share, of course, a general commitment to a progressive agriculture, but beyond that they do not share a great deal. The writers of the *General Views*, for example, are divided more evenly among the various rural professions than are, say, the contributors – most of them tenant-farmers – to the *Annals of Agriculture*, a periodical started by Arthur Young in 1784.[8] We can get a sense of what sort of differences of interest existed between writers from different rural professions from this criticism by William Marshall of Thomas Stone, the author of the first *General View* of Lincolnshire,[9] and a land-surveyor:

on...the APPROPRIATION of TERRITORY, he appears to have had considerable experience: and, on the GENERAL MANAGEMENT of LANDED PROPERTY, he, in the nature of his profession, possesses considerable information. But, out of his profession, we can seldom follow Mr Stone, with safety. He possesses, it is true, that sort of *general* knowledge of AGRICULTURE which men of his profession necessarily imbibe; and who are naturally led by it to consider the *improvements* of which an Estate is capable, rather than to study, in detail, the *business of practical husbandry.*[10]

For the purposes of this study, however, I am more interested in what these different sets of authors have in common than in what separates them; but it is important to note the divisions among them, because in other contexts they do become important, and because I do want to make it clear who it is I am writing about when I write of the rural professional class, and what separations that label might conceal.

Claudio Veliz, in an unpublished Ph.D. thesis,[11] has argued that the contributors of articles to the *Annals of Agriculture* represent what can be called the Farming Interest; a group composed for the most part of practical farmers, who lived on the land and derived all or most of their income from it, and who found themselves to a degree in opposition to the Landed Interest, of large, and principally titled, landowners – for reasons suggested earlier. The members of the Farming Interest might own their land, or lease it, and in either case their average holding would be between 200 and 800 acres; they were reformist in politics, and mainly because they saw that the obstacles to agricultural improvement were largely institutional – they wanted, for example, the commutation of tithes, and a greater freedom to enclose; they were literate, and willing to experiment in agriculture; and, although fairly prosperous, they lived thriftily, and conducted business with careful efficiency. Dr Jones, a contemporary writer quoted by Veliz, also gives an account of the characteristics of a member of the Farming Interest: he is, said Jones, a farmer engaged every day of the year in farming; a tenant, who managed his farm himself, without a bailiff or other delegate; he paid an adequate rent – low rents gave no incentive to improvement; and, finally, he did not perform manual labour himself, though quite capable of doing so. That Jones could describe a member of the Farming Interest so precisely does suggest that those who belonged to it were very conscious of themselves as composing a group, with a very specific identity.[12]

The Farming Interest was not, Veliz estimates, especially large at the end of the eighteenth century, though he guesses that some 3,000 could be said to belong to it; which, if they were concentrated mainly in England, averages out at about sixty or seventy literate and progressive farmers in each county – I should have thought a fairly substantial number. It was, anyway, certainly growing, and widely dispersed throughout the country; and though quite unable to influence government policy – unable indeed to persuade the Government to have a policy towards agriculture – it must have been fairly influential at a local level. Before 1775, for example, there were only two agricultural societies in England; between 1775 and 1800 another sixty were formed throughout the British Isles. Nearly all these societies subscribed to and published their own transactions in the *Annals of Agriculture*. In the first twenty-five volumes of the *Annals* are articles by 316 different authors; and of those who contributed five or more articles, two-thirds were farmers living full-time on their land. And it is most important to emphasise the literacy of the Farming Interest, which indeed extended a long way beyond the ability to write and to understand accounts of experimental farming. Those who write, write well, and many show themselves familiar with the Greek and Latin, as well as with the English, classical authors.

A great deal of what Veliz says about the contributors to the *Annals* is no doubt also true of most of the reporters for the Board of Agriculture, who have on the whole similar political interests, at least as far as agriculture is concerned, and a similar ability to write. But the reporters were not – as the passage quoted earlier from Rosalind Mitchison suggested – predominantly drawn from the ranks of the professional farmers, though they were drawn almost exclusively from the rural professional class considered as a whole. Of 57 reporters, 15 were or had been farmers, 9 were surveyors, 6 were agents, 5 'agriculturalists' – writers on agriculture who had usually farmed themselves; another 5 were parsons, 1 was a valuer, and there were a few others mostly of unknown profession.[13] The qualifications of many of them as agricultural reporters were often disputed; and even Arthur Young in his autobiography complains that many of the reporters scarcely knew the right end of a plough.[14] William Marshall claimed that almost all of them were deficient in practical experience, scientific knowledge, and familiarity with the region they were describing – all of which he regarded as indispensable qualifications for a reporter; he did not think, on the other hand, that the writing of the reports should have been entrusted instead to practical farmers: if a man can write well, argued Marshall, that is a strong reason to believe he cannot farm.[15]

In the literary activity of the agricultural improvers the divisions between them become particularly salient; and it is clear that a tenant-farmer living on his farm, and writing a short report of an experiment for the *Annals of Agriculture,* is in a very different situation from a surveyor, for example, with time to travel over an entire county, and write a 400-page report on what he sees. But as I have said, more important for our purposes is what the various agricultural writers of the time can be said to have in common, whatever the precise degree of their knowledge in the subjects they undertook to discuss; and the reporters do share with the contributors to the *Annals* a commitment to a progressive, efficient, and experimental agriculture in general, and in particular a set of attitudes to land, which we will begin to examine in the next section. If I have chosen to draw more of my material from the *General Views* than from the *Annals,* which are represented mainly by Arthur Young's contributions, this is because the *General Views* were the production of a wider selection of writers from the rural professions, and because, by their very nature, they suggest their writers' attitudes to the land more explicitly than do accounts of experiments with new crops and new rotations.

It is quickly apparent to anyone who reads the literature of the period which is concerned with agriculture, or any of the local country newspapers which grew in number and in circulation so remarkably from 1750 or so onwards (see below, p. 85), that there must have been, from about 1750 at least until 1815, a considerable increase in the numbers of those engaged in the rural professions, although it is of course impossible to give a reliable estimate of the amount of the increase. As I said earlier, I do not want to suggest that the various members of these professions made up an identifiable class, in a sense a sociologist would accept; although groups within it, such as the literate and progressive tenantry, did clearly feel themselves to have some corporate identity. It would certainly be dangerous to add together the various rural professions – quantity-surveyor, land-agent, tenant-farmer, solicitor specialising in rural affairs, and others – and to regard the sum of them as one 'professional class', in any wider sense than the one I have prescribed. Those engaged in the rural professions were divided by the specific nature of their occupations, of course, and also for example by where they lived.[16] A tenant-farmer would live on the land he farmed; a land-agent on the estate he managed, or in a market-town in the area of that estate, and he might be responsible for industrial and other non-agricultural undertakings of his employer; what we now call an estate-agent might live in a market-town, or in a large manufacturing city, from which professional services were offered to the country round, and where he might be involved in industrial and mercantile, as well as agricultural transactions. There are examples of valuers, again, whose offices are in London, but who travel out frequently to undertake extensive commissions in the country:[17] any very wide community of interest among professional men in such different situations would be very hard to establish. But it is certain that most of them did share, with each other and with the agricultural writers we have been discussing, a commitment to a progressive agriculture. They of all the groups in eighteenth-century rural England had probably the least at risk in the Agricultural Revolution – though this may not have been true of tenant-farmers – and certainly they had a good deal to gain by it: in the improvement of agricultural land their skills were indispensable. They must have understood that their own fortunes were dependent on an increasing productivity in farming; they were literate; and they could see the economy of their own region as part of the wider, national agricultural economy.

It is, as I have said, impossible to estimate by how much the rural professional class increased in size between 1750 and 1815, but if we think of the growth of this class in terms of one of the, so to speak, group activities its members undertook together, one which is particularly 'progressive' in its tendency, the enclosure of open-field land by Act of Parliament – and the number of such enclosures increased steadily during the time we are discussing – we will have an idea of one way in which the Agricultural Revolution transformed the social as well as the topographical map of rural England. An enclosure required, first of all, the services of lawyers to draw up the enclosure-bill; of paid enclosure-commissioners, to supervise the whole business of putting the act into execution and redistributing the land;[18] of solicitors to draw up the claims of those whose land was to be enclosed, and who could afford the services of a solicitor; of quantity-surveyors, to mark

Plate 5. Sandby: *An Ancient Beech Tree* (1794)

Plate 6. From *L'Encyclopédie* (Planches, vol. i, Paris, 1762):
Agriculture, Labourage

out the course of new roads, and to measure out the new allotments of land; and of auditors, to check through the commissioners'
accounts of the expenses of the enclosure. Also involved in most
enclosures were surveyors or valuers to adjust on behalf of landlords the rents of newly-enclosed and integrated farms; the land-
agent of the local large estate, if there happened to be one in the
area; and estate-agents, to negotiate sales of land – an occasional
local effect of enclosure was to make the market in land a good
deal more fluid than normally it was. It is worth pointing out,
however, that a number of the occupations I have listed here as
included among the rural professions might all be performed by
one man. A man who called himself, say, a quantity-surveyor,
might act as a valuer, an estate-agent, broker, enclosure-commissioner and other things besides; and the often long-drawn-out
nature of business transactions in the country – an enclosure might
take years to complete[19] – together with the growing facility of
travel in the period, made it possible for such a man to take on
numerous commissions at once,[20] in any of his different capacities,
and to offer his services in an area much larger than that of his
own county.

The determination of large landowners who had invested in
enclosure – an enormously costly process – to see a quick return
on the capital thus invested, helped also to create a new order of
tenant-farmers, literate, experimental, and business-men enough
to survive the rack-renting system and establish themselves in
rural society as men of some consequence, if not – in that they did
not own the land they farmed – on a footing with the gentry. The
tenantry, indeed, became increasingly important after 1760,
during the fifty years of high prices and profitable farming before
the slump of 1813; the increasing sophistication of tenant-farmers
was frequently noticed by poets of rural life, and a number of
riculturalists were quick to relate it to the effect of enclosures, and
improvements they encouraged in farming techniques and
management. Arthur Young, in his report to the Board of
ulture on farming in Oxfordshire (1809), writes: 'If you go
Banbury-market next Thursday you may distinguish the
rs from enclosures from those from open-fields; quite a
nt sort of men; the farmers are as much changed as their
dry – quite new men, in point of knowledge and ideas.'[21]
herwise bitter review of this report, William Marshall, the

other great agricultural writer of the period, quotes this remark without apparent disapproval.[22] To include the more sophisticated and progressive of the tenantry in what I have called the 'rural professional class' is not, I think, as arbitrary as it might seem: a good deal of the writing on agriculture produced during the period was anxious to suggest that to take up farming was, for a literate man with modest capital, to take up a profession; and the 'professional farmer' was so-called to distinguish him from the semi-literate tenant, and from the mere yeoman, as well as from the gentleman who took an intelligent interest in the management of his estates, and with whom the professional farmer no doubt felt more affinity.

The increase in the size and influence of the rural professional class, and in the sophistication of its members, was very directly related, in those areas of England where enclosure was widespread, to the growth of the enclosure movement; and there and elsewhere to the generally increasing emphasis on the proper management of land. The rural professional class, if not exactly a creation of the Agricultural Revolution, was inevitably on the side of agricultural improvement; and in this sense the agricultural writers of the period, themselves almost all drawn from among the rural professions, can be said to be representative of the members of those professions taken together; who could express in concrete form, in the landscape of parliamentary enclosure, those attitudes to land which the agriculturalists expressed in their writings.

II

The writers of the *General Views* were not primarily interested in land as land-*scape*, and it is not their aesthetic attitudes to land which are most important to us in this study. These attitudes are worth examining, nevertheless: the reporters do often give descriptions of the landscape of the counties they are surveying, and sometimes show themselves to be acquainted with the convention language and procedures of eighteenth-century landscape-descrption; and they do seem anxious to relate the aesthetic respons landscape evokes in them, to their more practical interest in improvement of agricultural land. The *General Views* bega appear in 1793, by which time the theories of the Sublime and of the Picturesque were becoming more generally understood; and the reporters can be divided into those still innocent of the new aesthetic theories, and those who know themselves to be corrupted by them – the word is not too strong.

For many of those who had managed to keep themselves ignorant of new tastes and styles, the problem of relating their aesthetic and their practical interests was of course no problem at all: a beautiful landscape was, for them, a *paysage riant*, a landscape carrying with it associations of productivity and opulence. This solution, if it can be called that, was one of course proposed by the majority of writers on land until say 1780, and poets among them. *The Seasons*, which did not for the eighteenth-century reader reveal a nature as hard to dominate as it does for me, was clearly very popular among agricultural writers, who often quoted passages in it descriptive of this or that branch of agriculture, as they did also passages from Dyer. Typical enough of the tendency to equate beauty with utility are these lines by John Langhorne:

> What pleasing scenes the landscape wide displays!
> The 'enchanting prospect bids for ever gaze...
> To social towns, see! wealthy Commerce brings
> Rejoicing Affluence on his silver wings.
> On verdant hills, see! flocks innumerous feed,
> Or thoughtful listen to the lively reed.
> See! golden harvests sweep the bending plains;
> 'And Peace and Plenty own a Brunswick reigns.'
> ('Studley Park', lines 83–4, 91–6)[23]

John Langhorne is a much under-read poet, and a witty one, as his idea of flocks as 'thoughtful' suggests; and in particular here the reference to Pope's *Windsor Forest*[24] – Langhorne is fond of thus quoting, and turning the quotation against its author – reminds us that Pope more eloquently than anyone proposed the equation of beauty with utility,[25] a fact not unrelated to the dislike the picturesque critics began to conceive for him.[26]

Naturally enough, the reporters to the Board of Agriculture often accept the equation of beauty with utility, though with more or less idea of the difficulties it involved. Perhaps the most straightforward example of this acceptance is to be found in this passage, by James Donaldson, the author of the first *General View* of Northamptonshire:

The surface of this county is as peculiarly advantageous for cultivation, as it is delightful and ornamental. In no other part of the kingdom, perhaps, are more agreeable and extensive landscapes to be seen. Here, there are no dreary wastes, nor rugged and unsightly mountains to offend the eye, or to intercept the view. The surface is nowhere so irregular, but it can be applied to every purpose of husbandry and tillage. Every hill is cultivated, or may be kept in a profitable state of pasturage, and every inequality in the surface contributes to its ornament and beauty.

The upper and middle parts of this county are richly ornamented with extensive woods, which are intersected with numerous vistas and beautiful lawns. The various avenues of trees, extending in many parts for miles together, the rivers and streams winding along the vales, and answering the necessary purposes of machinery, agriculture, and trade...present a prospect beautifully diversified and highly picturesque, and which cannot fail to delight the eye, and enliven the heart of every spectator.[27]

This must have seemed at the time it was written an old-fashioned piece of description, and indeed its most obviously anti-sublime sentence – the one about 'unsightly mountains' – is taken over almost verbatim but without acknowledgement from John Morton's *Natural History* of the county, published over eighty years earlier.[28] Donaldson still thinks in terms of a Renaissance perspective, of straight lines to the horizon: there are no mountains to 'intercept' the view; and his idea of an ornamental landscape is still based on Le Nôtre's, of woods 'intersected' with avenues and vistas. Donaldson was, in point of fact, a surveyor, and thus no doubt more acquainted with the straight lines of the theodolite than with the 'circling landscape' as it appeared in a Claude-glass. There is no need to point out, perhaps, in a passage which has so little to conceal, the presence in it of the equation we are considering: it is obvious, for example, that 'every inequality' in the surface is acknowledged to be beautiful precisely because it is not so irregular as to prevent its being ploughed. It is true that a sort of distinction between the beautiful and the useful is proposed, obliquely enough, in the first sentence; and again in the last, where it is what is beautiful that 'delights the eye', and the thought of what is useful that 'enlivens the heart'; but it is a frequent technique of writers such as Donaldson – and a particularly useful one, when for instance they are describing the landscape of parliamentary enclosure – to start off as if beauty were one thing, and utility another, and then to discover with some delight that in the particular landscape they are considering no such separation has to be made. This involves a complete ignorance or a complete rejection of the

Picturesque: the word 'picturesque' in this passage by Donaldson is not used in its specialised sense at all, but in the old-fashioned way, to indicate that to think of a landscape as beautiful is to think of it as a picture.

It is particularly when they write of the differences between open and enclosed country that writers on agriculture are most willing to identify a beautiful landscape with one which is well-farmed. William Cobbett, who can be thought of as, in some respects, a representative of the Farming Interest, repeatedly makes this observation, and writes, for example, of 'those very ugly things, common-fields';[29] and then riding out of Royston, remarks: 'The fields on the left seem to have been enclosed by act of parliament; and they certainly are the most beautiful tract of *fields* that I ever saw.'[30] In the same spirit Arthur Young commends the beauty of a quickset hedge, which turns out to be the same as its impenetrability: it is beautiful because it will not let wind into the field, or cattle out.[31] And those agricultural writers who are aware of the structures Claude, for example, applied to landscape, sometimes suggest that open fields are unaesthetic because they do not allow themselves to be properly composed into a pictorial landscape. We saw in the last chapter (see above, p. 32) how the Rev. James Tyley, author of a Latin poem on the enclosure of Raunds, in Northamptonshire, complained that such fields, stretching to the horizon without division, 'strained and tortured the sight'.[32] Arthur Young, riding near Orleans on the first of his French tours, makes the same charge though less dramatically: 'One universal flat, unenclosed, uninteresting, and even tedious, though small towns and villages are everywhere in sight; the features that might compound a landscape are not brought together.'[33] Thomas Batchelor, author of the second *General View* of Bedfordshire,[34] can write in his poem, 'The Progress of Agriculture' (my italics):

> But, Industry, thy unremitting hand
> Has chang'd the *formless* aspect of the land...
> And hawthorn fences, stretch'd from side to side,
> Contiguous pastures, meadows, fields divide.[35]

Of the reporters to the Board, perhaps only William Pitt, who wrote the second *General View* of Northamptonshire,[36] can occasionally allow the sight of open fields into his idea of what can be called beautiful: '*even* the open common fields...' (my italics), he writes, 'increase the variety and add to the general appearance of beauty and fertility'.[37] The argument is that the fields, because they add to the variety of the landscape, must add to its beauty; and because they add to its beauty, they must add to the impression it gives of fertility.

The rather transparent attempt William Pitt has made is to unite his practical interests with an idea of beauty which is dependent not on an association, whether conscious or not, of beauty with utility, but on a specifically abstract aesthetic. One or two of the other writers of the *General Views* can be seen making the same attempt: W. T. Pomeroy, the first reporter on Worcestershire,[38] is first careful to point out that, in that county, 'there are no tracts . . . so barren . . . as to be without an agreeable, and profitable verdure';[39] and then continues:

On a nearer view, from the central hill, which rises more particularly to the east of [Worcester], a most beautiful landscape presents itself: the whole of the background...appears to be one continuation of noble hills; forming, as it were, the frame of the delightful picture that presents itself in the centre, diversified with all the beauties of hill and dale, wood and water. If the Aberley and Whitley hills occasion some irregularity in the frame, they will scarcely be thought to take off from the beauty of the piece; these, and the adjoining hills, rising with a bold front, and most of them cultivated to their summits, recall to the mind the enthusiastic description of Italy; and the sheep, hanging as it were, from the brows of others, illustrate the much-admired idea of the Roman bard.[40]

The nearest we approach in this passage to an idea of beauty as utility is the reference to hills 'cultivated to their summits', which itself brings with it an aesthetic association, of the landscape of Italy. But for the most part, it's clear that Pomeroy is making here a for him quite unproblematic separation of the ideas of beauty and utility. The landscape is not for him beautiful, as it might have been for Pope early in his career, simply because it is well-cultivated: Pomeroy's aesthetics are more abstract than that, and although it cannot be asserted that he is consciously attempting here to describe a landscape in the manner of Claude, it is clear that it is in terms of the sort of structure that we examined in the first chapter that he considers the Aberley and Whitley Hills, the bounds of the landscape, 'occasion some irregularity' in the frame of the picture. On the other hand we hardly feel any strong connection here, as we do in Thomson, between the idea of cultivating a landscape and the idea of describing – that is to say, composing and controlling – it. That sense we do get more from this passage by Thomas Ruggles, the author of a series of letters on picturesque farming,[41] and, by virtue of the degree of interest he takes in aesthetic matters, a particularly unrepresentative member of the class whose attitudes we are examining. This is Ruggles's description of the view from Hagley,

> where the beauty of the landscape strongly calls the mind to reflect on the goodness of him who created such enchanting objects of vision, as at once, from an inclosed and thickly-wooded fore-ground, where all that the eye can enjoy, commanding a range of highly-cultivated country, interspersed with a vast variety of objects, closed at an immense distance by the Welsh mountains bursts on the view...[42]

The syntax of this preserves, with deliberate artifice, that of Thomson's original: and the enjoyment Ruggles's 'eye' derives from looking over enclosures and highly-cultivated country is clearly related to the pleasure it takes in organising the landscape as a whole.

Not many agricultural writers achieve, as Pomeroy does, a separation of the aesthetic and the practical so complete as to allow them to describe landscape in so consciously *pictorial* a manner. Arthur Young, for example, who was a connoisseur of landscape and an admirer of Claude, could never manage to describe an agricultural landscape without remarking on the nature of the soil, the quality of the crops, and the likely condition of those who worked the land. It was only when describing a land-scape-garden that he was able to adopt the manner of Claude, in this passage for example, an account of Lord Belvidere's place near Mullinger, in Ireland:

> It is one of the most singular places that is any where to be seen, and spreading to the eye a beautiful lawn of undulating ground margined with wood. Single trees are scattered in some places, and clumps in others; the general effect is so pleasing, that were there nothing further, the place would be beautiful, but the canvas is admirably filled. Lake Ennel, many miles in length, and two or three broad, flows beneath the windows. It is spotted with islets, a promontory of rock fringed with trees shoots into it, and the whole is bounded by distant hills.[43]

It is particularly easy, of course, to discover a composed land-scape in a landscape-garden; but Young does a lot of the work of organisation himself, and understands the landscape outside the park as part of 'the canvas'; so that it isn't any lack of aesthetic know-how that prevents him from adopting the structures of

Claude when describing a prospect of cultivated land. And that he never does describe a cultivated landscape as a composition tells us a good deal about his attitudes to matters of taste in general, and to landscape-gardening in particular, of which he was very fond. For Young, a garden was a tract of land by definition not useful, given over to beauty at the expense of utility: the only way in which it could be said to express the idea of utility was, that for it to exist at all argued a certain prosperity in the country round. And so it was only in a landscape-garden that he was able openly to acknowledge the separateness of what he did in fact feel to be antipathetic notions, of beauty and utility, and to indulge without any sense of guilt his admiration of abstract beauty – and that he did feel guilty about this admiration I hope to show in the next section. William Cobbett, on the other hand, is quite able to see in a garden, no less than in an agricultural landscape, 'utility and convenience combined with beauty',[44] and William Marshall, almost a functionalist among experts on landscaping, argues that an expanse of grass before a house is more *useful* if not too cluttered with trees:[45] a pleasantly naive idea to be advanced by a man so downright and practical as Marshall, who could not see that (as Christopher Hussey points out in another context)[46] a lawn which, though it reminded you of a pasture, was not in fact employed as one, was not thereby more useful than a picturesque garden of the type Payne Knight approved, where weeds as well as trees flourished and were encouraged.[47]

III

There were a good number of agricultural writers who were aware of the theories of the Sublime and the Picturesque – which, insofar as for the purposes of this chapter they may be said to represent the same taste, for uncultivated landscape, I shall from now on refer to by the one term, *Picturesque*. And those writers who were thus aware did of course find it a great deal harder to accommodate their aesthetic interests to their attitudes as practical agriculturalists, and it is not too much to say that as agriculturalists they felt themselves to be corrupted by the Picturesque. As we saw in Chapter 1 (see p. 62), the movement of taste away from the landscape of Claude, the *paysage riant*, and towards the landscape of forests and mountains, was a movement from that which can be cultivated, to that which resists cultivation. William Gilpin was quite explicit that this was so, and when he imagined himself as arguing with those who did equate beauty with utility, would use their own language metaphorically, and turn it against them: land which was *merely* fertile he called 'a barren prospect', and explained: 'I mean *barren* only in a picturesque light; for it affords good pasturage; and is covered with herds of cattle; and a beautiful breed of sheep, with silken fleeces, and without horns.'[48] 'We hardly admit the cottage',[49] he wrote elsewhere, and 'as to the appendages of husbandry, and every idea of cultivation, we wish them totally to disappear'.[50] And another theorist of the Picturesque, Archibald Alison, argued: 'The sublimest situations are often disfigured, by objects that we feel unworthy of them – by traces of cultivation, or attempts toward improvement.'[51] The Picturesque was, of course, one aspect of eighteenth-century primitivism and of the desire to find in nature a force powerful enough to resist the advance of an increasingly rationalist and scientific civilisation, and clearly any agriculturalist who approved the theory would find it hard to relate to his prior commitment to a progressive agriculture.

Almost none of the reporters who have discovered the Picturesque is able to make the connection at all comfortably: the only thoroughly successful attempt is made by John Billingsley in his *General View* of Somerset: 'These woods are very romantick and picturesque, and being secured from the south west breezes, the growth is very rapid, and the profit greater than any will believe who have not had experience thereof...'[52] William Pitt is more typical, and in his report on Leicestershire, 1809, is anxious, or is trying to appear so, for a 'rational, desirable, useful, and much to be wished for triumph of utility over taste'.[53] But perhaps the two who feel themselves particularly corrupted by the theory are Arthur Young himself – though in his other writings more than in his reports – and John Clark, author of the first Herefordshire report,[54] who also wrote an essay in which he argued for the authenticity of Ossian's poems,[55] a common indulgence of amateurs of the Picturesque.

Clark's description of the landscape of Herefordshire begins correctly enough, and presents it as a *paysage riant*: 'the wide flats', he writes, 'are clothed in nature's fairest robes, and enriched by a profuse distribution of her most chosen gifts'.[56] But soon the hills raise their 'mild heads', and when they do it is to 'invite the traveller to partake of an air less luxuriant and satiating than that of the plains below'.[57] The atmosphere on the plains, apparently, is 'so loaded with the riches which it collects from the sweet scented herbs around, that the inhailed air gives a glow of health and vigour to the surrounding vegetables on which it breathes'.[58] This atmosphere soon enough begins to cloy: 'The idea of *richness* is *rather prevalent,* and apt to overawe the mind by that self-sufficiency, and those assumed airs of superiority, of which it is, perhaps, not easy for Wealth to divest herself. Cornfields, meadows, orchards, extended lawns, and hop-grounds, satiate the eye by one continued scene of luxury.'[59] What Clark finds oppressive is what he apprehends by taste and smell: it is the richness of the atmosphere that at first overpowers him; but in that last sentence he returns to a more conventional critical position, and suggests that the landscape, because of the idea of richness it proposes, satiates as well 'the eye', and thus cannot be properly composed.

It is hard not to adopt a patronising tone towards Clark, whose 'fine writing', says Marshall, 'too frequently involves his good sense in a degree of obscurity; or, by exciting a smile, it is passed over unheeded'.[60] But it would be a pity if his enthusiastic style obscured, what is, if not exactly a complexity in the way he apprehends landscape, at least a confusion which interestingly reveals what he felt to be the threat implicit in a cultivated and luxuriant landscape, and suggests very precisely the nature of his interest in the Picturesque, and in the less luxuriant atmosphere of the upland. And unusually for an agricultural writer, Clark does come very close at one point to stating an open preference for what resists cultivation: 'no barren spot', he says, 'that by the humility of its deportment would form a contrast to the general claim to pre-eminence'.[61] Certainly Clark finds it impossible to pretend that the notions of taste and of utility are anything but antagonistic towards each other; as when he is grateful that there is no forest in Herefordshire, 'which,' he says, 'in such a soil, would be apt to throw a gloom over the dejected mind, from the unpleasant reflection, that the gratification of the eye was purchased at too high a price, by excluding the operation of the plough and the scythe from the spot where it grew, thereby lessening the more substantial and the more requisite comforts of society, by lessening the means of subsistence'.[62] Clark does, in fact, take considerable pains to suppress his interest in the Picturesque, and when that interest re-emerges it does so in language which suggests that his deliberate amnesia has taken a form analogous to sexual repression. After saying, a few lines above, that the barren spots in the landscape of Herefordshire were pleasantly humble in contrast to the opulence of the fields and orchards, he then denies that there are such barren spots in the landscape at all. 'It is', he says, 'of very little importance from what station [the agricultural wealth of the county] is viewed, so that it can be seen; for when there is no natural nakedness to cover, nothing can be seen from any position, which the traveller would not wish to view.'[63]

The idea of an uncultivated landscape is here operating on John Clark's imagination in a way exactly opposite to the way it operated on Thomson's (see above, p. 31). For Thomson, the luxuriance, the opulence of the vast savannahs offered a liberation from the 'little scenes of art' he found in Europe; and he is able to respond without reservation to the 'exuberant spring' and the rivers like 'fattening seas' of the tropics. For Clark, it is cultivated land which is luxuriant; but it imposes its luxuriance on him in such a directly physical way, that he quickly feels the heady atmosphere of lawns and orchards to be oppressive, and indeed the phrase he applies to them – 'one continued scene of luxury' – would be more naturally descriptive of an orgy than of agricultural land. He prefers at first, therefore, the land which is not thus fertile, but *barren* – a preference, however, which an agricultural writer cannot properly admit to, and one which Clark soon feels obliged to disown. The fertile land is *clothed*, of course, 'in nature's fairest robes', its wealth cannot 'divest' itself of its airs of superiority; and by contrast the barren land, which at first was humble – that is, not over-dressed – would now, if it had not completely disappeared from the landscape, be *naked*, shameful, not to be looked on; and furthermore, its nakedness would be *natural* – the word suggests that the only decent land is that which the *art* of agriculture has dressed.

Arthur Young's *Tours* – those of France, Ireland, and the North of England in particular[64] – are full of descriptions of picturesque landscapes, but he seems to have felt not much more at ease than Clark in his situation as an agriculturalist with a taste for uncultivated landscape. And so he seeks to justify this taste, by balancing each description of landscape with another description, immediately following, of cultivated land. This is Arthur Young in Ireland:

The Glen is a pass between two vast ridges of mountains covered with wood, which have a very noble effect, the vale is no wider than to admit the road, a small gurgling river almost by its side, and narrow slips of rocky and shrubby ground which parts them: in the front all escape seems denied by an immense conical mountain which rises out of the Glen, and seems to fill it up...Passing from this sublime scene, the road leads through chearful grounds all under corn, rising and falling to the eye, and then to a vale of charming verdure broken into inclosures...[65]

The way Young shifts from the 'sublime scene' to the 'inclosures' at the end of the passage is not in this single instance especially striking. This is, after all, the description of an actual place, and no doubt the road does lead, as Young says it does, thus directly from one to the other. And neither does there seem to be either any particular *moral* opposition between the two varieties of landscape: the agricultural land, indeed, is described mainly in abstract visual terms: the corn-fields 'rising and falling to the eye', and the vale 'broken into inclosures' – the word 'broken' there could be a term either from aesthetics or from agriculture.

A few pages later, however, Young again describes a 'sublime' landscape, which he again immediately balances with a view of agricultural land: 'the high lands almost lock into each other, and leave scarce a passage for the river at bottom, which rages, as if with difficulty forcing its way. It is topped by a high mountain, and in front you catch a beautiful plat of inclosures bounded by the sea'[66] – and this habit, of turning from the sublime and the barren to agricultural land, and especially enclosed land, occurs so regularly, and so often, in those of Young's tours that led him into mountain country, that it becomes hard to believe that in each case the productive landscape is not being introduced to distract us from the unproductive landscape Young in one way prefers. In the *Northern Tour* the procedure is used especially often, and in one passage in his account of that tour Young finds himself above a valley 'one would have taken for...a sample of terrestrial paradise'.[67] This paradise, however, is not a *paysage riant*, offering up the gifts of nature in even more abundance than a properly enclosed and cultivated landscape could do; instead 'many rugged and bold projecting rocks discovered their bare points among thick woods which hung almost perpendicularly over a deep precipice'[68] – the more one looks at his language, the more one speculates about the precise nature of Young's guilt at having a taste for the Sublime. And Young is able, in this landscape too, to discover 'five or six grass enclosures of a verdure beautiful as painting can express'.[69]

No real reconciliation of course is possible between the interests of the practical farmer and the picturesque writer, although this technique of Young's does allow them to coexist, and indeed insists that they do. There is, however, one area of picturesque theory which specifically did attempt to reconcile the demands of taste and those of utility, in the *ferme ornée*, a sort of practical man's version of the landscape-garden. Thomas Ruggles, in his letters on 'picturesque farming' already referred to (see pp. 61 and 77), suggests what sort of improvements the 'picturesque farmer' can make, which will be 'consistent with general utility and profit'.[70] In practice, Thomas Ruggles was too committed an agriculturalist to discover that taste and utility were often in disharmony, although, like James Donaldson, he does seem pleased to find them so frequently in accord: thus, for example, he suggests that 'it will not be found consistent, either with profit, or the beauty of the landscape, totally to expel summer fallows';[71] and elsewhere he remarks that 'the language of taste and economy is in this instance the same, viz. the smaller the quantity of dead wood in your fence, the less does it hurt the sight'.[72] At times, however, the conflict is undeniable, as for example when Ruggles suggests a series of expedients by which the necessarily rectangular shape of an arable field can be disguised.[73]

It cannot be said that John Clark, for example, and Thomas Ruggles, were at all typical of the rural professional class in the interest they display in the Picturesque – at the close of one of his letters, Ruggles apologises that his subject 'naturally leads the language astray from that sobriety of expression which becomes the farmer',[74] and he seems to have felt, in a quieter way, some of Young's embarrassment at his own taste. Nevertheless, too many agricultural writers of the period reveal an aesthetic interest of one sort or another in landscape for us to believe that such an interest was untypical of the rural professional class as a whole. The different attitudes to landscape we have examined in this chapter are all drawn from the same range of attitudes we discussed in Chapter 1, and it is important to remind ourselves again that they do all have the same effect of denying the individuality of the place to which they are applied. The majority of agricultural writers, of course, do hold more firmly even than do the pre-picturesque poets to the idea that the beauty of a landscape is directly related to its productivity; and in this sense their attitudes to landscape are less 'abstract' than those of the eighteenth-century aestheticians, We are dealing, however, with a class of agricultural 'improvers', at a time when 'improvement' could be used almost synonymously with 'enclosure'; and to enclose a place, just as much as to make it into a landscape-garden, means to work it into a structure more or less ordained elsewhere – and thus – as far as that place is concerned – an arbitrary one.

IV

I suggested in my last chapter that the various attitudes to landscape we had been considering – whether Thomson's, Lyttelton's, or Gilpin's – were all the expressions of an attempt to occupy, so to speak, the place to which they were applied; to appropriate it and to destroy in it what was unknown. For many writers – Gilbert White, for example, in his poems (see above, p. 40) – this appropriation was so habitual as to create no resonance, and we never feel any sense implicit in their work that the places they describe had any particular mystery or individuality to be destroyed. But both Thomson and Gilpin feel nature in some way as powerful and mysterious, and so also do the admirers of the Picturesque among the agricultural writers we are discussing; and the effort of all these writers is to be able to control whatever power nature seems to them to have, by coming to *know* the natural landscape according to one system or another. And in this they can be seen as part of a wider movement in the eighteenth century, to *explain* the countryside, open it out, and to make each particular place more available to those outside it.

This movement can be traced for example in the growth in the number of provincial newspapers during the period, and in the wider circulation of local newspapers. In the period before about

1750 the average provincial newspaper – those published, for example, in Cambridge or Northampton or Stamford – would be distributed within a relatively small radius of its town of origin; but the practice was growing of engaging itinerant newsmen to distribute papers,[75] so that the circle of influence of each country town which produced a newspaper was becoming wider and embracing more and more outlying villages. Perhaps by the middle of the century the areas in which the several newspapers circulated were tending to overlap, so that the literate inhabitants of the countryside became in a sense freer of their dependence for information on one particular town, and more aware of themselves as part of a wider area, in which would circulate newspapers from different provincial towns. By 1756 the editor of the *Bath Advertiser* was claiming that the paper was 'constantly and regularly distributed through a Space of Country near Sixty Miles in one Direction, Westward, and above Seventy Eastward; and so in Proportion all around';[76] and in 1764 the *Cambridge Journal* was distributed by 'seven men, at a great Expence, who carry this Paper through the Counties of Cambridge, Huntingdon, Bedford, Hertford, Northampton, Leicester, Rutland, Nottingham, Derby, and part of Norfolk, Suffolk, and Essex'.[77] By the turn of the century the *Cambridge Chronicle* carries advertisements of property for sale in places as far north as Gainsborough, and as far south as Great Bentley in Essex. These provincial newspapers did not usually contain a great deal of national news, and did not often provide editorial comment on political events. An analysis of a sample issue of the *Stamford Mercury* (30 May 1800) reveals fairly unambiguously the real function of these newspapers, and who read them. Of the 20 columns in that issue, less than $4\frac{1}{2}$ were filled with national news, and less than 2 with local news. Of the remaining $13\frac{1}{2}$ or so columns, $1\frac{1}{2}$ contained intelligence about agricultural prices at various markets; rather more than $4\frac{1}{2}$ contained public and legal notices, many of them concerned with the progress of local enclosures; and more than $7\frac{1}{2}$ were filled with privately inserted advertisements, many of them advertising land, houses or businesses for sale or to let. The prosperity of the *Stamford Mercury*, at least, clearly depended on the facility it gave to the commercial and professional classes to communicate amongst themselves, and to widen the circle in which they could transact their business.

The improvement in the quality of roads is another factor in this opening-out of the countryside in the eighteenth century – an increasing number were taken over by turnpike trusts, according to Lord Ernle some 452 between 1760 and 1774, and another 643 between 1785 and 1800[78] – the two periods correspond roughly with the two periods of greatest agricultural prosperity at the end of the eighteenth century. The trusts were not perhaps greatly successful – it was hardly possible to make enough by tolls to keep a main road well maintained – and the turnpike-system did not improve the general condition of roads throughout the country to any very remarkable degree; at the end of the century it was still probably the rule to find a good few miles of turnpike followed by many more of road maintained by the different parishes it passed through, and mostly in disrepair. But certainly the establishment of the trusts – and the passing of the two Highway Acts in 1773[79] – do reflect what was a very considerable concern with the facility of travel, with mobility, which were reflected also in the greater efficiency of the coaching services after 1784, when John Palmer's mail coaches began to operate.[80]

This concern was largely a matter of economic interest: a greater frequency of exchange between villages and market-towns could encourage, for example, a greater diversity of agriculture; for as long as roads were bad and villages thus isolated, every village had to grow corn for its own consumption. And this points to an important effect of the concern for mobility in general and of the turnpike-system in particular: a good road-system would encourage every village to think of itself no longer as primarily concerned to grow its own food for its own needs, but as putting its agricultural produce into circulation, and thus as being more dependent on national prices and more part of the national economy. Furthermore, for a parish to have the maintenance of its own main road taken over by a trust could well have meant that, whereas before the road had been seen as serving primarily an internal need, to connect one part of the parish with another, it would now be seen mainly as connecting say one market-town to the north with another to the south, and would thus reduce the particular parish to the status of a landmark on this longer and more important journey. The parish would become less and less the centre of the area it saw around it, and more and more a part of an extended network of directions which had no centre except perhaps in the metropolis. One way in which this can be understood is by

86

comparing the maps made of counties at the end of the seventeenth century with those made at the end of the eighteenth. The former usually show villages as isolated dots without connecting roads; the latter are, in effect, road-maps.

The reporters to the Board of Agriculture almost all show themselves anxious to open out the countryside, by making it more accessible to the traveller, and by making individual villages more obviously part of a national economy. They are all much concerned with mobility, so that one of the most frequent criteria they apply in forming their opinion of an area is the facility with which it can be approached and crossed. The Reverend St John Priest, author of the second report for Buckinghamshire,[81] makes a complaint which a number of other agricultural writers also make: 'in the *passages* through lands under the open-field culture, not only the roads are bad, but the difficulty of discerning public roads from mere drift-ways, or from passages to lands of different proprietors, is so great, that without a guide, some of them cannot be travelled by a stranger with safety'.[82] This gives a very clear idea of how the countryside – and especially the open-field landscape – could be thought of as mysterious and hostile. The system of roads in an open-field parish – as we shall see in Chapter 3 (see below, p. 101) – is in the first place for the circulation of men and cattle within the parish, and often, if a way exists through several parishes from one town to another, it is not a direct route but the result of various such internal road-systems meeting at the parish boundaries and thus interlacing. And so there will often be no particular distinction between a road that will in fact lead the traveller, however indirectly, out of the parish, and one which leads the farmer to his land and the labourer to his work but takes the traveller nowhere. But Priest's idea of a road is that it should be threaded through one village and another like a string through beads: he thinks of the road as in some sense prior to the villages on it, and not of the villages existing separately first and then pushing out such connecting threads as were found necessary for their own economy – or simply that the road from *A* to *B* came to be *that* only by the almost chance conjunction of the interior roads of two settlements. For Priest the road-system of an open-field village is a labyrinth, whose secret cannot be learned without a guide, and which it is positively dangerous to enter without one.

A number of other reporters make substantially the same complaint as Priest: William Pitt for instance writes of the cross-roads in Leicestershire that they are 'not to be called roads, for they are nothing more than passing through the different closes (fields) upon the turf, and in many of them not the least track of a wheel is to be seen for miles together'.[83] Among other writers, the Reverend James Tyley found open-field land similarly bewildering to pass through, and writes of the need to use 'the lofty spire of a church' as landmark 'in places hideous by neglect and unworn by traffic'.[84] Arthur Young tells of a common near Grimsthorpe 'with roads pointing nine ways at once, but no direction-post'.[85] On the other hand he is full of enthusiasm for travelling in Oxfordshire, where, he says, 'A noble change has taken place, but generally by turnpikes, which cross the county in every direction, so that when you are at one town, you have a turnpike road to every other town. This holds good with Oxford, Woodstock, Witney [&c.], and in every direction, and these lines necessarily intersect the county in almost every direction.'[86] There is nowhere in the county, in short, not now accessible, nowhere that cannot be visited and known.

'Good roads', writes the Rev. A. Young in his second Sussex report, 'are an infallible sign of prosperity',[87] and he speaks of the 'general impetus' given by such roads 'to circulation, and fresh activity to every branch of industry'.[88] He enthuses over 'the animation, vigour, life, and energy of luxury, consumption, and industry, which flow with a full tide through this kingdom, wherever there is a free communication between the capital and the provinces'[89] – the degree of activity on the roads in an area becomes a standard by which the mental alertness of the population can be measured. This idea, and that of the importance of circulation generally, is a recurrent theme in Arthur Young's *Tours* of France. At the beginning of his first tour, he notices the lack of traffic to and from Paris, and later he was 'confirmed in the idea that the roads immediately leading to that capital are deserts, comparatively speaking, with those of London. By what means can the connection be carried on with the country?'[90] In Mirepoix, a town then of 15,000 inhabitants, 'nothing like a cabriolet of any sort was to be had...circulation is stagnant in France'.[91] And Priest in his Buckinghamshire report explains the need for good roads in terms of the change from the old to the new agriculture. 'Formerly', he says, when all lands were in open-field culture, and when farms produced little else but subsistence for their own neighbourhoods...when the means of getting from one parish to that adjoining, and returning back again in the course of a day, was all that was requisite...at these times bad roads were congenial with the times, but at the present day, when farmers are enlightened...and when necessity compels them to think of distant markets [which] have such communications with one another, that one can within a day or two regulate those of the whole island; a Surveyor of Agriculture is astonished to find so many roads in the state described...[92]

This passage places the need for good roads once again in the context of a general opening-out of the country, and argues that the expansion so to speak of the mental horizons of farmers – who now think in terms of 'distant markets', and are aware of how these are all parts of a national economic structure – has given them the sense of inhabiting a wider space than that of 'their own neighbourhoods'.

It must be true that the sort of attitudes to land we have seen expressed in this section involve as considerable a detachment on the part of those who held them from the places they describe as do the structures employed by Thomson and the theories of William Gilpin. The concern to be always moving through a place, to see it never primarily as a place-in-itself, but always as mediated by its connection to one place to the east, and another to the west, produces a sense of space which is defined always by this linear movement, so that to stop at a place is still to be in a state of potential motion, on the look-out as Arthur Young clearly was in Oxfordshire for the road to the next town. This detachment produces its own kind of sophistication, in the sort of knowledge it produces of land described, as can be seen from this passage of William Marshall's 'travelling notes', which he would make while 'traversing different lines of road'[93] in a district. The passage represents one day's ride, and I have been reluctant to cut it because as I hope will appear there is very little here which does not contribute to the particular sense Marshall arrives at of the land he is passing through.

15th, July, 1810

Leave Epworth (a small Market Town) by a gradual descent toward the west.

Skirt a common field of many crops (rich and beautiful) surmounted by wind mills. The soil reddish; the crops large and clean; exemplary feudal husbandry. Much flax and hemp observable.

Pass down a straggling street, a mile in length, and enter on a flat sandy passage, similar to that crossed at the south end of the island [of Axholme].

All modern inclosure. The crops chiefly rye, potatoes, and *flax* (on this moory land!)

Cross a large embanked drain; accompanied by a catch-water sewer.

Still a dead-looking sandy soil. Yet meslin and flax.

Cross another drain; and appear to enter upon a somewhat higher ground, but still heavy sandy road: and the substratum (seen in a pit) a depth of sand.

Much lime in heaps, on fallow: – the first seen in travelling five hundred miles.

Some sheep and young cattle, in ley grounds; – the only stock observed, since entering the flat!

Still recent inclosure.

Continue to rise (if the eye does not deceive) a gentle ascent of sandy land.

Good rye. Quere, after limed fallow? And still large fields of flax! – and mostly good, for the season.

Pass Standtoft Grove: – a house embosomed in trees.

Turn northward, on a raised drain-bank-road.

Still rye lands appear on the left. On the right, an extent of rushy pastures, very thinly stocked: – horses and a few sheep. The ground, apparently, has formerly been under the plough.

Reach better land, and good wheat.

Cross the 'Old Dun', – highly embanked; and enter YORKSHIRE. Turn, westward, on a good gravel road: that between Doncaster and Barton.

Now, charming crops of corn and flax.

Fields of rape, ripening.

Good short-horned cattle.

Still lime on fallow.

Heaps of bog-wood, on fallow ground; as stone heaps are seen on stony lands; – dug out of the substratum (an ordinary sight in the fens of Cambridgeshire, &c.) see one fence made, and another making, with the larger roots, placed in close array: – a ragged, tolerable fence: – a proof, this, of the fenny nature of the land. Yet the substratum, here, would seem (from the slight views caught of it) to be of a brownish colour. – Quere, moory mold mixed with natural warp?

Charming crops of corn: – yet still water fences prevail; though marks of oldish modern enclosure are observable.

Still in an extended flat of rich soil, and good arable crops.

Many cattle seen on the left.

Still pale, silt-like soil, highly fertile: – the wheat crops, here, are unable to stand.

Leave the high road; and turn north-west-ward, towards Thorne.

A field of beans: – the first from the Isle of Axholm. – Quere, is the whole flat covered with alluvion, natural warpe? The first deposit *sand*, – the next, *silt*, – the farthest from the source, *silty clay*? But this by the way. Much study on the spot, examined as a whole, would be required to determine this interesting, though not very important point.

Still among embanked drains; and doubtlessly still on water-formed lands.

A flag-path (for horses and foot-passengers) by the side of the road again

(an ordinary accompaniment through the Island of Axholm:) a proof of the
strength and retentiveness of the soil.

Cross a canal; and pass a well herbaged common.

Old enclosure and hedge trees, about Thorne.[94]

This passage is fairly typical of the descriptions of land produced by a number of itinerant agricultural writers contemporary
with Young and Marshall, although most write in a more continuous prose, and few are as observant as Marshall. What seems
to me most remarkable about Marshall's method is that he takes
with him on his journey no local knowledge at all – he does not
relate what he sees to any prior expectations about what he *would*
see – and what he learns about the land between Epworth and
Thorne is derived only from his general agricultural knowledge,
and what he can observe. The knowledge he arrives at of, for
example, the soils he encounters, depends on no local knowledge
of the surface geology of the area, but on a series of observations
which finally reveal to Marshall the complete geological structure
of the area. Thus after descending out of Epworth through reddish
soil, he continues on 'a flat sandy passage'; soon after, he has the
impression of again coming on to higher ground, 'but', he remarks,
'still heavy sandy road: and the substratum (seen in a pit) a depth
of sand'. He includes here what seem to be to him, at this stage,
puzzling and contradictory impressions, as he does again later
when he comes across two fences made of bog-wood, 'a proof,
this, of the fenny nature of the land. Yet the substratum, here,
would seem (from the slight views caught of it) to be of a brownish
colour.' The attempt to reconcile these contradictory impressions
leads him to produce, as he proceeds, a conjectural soil-system of
the whole area to explain what he has seen on the length of his
journey so far.

The parentheses in Marshall's remarks about the soil – '(seen in
a pit)', '(from the slight views caught of it)' – are there to answer
the question, how do you know? – and all the knowledge Marshall
arrives at in this passage is derived from observations of that sort;
observations, too, of a man who is always moving, who will not
stop to check his impressions, or to ask for information, because
his interest is in, precisely, the sort of knowledge that he can get
of a place simply by riding through it, as a stranger, and by ignor-
ing the sort of particular knowledge that the inhabitants could
offer him. The knowledge he wants is the sort that can synthesise

the various impressions he receives – the places he passes through – into an idea of them as parts of one diverse but unified area. He is fully aware of local differences of topography, of agricultural practice, from village to village, but that awareness does not lead him to consider each village as unique, as the inhabitants of each might consider it: the attempt is always to locate the different villages in one more or less homogeneous district, with its own general characteristics. And there are more connections here than is perhaps apparent to anyone not familiar with writing on this sort of subject: thus for example Marshall at first sees very little stock on the flat; and it is the consequent lack of manure which explains the presence of lime on the fallows – 'the first seen in travelling five hundred miles'. There is nothing in these notes which is, finally, random: they all contribute to produce an enlarged view of the agricultural structure of the region, first, and of the whole country; and Marshall's ability to grasp this structure is crucially related to the fact of his mobility; and not just to the vast experience that mobility obviously provides, but to the detached way of experiencing a place that it encourages.

The knowledge of geography of all the agricultural writers of the period is of this sort – the ability to think of a place almost completely in terms of its relations with other places. This is of course partly related to the particular way they worked as reporters – that is, as tourists – but that does not mean that in this ability they were uncharacteristic of the rural professional class as a whole. Certainly Marshall himself was very doubtful about the sort of attitudes most tourists took with them: the worst reports to the Board he condemns as the products of 'transient tours of enquiry',[95] and though what he is usually objecting to when he makes this charge is the habit of not observing for oneself the agricultural practice of a county, but of asking local farmers to describe it,[96] he also suggests that the sort of knowledge arrived at by the method we have just seen him practise himself is of limited value. 'A mere tourist', he says,

may catch certain facts which pass under his eye while travelling: and, in this way, he may gather some general ideas of the nature of a country, and a few particulars of practice that may happen to be going on, *at the time of his tour*; and such facts may be entitled to public notice, *as far as they go*. But let him not claim, on such slight pretensions, a right to make a *general Report* of the nature and practice of the country or district thus passed over.[97]

Marshall argues that such a report can be properly made only by a resident in the region in question;[98] but he did not always follow this ruling himself, and his opinion was anyway not shared by most other agricultural writers.

In his tours of France, Arthur Young several times defends the sort of knowledge a tourist can gather. He complains of the quality of the inns in the Midi, and goes on:

There have been writers who look on such observations as rising merely from the petulance of travellers, but...such circumstances are political data. We cannot demand all the books of France to be opened in order to explain the amount of circulation in that kingdom: a politician must therefore collect it from such circumstances as he can ascertain, and among these, traffic on the great roads, and the convenience of the houses prepared for the reception of travellers, tell us both the number and the condition of those travellers.[99]

In England, he argues, 'in situations absolutely cut off from all dependence, or almost the expectation of what are properly called travellers, yet you will meet with neat inns...and a refreshing civility!...Are no political conclusions to be drawn from this amazing contrast?'[100] According to Young, an observant tourist is able to come to a valuable understanding of the places he visits, and indeed (the implication is) a better one than could be derived from books. The condition of the traveller, of the tourist, Young elsewhere goes so far as to suggest, is becoming the normal condition of the literate in England, and he is amazed that this is not so in France: 'The French must be the most stationary people upon earth, when in a place they must rest without a thought of going to another. Or the English must be the most restless; and find more pleasure in moving from one place to another, than in resting to enjoy life in either.'[101] This is rather an extreme statement of course; but it is true in this sense, that the idea of space I have suggested in this section as characteristic of the rural professional class is one which regards the individual place always as part of a larger area, and this idea is arrived at particularly by the ability to move with ease across wide tracts of country. This ability involves, as I have said, a detachment from the individual place, and indeed an appropriation of the individuality of each place the traveller passes through – and in this way is related to all the various generalising attitudes to land we have been examining in this chapter and the last.

V

The writers on agriculture we have been considering all agreed that if agriculture was to progress the process of converting open fields into enclosures would have to be completed; and finally in this chapter I want to discuss what sort of attitudes to land are involved in this advocacy of enclosure. Enclosure can be of two main kinds: there is the simple taking-in of the common grazing land of a parish, whether to extend the cultivated area, or to stock it more efficiently; and there is the division and redistribution of the arable land of a parish lying in open field, whether to maintain it as arable, or to convert it to pasture. An enclosure by Act of Parliament might involve both processes, but the appropriation and enclosure of the common alone was quite normal in parishes where the arable land was already enclosed.

I suggested in Chapter 1 that the enclosure of uncultivated land, with the object of cultivating it, was a way of bringing it into that part of the landscape which because it was cultivated was known, and no longer hostile; and I suggested also that in this the enclosure of common land was analogous to the procedures used by poets and painters of landscape in the eighteenth century. There is no particular need to make the point any differently here, except perhaps to notice that the idea of a connection between the *cultivated* and the *civilised* is very frequently present in writing about enclosure: the two authors of the first *General View* of Hampshire remark of the landscape of that county: 'We are sorry to observe such immense tracts of open heath, and uncultivated land, which...reminds [*sic*] the traveller of uncivilised nations, where nature pursues her own course, without the assistance of human art...'[102] The enclosure of open-field land is usually an operation on a larger scale than that of common grazing land, and one in which as I suggested at the beginning of this chapter representatives of almost all the rural professions would normally be engaged. To enclose an open-field parish means in the first place to think of the details of its topography as quite erased from the map. The hostile and mysterious road-system was tamed and made unmysterious by being destroyed; the minute and intricate divisions between lands, strips, furlongs, and fields simply ceased to exist: the quantity of each proprietor's holding was recorded, but not among what furlongs it had been distributed. Everything about the place, in fact, which made it precisely *this* place, and not that one, was forgotten; the map was drawn blank, except for the village itself, the parish boundary, and perhaps woodland too extensive or valuable to be cleared, and streams too large to be diverted. The enclosure-commissioner would then mark in the new roads he was to cause to have made to the neighbouring villages, running as straight as the contours of the land would allow. The allotment to the Church in lieu of tithes was next marked out, and then the allotments of the other proprietors, all these allotments to be sub-divided as far as possible into rectangular fields of more or less uniform size. In this way the map was re-drawn, and the new topography would begin to be realised on the actual landscape.[103]

I shall be discussing the process and effects of one particular enclosure later in this book, but it is worth pointing out here a few general implications of parliamentary enclosure. There is a sense in which an open-field parish in the late eighteenth and early nineteenth centuries could be said to have a different geography according to who was looking at it: thus, for those of its inhabitants who rarely went beyond the parish boundary, the parish itself was so to speak at the centre of the landscape, and every place outside a point on the circumference of the parish, or beyond the horizon. The roads, as we saw earlier, were for them primarily an internal network, to connect different places within the parish. For those inhabitants accustomed to moving outside it, however, and for those travellers who passed through it, the parish was simply one of many in a district defined not by some circular system of geography but by a linear one, as part of a complex of roads and directions which 'intersected' each other. The topography of an open-field parish was essentially the expression of the first system, that which saw the individual place as an integral, a self-contained unit, connected as much by chance as by necessity with other places outside it; it was an expression of the way agriculture was carried out in the parish, at one time in its history at least, and while it lasted it ensured that no very revolutionary changes in agricultural practice could occur. This obligatory submission to the ancient and the customary was no doubt part of what made open-field parishes – thus turned in upon themselves – so mysterious to the improver, and so closed to the traveller; and the effect of enclosure was of course to destroy the sense of place which the old topography expressed, as it destroyed that topography itself. The new topography – of integrated holdings, of heath perhaps enclosed and cultivated, of moors drained, of roads leading emphatically *out* of the parish – was a structure which could be and was applied in some form or another to all open-field parishes undergoing enclosure. And its tendency of course was to destroy the individuality of the parishes to which it was applied – and which were individual to the inhabitants, not because one parish was especially different from all the others, but because the inhabitants of a parish who rarely travelled outside it could know only one parish at all well. An enclosed parish was opened out by its enclosure and made part of a much wider geographical area; its new landscape was a complete realisation of all those attitudes to land we have seen as characteristic of the rural professional class.

If I may anticipate my argument here by a chapter, I would like to refer briefly to the situation John Clare found himself in when, in 1809, his own parish of Helpston began to be enclosed. I shall argue later that Clare's sense of place was much the same as that expressed by the open-field landscape; but it is worth noticing here that as a poet Clare inherited a tradition of landscape-poetry – the first poet of landscape he read, and probably his favourite, was James Thomson – which worked either by applying a more or less arbitrary visual structure to a view, or by applying to it a set of rules and concepts which, whatever the intention behind them, had the effect of *judging* the place by more or less arbitrary and external criteria, and of comparing it always with other places. The effect of these procedures on the individuality of the places to which they were applied was thus very similar to that of the landscape of parliamentary enclosure on that of an open-field parish; and in particular for Clare the new topography of Helpston was a structure arrived at elsewhere and imposed on the parish, which worked against Clare's own sense of place, and which had also an aesthetic sanction, in the theory generally held by the members of the rural professional class responsible for enclosure, and by some poets at least, that an enclosed landscape was more beautiful than an open-field landscape. I hope to establish later in this book that much of Clare's poetry is an attempt to assert his

96

own sense of place against that expressed by the tradition of rural poetry, and by the new landscape of Helpston, and that this meant also that he had to discover a new way of describing landscape, one which did not express precisely the sense of place he was writing to oppose.

3. The sense of place in the poetry of John Clare

The village of Helpston, where John Clare was born in 1793 and where he lived until 1832, is about half-way between Peterborough and Stamford, 'on the brink of the Lincolnshire fens', as Clare described it,[1] and in the Soke of Peterborough – until recently the most easterly part of Northamptonshire, but now half of the new county of Huntingdon and Peterborough. The parish is an oblong, very much longer than it is wide, which runs northward from the heath and woodland above the fifty-foot contour down to the flat, fenny meadows at the edge of the Welland valley; and thus it encloses within its boundary two very distinct types of landscape. For although there is only one corner of the parish where the land rises above 100 feet, to drive through Helpston from the south is to become aware of a very sudden falling-away of the land, which registers itself hardly at all as an actual physical drop, but as a sudden meeting of the landscape of limestone heath and level fen: the houses, as you drive through the village itself, begin opposite a large wood and end, only half-a-mile later, on the alluvial soil which stretches from the north and east of Helpston unbroken to the Wash. The landscape of the limestone heath, said Clare, 'made up my being'.[2]

Until the beginning of the nineteenth century, the land in the parish lay in open field; that is to say, the land was divided into three large fields, in turn divided into furlongs, themselves made up of the 'lands' which were the basic unit of land-tenure in parishes farmed on the open-field system. A 'land' was a long piece of ground,[3] ploughed into a ridge, running the whole length of a furlong – often about 200 yards – and anything between ten or twenty times longer than it was wide.[4] The total holding of a landowner in the parish was made up of lands distributed more or less equally among the three fields.

The open-field system does not seem to have been general all over England before the enclosure movements of the sixteenth century and after, but was confined within a broad band of country which stretched from Durham and Yorkshire south-westward to Hampshire and East Dorset, including all the Midland counties of England, but not Lancashire, Cheshire, or most of East Anglia. In France the areas of open-field farming were similarly limited, and stretched from east of Normandy across the northern half of the country to Lorraine. This champion country, *champagne* in France, was always understood to be very separate, in point of its topography, from the woodland country, *bocage*, of small enclosed fields, scattered settlements, and more or less compact farms. The champion country was, as Maurice Barrès described it in Lorraine, 'uncluttered':[5] the eye moving over the long sweep of arable was engaged by very little – a clump of wood here, a tract of waste there – on its journey to the horizon: most important of all, there were very few permanent fences or hedges, except around the small enclosures near the village and attached to the farmsteads concentrated there. In woodland country, on the other hand, there were hedges everywhere, thick and well-wooded; and the successive hedgerows, one behind the other across the landscape, appeared often so dense that the effect of riding through woodland country, as various writers noticed, was of riding through a forest. A parish enclosed by Act of Parliament, with its hedges well established and planted with trees, might present something of the same impression.

It was often thought that the open-field system, confining itself as it did in England to that broad oblique band from Durham to Dorset, and in France to the northern plains, had been developed as a response to the particular climatic and geological conditions, whatever they were, that prevailed in those areas; it seems perhaps more likely now that the system was one arrived at by a people who were herdsmen before they became cultivators of the soil, and who began growing crops on land as it were borrowed from the cattle, and which had earlier been uniquely their preserve. Looked at in this light the topography of an open-field parish such as Helpston emerges as peculiarly consistent and inevitable in its arrangement. The first necessity which is expressed, so to speak, by the topography of an open-field parish, the pattern of its roads and the arrangement of its fields, is for the cattle to be fed throughout the year: on the often sizeable tracts of common land and waste which lay within the boundaries of most open-field parishes in England, but also on the arable fields when they were lying fallow, on the stubble after the corn-harvest, and on the aftermath on the meadows after the hay-harvest. And from this need to pasture cattle on the arable land – not only because there was not enough common or waste to support them, but also of course because of the need to manure the fields – and from the characteristic, elongated shape of the arable 'land', excessively narrow and awkward to enclose, it is possible to deduce the reasons for the other features peculiar to the open-field system of farming, and in particular the collective obligations enjoined upon the farmers. Thus it was necessary for all the land which was to become fallow in any particular year to be located in the same field, and to become fallow at the same time, so that the cattle could range over the empty field without risk of spoiling or feeding upon standing crops. It was necessary, too, for the same crops to be grown in each of the other fields, so that they could be harvested at the same time, and the whole of each field thus left free for the cattle to graze. This system of compulsory rotation and the distribution of holdings among the various fields of the parish encouraged the concentration of houses and farms at the centre of the parish, with the fields – two, three, or sometimes four – spread out around them and all equally accessible. Furthermore, the practice of grazing all the cattle together in the same area of the parish made it possible for the whole herd to be entrusted to one herdsman, who would lead them together to wherever it was permitted for them to graze at this time or that; and this too encouraged the concentration of farms at the centre of the village, where the cattle could easily be assembled each day.

I said in Chapter 2 that the landscape created by parliamentary enclosure was the result of applying a very rigid pattern to the land being enclosed; it is no less true that the idiosyncratic topography – as it appeared to eighteenth-century agricultural writers – of the open-field parish had originally been arrived at by imposing on the land a pattern hardly at all less rigid. The plan of an open-field parish, according to the French historian Roger Dion,

s'est indifféremment imprimé sur toutes les variétés de terrains que peuvent offrir nos plaines et nos plateaux. La délimitation des champs, la disposition des chemins et des habitations, en un mot les lignes maîtresses de la figure qu'on obtient en traçant sur le papier le plan d'un terroir cultivé et habité, furent arrêtées d'après des conceptions *a priori*, qui s'étaient imposées souverainement à des groupements humains très étendus.[6]

The map of Helpston before the enclosure (see Map 1 below), as far as it can be reconstructed,[7] confirms this idea of a plan based on *a priori* conceptions. The homes and farmsteads are almost all concentrated in the compact village, which lies more or less at the centre of the parish, the three arable fields spread out around it. The houses are arranged round the island containing the church and the glebe farm, along the road to the Parks (a tract of rough pasture in the neighbouring parish), running from the centre of the village west to King Street, and along the road running southward towards the heath. This second road, the widest in the parish, was the main road along which the cattle travelled from the village out to the largest of the commons to which Helpston had access, the Snow; and this probably explains why of all the roads in the parish it was the widest, and seems to have been the only one fenced along most of its length. After leaving the village, the road comes to the stream fed by Round Oak Spring in Heath Field, and to the right-hand turning along a drift road leading to the Snow; and south of this turning the main road continues, wide and fenced on either side, to the rough-grazing land of Helpston Heath (also called 'Emmonsailes' or 'Ailesworth' Heath – Ailesworth was the parish immediately south of Helpston), where some common grazing was still permitted at the time of the enclosure, although by 1772 at least, the larger part of the heath-land which lay within the parish boundary had been appropriated and fenced by the Earls Fitzwilliam, the Lords of the Manor.[8]

There is no road leading eastward out of the village, and the road to the west, Parkway, is marked by dotted lines on one eighteenth-century map, and does not appear at all on another:[9] the cattle would not normally be led out of the village to east or west unless it was to graze on the fallows or the mown meadows, in which case there was no need – as there was on the southward road – to keep them away from crops or the sown areas of the arable. To the north, however, the Nunton road is again clearly defined, and leads to the long meadows where the cattle might graze after the hay-harvest, and to which they might have to be led through fields of standing crops.

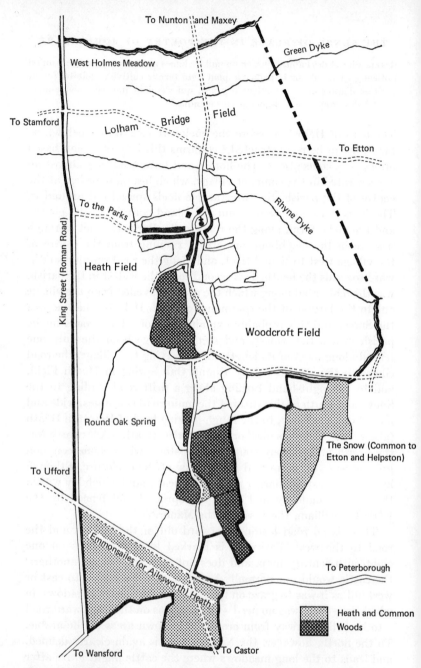

Map 1. A sketch map of the parish of Helpston in 1809, before the enclosure (approximate scale: 1 mile = 2¼ in.). The irregularly-shaped patches of land around the village itself, and on either side of the road to Castor, are old enclosures; the rest of the unshaded area within the parish boundary is open-field arable, with some meadow-land. It is impossible to fix precisely the boundary of the parish in its north-east corner: it picked its way between the furlongs in Lolham Bridge Field and in Etton fields (see note 7, page 225).

Crossing the parish to the north of the village, and running between Glinton in the east and Bainton in the west, is the old Stamford road; across the south of the parish ran another 'Stamford Road', also sometimes referred to as 'the way to Peterborough'. These roads cross the parish deliberately enough, but soon lose themselves in the neighbouring parishes and reach their destinations only very indirectly; although they are not especially important in the internal system of circulation within the parish, they no doubt first grew up to serve some local needs, and were not particularly designed as cross-roads. It was, presumably, by these roads that the inhabitants of Helpston had access to the towns to the east and west, and it is perhaps worth pointing out that they neither of them pass directly through the village itself, and thus do not encourage that notion I was speaking of in the previous chapter, of the village as a landmark between two other places, to pass through and not to stay in.

I said in the previous chapter that the characteristic sense of space which the topography and organisation of an open-field parish created was circular, while the landscape of parliamentary enclosure expressed a more linear sense. Perhaps I am in a better position now to explain what I mean. In the first place, the village of Helpston is at the centre of the parish, where the three fields of the parish come together: they form around the settlement a rough circle, which represents the area in which the villagers work and move. Around the village at the centre the crops rotate, and indeed it is fair to say that the fields, too, rotate about the hub of the village, as for example one year the wheat-field might be to the north of the village, then to the east, then to the south, and so on. The roads, too, that lead out of the village, are not primarily thought of as leading out of the *parish*, also, towards the neighbouring villages or towards Peterborough or Stamford. They are, as according to Dion the roads in open-field areas usually are, 'aménagés pour la circulation des troupeaux',[10] and the word *circulation* there can be taken in its root-meaning; the cattle move around the circle of the parish as they graze in turn the fallows, the commons, the meadows, the stubble, the fallows again.

This brings me to the last point I want to make here about what I am trying to argue as a characteristically open-field sense of space, and it is one which seems to be particularly important in relation to the idea of landscape we find expressed in Clare's poems. Compared with the landscape of the woodland country, the most obvious visual fact about the champion country was its simple openness: except around the villages themselves, or where occasionally a large block of lands had all fallen into the hands of one farmer and had at some time been enclosed by him, there were few if any permanent fences to obstruct the view across the fields. On a manuscript map[11] of Helpston and its neighbouring parish Etton, drawn in 1772, the open fields are simply blank spaces and the only lines are those delineating old enclosures and roads; it was the appalling openness of these infinite spaces, 'unbroken tracts' that, according to the Reverend James Tyley, 'strained and tortured the sight'.[12] Furthermore, each field in the parish was, as we have seen, at any one time covered with the same crop, or else uniformly fallow. Another French historian, Georges Lizerand, describes what must have been the visual effect of this open and uniform landscape, as against the *bigarrure*[13] which presents itself in France nowadays, in those areas where the open-field layout to some extent has survived, but where each farmer is free to pursue his own rotation indifferent to that pursued by his neighbours on the fields around his own:

La masse des emblavures recouvre les mouvements du sol comme le ferait un grand manteau et elle les adoucit. Elle n'exclut pas le coloris, mais elle le réduit à quelques nuances; ainsi, à la fin du printemps, le vert bleuté des blés, le vert gris des seigles, le vert plus clair des mars, tranchés par le 'sombre', la teinte de la terre en jachère. Dans cette campagne simplifiée, où le regard n'est arrêté par aucun arbre, cela compose un paysage aéré et véritablement grand, que renforce encore le cercle de l'horizon reculé.[14]

The coming-together of these two characteristics of the open-field landscape – its openness, and its uniformity – created a visual effect, peculiar to the areas of open-field farming, which was often noticed by old writers on agriculture. William Marshall observed that 'at all times, the manager of the estate was better enabled to detect bad husbandry…by having the whole spread under the eye, at once, than he would have been, had the lands been distributed, in detached, inclosed farmlets';[15] and an eighteenth-century French writer, quoted by Marc Bloch, remarked that, where field succeeds field with nothing to show where one property ends and another begins, unless some rising ground intervenes 'the husbandman sees at a glance all that is happening on the parcels he possesses in a single *quartier*, or even over the whole field'.[16] That the same crops had to be grown on any particular field in any particular year meant also, of course, that almost the entire labouring population of a village would be engaged in working the same field at the same time: at the time of spring ploughing, for example, the ploughing and sowing would all be being performed in one and the same field. That field would thus present itself to the observer as a scene of continuous and simultaneous activity, carried on in all parts of the field yet visible 'at a glance', and in which almost the entire village was engaged. Obviously enough, this impression, of seeing 'at a glance all that is happening', must have been far more a characteristic of open-field landscape than it could ever have been of the landscape of compact farms and small enclosed fields – whether in old-enclosed country, through which one rode as through a forest, or in parishes enclosed by Act of Parliament.

By John Clare's time, Helpston was not still farmed on quite such communal, unindividualistic lines as my account of the topography of the village might suggest, although in all its more important aspects the open-field system was still maintained. No doubt the large farmers at least felt themselves to be a good deal nearer to Peterborough and to Stamford than their predecessors had. Various changes had taken place, too, in the organisation of land, which the maps do not reveal but which can be deduced from, for example, the acreage returns of 1801,[17] the minutes of vestry meetings in the years immediately before the enclosure,[18] and the terrier of his lands in Helpston which Earl Fitzwilliam submitted along with his enclosure-claim to the enclosure-commissioners.[19] From these it appears that, in the first place, the three fields of the village were, at least by 1801, thought of as four, and this had enabled a more sophisticated system of rotation to be introduced.[20] Although no new land had been enclosed around the village for several hundred years, there seem to have been 'field closes', probably fenced off from the furlongs around, but open to be grazed when the fields were open.[21] It is clear, too, that a form of convertible husbandry, the variety that W. G. Hoskins has discovered on the open fields of Leicestershire,[22] was being practised in Helpston by 1800, and under certain conditions the owners of lands in the fallows were able to take them in and sow them with clover, artificial grasses or turnips, which the herdsman made sure the cattle did not invade.[23] In these ways the parish must have presented a rather less uniform appearance in 1800 than it had perhaps in 1600; but the point remains that the open-field system was so self-contained, so intricate, that it could never be much modified in its main principles, of compulsory rotation and collective grazing. As long as the land was distributed as it was, the methods of farming could not be much changed; and as long as the topography of the parish remained an expression of open-field farming practice, the characteristically open-field sense of space – circular, restricted by the boundary of the parish – was bound to survive, and the wider, mobile, linear sense of space of the rural professional class could not be properly imprinted in the consciousness of the villagers.

The Act of Parliament for the Enclosure of Helpston was passed in 1809,[24] and the final Award was published in 1820.[25] The gap between the Act and the Award is unusually long; but in fact the new landscape of Helpston was fully marked out long before the Award was published. The new public roads were staked out by the middle of 1811, the new allotments of land by the beginning of 1812, and the minor and private roads in the summer of 1813.[26] The actual work of enclosing must have been started by 1813 at the latest, and was probably more or less completed by 1816, when a vestry meeting in Helpston drew up new bye-laws for the parish,[27] to accord with the new organisation of land within it.

The topography of the parish today is largely what the enclosure of 1809–20 made it (see Map 2 below)[28] – the houses at the edges of the village, and of course the railway, are of a later date, but the pattern of the roads, the shape of the roads, and the balance of field land, meadow, and woodland, are still pretty much as they were designed to be by the Award. The Act was a very comprehensive one, and provided for the enclosure not only of Helpston but of Maxey to the north, and of Etton, Glinton, Northborough and Peakirk to the east, and this allowed the commissioners to think of these six parishes as forming together one large area of land rather than six small ones. In this idea they would have been encouraged, too, by the fact that the Fitzwilliam estate spread out over all six parishes, and the point of enclosure was, at least as much as anything else, to rationalise the layout of that estate.

The attention of the commissioners was first turned to laying

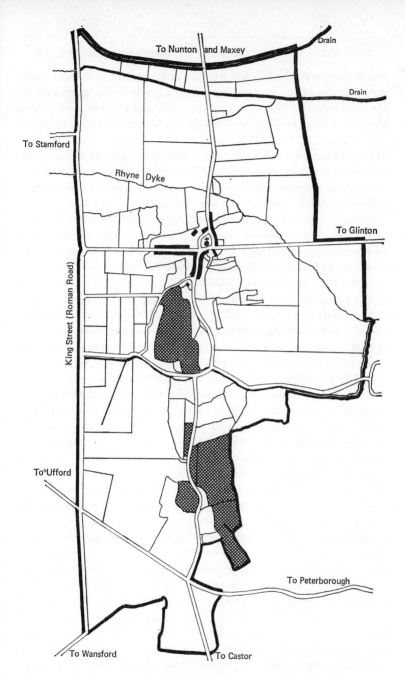

Map 2. A sketch map of the parish of Helpston in 1820, after the enclosure (approximate scale: 1 mile = $2\frac{1}{4}$ in.). The shaded area is woodland; the unshaded area within the parish is divided into more or less rectangular fields, which would in turn have been sub-divided by their various proprietors (see note 28, page 227).

out a new system of roads for the area; and in this their main innovation – as can be seen from Map 2 – was to lay a ruler along the map between the villages of Helpston and Glinton, and to join them by a long, straight road which was to become the main route out of Helpston towards Peterborough, linking up with the turn-pike road already passing between Peterborough and Glinton. At Helpston the new road from Glinton met the old road to the Parks; and whereas before the old road had reached King Street rather indirectly, picking its way no doubt around the edges of furlongs in Heath Field, now the commissioners took the kinks out of it, and thus produced one single straight road, leading from Glinton through Helpston to King Street. This road became the new road to Stamford, though it did not in point of fact lead there very directly; and the old Stamford road, running across the north of the parish through Lolham Bridge Field, was 'stopped up and destroyed as superfluous and unnecessary'.[29] The road to Nunton and the road running south to Castor the commissioners left as they were, except that all the public roads in the village were now to be of a proper width and properly hedged. It is apparent, too, from Clare's writing, that a very considerable number of footpaths through the old arable fields were 'discontinued' at the enclosure, but it is not possible to determine the precise course of these: the fields, for all their numerous divisions into furlongs each with its individual name, their footpaths and green balks, were to the commissioners the blank, empty spaces they appeared to be on Earl Fitzwilliam's map; thus the commissioners do not explain in the Award what features of the old topography they have eradi-cated, but only the features they have allowed to stand, or intro-duced themselves into the landscape.

Across the northern boundary of the parish the commissioners caused to be dug a long drain called Maxey Cut; and more or less parallel with it, a little way to the south and where before a stream had run through the Long Meadow, they made another long drain, slightly narrower. These two ditches stretched from King Street in the west to the River Welland at Peakirk Moor in the east; and thus served to drain a long strip of land running through all six parishes involved in the enclosure. Green Dyke, a stream which led eastward from a pond in the meadows at the north of Lolham Bridge Field, was stopped at source, as may have been also the stream leading from Round Oak Spring in Heath Field; and the ditches made by both streams through the fields were made more regular and incorporated into the new drainage-system of the parish.[30]

The most obvious effect, however, that the enclosure had on the topography of Helpston must have been on the old arable fields and common grazing-land. The enclosure was a somewhat unusual one, in Helpston at least, in that owing to the very considerable variety of soils in the parish – from the good soil in the north to the 'very fleet soil on a ragg-stone', as one surveyor described it after the enclosure,[31] in Heath Field – it was decided to distribute the holdings of the larger farmers, as before, around the different areas of the parish, but now of course in much larger allotments. Thus the farms were not compacted as they usually were by an enclosure, a fact often still remarked on as curious by the local population. But still as after any enclosure the land in the parish was divided into square parcels, which were quickly fenced and hedged, and then allowed to be put under any course of husbandry that the owner of each might choose. In some enclosures of open-field land by Act of Parliament, a great deal of the work of enclos-ing had already been done by the farmers themselves, either by agreement amongst themselves or by some form or another of coercion, and the Act was merely to confirm their work, and perhaps to clear up one or two remaining slips of open-field land. In Etton, for example, about two-thirds of the parish was already enclosed by 1809, and had been for centuries; in Helpston, on the other hand, four-fifths of the land was still open at the time of the enclosure; and the new pattern of the fields – square-shaped and straight-hedged – was laid over almost the whole of the parish like a grid. The openness and the old uniformity of the fields dis-appeared together, to be replaced by a very different uniformity; and by its new straight highway to Peterborough, and its new system of land-drainage, Helpston was made a part of the large, flat, fenny area of the Soke to the north and west, its face turned outward towards Milton Hall, the seat of the Fitzwilliams in Northamptonshire, and towards the expanding town of Peter-borough.

I

There are three poems by John Clare which were apparently written during the period of the enclosure, or just after it, and which describe the effect of the enclosure on the old landscape of Helpston. 'Helpstone',[32] a poem in imitation of *The Deserted Village*, was written, according to Clare, in 1809, but as a large part of the poem is about the effects of the enclosure, he must have been adding to it at least until 1815 or so; it was published in his first collection[33] of 1820. The second poem, 'Helpstone Green',[34] was published in 1821,[35] but the form and style suggest that it also was written about 1815. The third poem and by far the best, 'The Lamentations of Round Oak Waters',[36] remained unpublished until 1935; but J. W. Tibble, who produced in that year an edition of Clare's poetry in two volumes, suggests that it was probably written in 1818.

What are probably, then, the two earlier poems, 'Helpstone' and 'Helpstone Green', are both very dependent on Clare's reading in the poetry of the previous century; on Goldsmith, most obviously, but there is something of Gray in them – the Gray of, for example, the 'Sonnet on the Death of Richard West', and of the Eton College ode[37] – and of that line of eighteenth-century landscape-poetry which shows the influence of the early Milton: of 'Il Penseroso' in particular. These debts, of theme, of tone, make Clare's two poems, as poems about the enclosure, very confused, and their effect seems to have been to distort what seems to have been for Clare, the real significance of the enclosure. In 'Helpstone Green', for example, Clare begins by writing of the 'long waving rows of willow', and of the 'hawthorn bowers',[38] cut down since the enclosure; he goes on:

> Whene'er I muse along the plain
>   And mark where once they grew,
> Remembrance wakes her busy train
>   And brings past scenes to view:
> The well-known brook, the favourite tree,
>   In fancy's eye appear,
> And next, that pleasant green I see,
>   That green for ever dear.

(lines 17–24)

We are thus invited to expect to find, in the next stanza, that not

110

only have the willows and hawthorn disappeared from the landscape, but that the green, too, has gone; but this piece of information is withheld for the space of a further stanza, and instead we read:

> O'er its green hills I've often stray'd
> In childhood's happy hour,
> Oft sought the nest along the shade
> And gather'd many a flower,
> And there, with playmates often join'd
> In fresher sports to plan:
> But now increasing years have coin'd
> Those children into man.
>
> (lines 25–32)

The poem has lost its original direction, and now, instead of showing us how the landscape has been changed, this last stanza seems to place the poem in that tradition of the poetry of melancholy – the sonnet on Richard West is in the same tradition – which opposes the *permanence* of the natural landscape against the transience of youth: the stanza might be taken from a poem which says that the green remains as it has been, but that the poet can never again see it as he saw it when a boy.

The same sort of confusion occurs also in the better of the two poems, 'Helpstone':

> Hail, scenes obscure! so near and dear to me,
> The church, the brook, the cottage, and the tree:
> Still shall obscurity rehearse the song,
> And hum your beauties as I stroll along.
> Dear, native spot! which length of time endears,
> The sweet retreat of twenty lingering years;
> And, oh! those years of infancy the scene,
> Those dear delights, where once they all have been,
> Those golden days, long vanish'd from the plain,
> Those sports, those pastimes, now belov'd in vain;
> When happy youth in pleasure's circle ran,
> Nor thought what pains awaited future man...
> These joys, all known in happy infancy,
> And all I ever knew, were spent in thee.
> And who but loves to view where these were past?
> And who, that views, but loves them to the last?
> Feels his heart warm to view his native place,
> A fondness still those past delights to trace?
> The vanish'd green to mourn, the spot to see
> Where flourish'd many a bush and many a tree?
>
> (lines 30–42, 51–8)

I think that, even with *The Deserted Village* kept firmly in mind –
and it is hard enough to put it out of mind, in a passage which
insists so firmly on its connection with Goldsmith's poem – it is
impossible for us not to be surprised when, as we read these lines,
the phrase 'past delights' turns over in the palm of our hand and
comes to refer, not to the youthful pastimes Clare is now too old
to enjoy, but to the green and to the trees which were once the
scene of those pastimes. It's partly perhaps that the convention
of the wanderer returning to the scenes of his childhood, which
Goldsmith uses in his poem, is more often used to express this
other theme, of the permanence of nature and the transience of
youth. In any case, the poem we do expect, after reading the first
dozen or so lines of the paragraph I have quoted, is the one which
says that the landscape is still as it was, but that the cares of
manhood now make it seem to Clare less than the Paradise it once
was; this is a poem Clare wrote often before about 1820 – this
stanza, from 'Childish Recollections',[39] will serve as an example:

> Though in the midst of each endear'd delight,
> Where still the cowslips to the breezes bow,
> Though all my childish scenes are in my sight,
> Sad manhood marks me an intruder now.

> (lines 33–6)

But in 'Helpstone' we find instead that the landscape, which at
the beginning of the paragraph seems to be a present fact for
Clare, exists now only in his memory of the village before the
enclosure. And so both this poem and 'Helpstone Green' present
us with two alternative, opposed versions of their content: is
Clare's nostalgia primarily for the old landscape of Helpston, or
for his childhood, the memory of which the landscape can revive
but which it cannot restore?

It is fairly clear that what Clare wants to do is to twist these
two strands of meaning into one, by saying that his childhood was
so bound up in the old landscape that, when the landscape disappeared, his childhood disappeared with it; but this is a particularly awkward argument when Clare is, as I have said, so thoroughly
dependent in these poems on that tradition of the poetry of
melancholy which opposes the permanence of nature to the
transience of youth; and we are, anyway, entitled to ask whether,
at twenty or at whatever age he was when he wrote 'Helpstone',
Clare would still have been able to see the landscape with the

careless eye of childhood had the enclosure never taken place.

Clare's most recent editors, Eric Robinson and Geoffrey Summerfield, have proposed that there is, running through all Clare's work, a 'pattern of imagery'[40] which would, perhaps, make more sense of these poems, and of the uneasy relationship they have with the poetry of the eighteenth century, than I have been able to do; and particularly of 'Helpstone', the last paragraph of which begins:

> Oh, happy Eden of those golden years
> Which memory cherishes, and use endears...

(lines 141–2)

According to Robinson and Summerfield:

If the countryside about Helpstone was not only the map of Clare's boyhood but also part of a rural landscape cruelly altered by enclosure, it was something even more significant. Helpstone was Clare's Paradise, his Garden of Eden...In the landscape of Eden before the Fall, Clare's boyhood love, Mary Joyce, is present – she is the Eve of Clare's Adam...Mary and Helpstone, Nature before enclosure, Eve before the Temptation, Eden before the Fall, childhood before the onset of adult trials and deceptions, were therefore a unity in Clare's mind.[41]

It is clear that this sort of scheme, if it is really present as a 'conscious pattern of imagery in Clare's poetry', would do much to resolve the confusions I find in the poems we have been looking at: we could say that Clare felt himself and Mary innocent as long as the landscape of Eden remained unenclosed, but that they fell with the trees at the enclosure. The main difficulty of this interpretation – beyond the fact that, after all, Clare is obviously saying no such thing in 'Helpstone' at least – is that, as far as we can see from the examples Robinson and Summerfield have so far produced to substantiate their theory, the imagery of Eden seems to be applied to the landscape of Helpston indifferently whether it is still open or enclosed; and in 'Helpstone' itself the lines about Eden that I have quoted, although they apply in this case to the landscape of Clare's childhood, are followed by a passage in which Clare prays that he may in his old age return to Helpstone and die there; certainly in these lines there is none of the sense of alienation that Robinson and Summerfield speak of, and which Clare himself certainly claims to feel elsewhere in the poem. Ironically enough, the last lines of the passage about Eden, which are also the last lines of the poem –

> And, as reward for all my troubles past,
> Find one hope true – to die at home at last!

(lines 155–6)

– are borrowed directly from Goldsmith's

> I still had hopes, my long vexations past,
> Here to return – and die at home at last;

(The Deserted Village, lines 95–6)

but whereas Goldsmith's hope cannot now be fulfilled, Clare has not been so thoroughly expelled from his Eden that he cannot look forward to a comfortable old age there. I think we have to conclude that Clare was, at this stage, simply unable to organise his response to the enclosure or to Helpston; and that there is no scheme of imagery that will help him out of his confusions, of the difficulty he finds in distinguishing between his own meaning and that of the poets he is imitating.[42]

But here and there in both these poems are lines and passages which are a good deal less dependent than those we have so far looked at on the conventions of the poetry of rural melancholy:

> In those past days, for then I lov'd the shade,
> How oft I've sigh'd at alterations made,
> To see the woodman's cruel axe employ'd,
> A tree beheaded, or a bush destroy'd:
> Nay e'en a post, old standard, or a stone
> Moss'd o'er by age, and branded as her own,
> Would in my mind a strong attachment gain,
> A fond desire that there they might remain;
> And all old favourites, fond taste approves,
> Griev'd me at heart to witness their removes.

(lines 69–78)

In these lines from 'Helpstone', Clare has approached the en-closure much more directly; there is no attempt to connect the landscape with a conventional melancholy of Clare's own; and the tone of nostalgia that does come across is a part, I would argue, of Clare's very individual sense of place, of his particular attachment to Helpston as itself individual, as 'local' in the sense that its landscape is not seen by him as part of 'nature' in general. It's clear, I think, that in these lines the sort of attachment to the objects of the landscape that Clare is describing is quite different from the sort of regret he was feeling earlier, when the identity of the old landscape was dependent on its having been the scene of

Clare's childhood. Here it is the simple fact that the trees and stones in the landscape were *there*, where they were, that caused Clare's attachment to them, and causes him to regret their destruction now. And this sense of place appears briefly also in 'Helpstone Green', where Clare writes that now

> ...the thick-cultur'd tribes that grow
> Will so efface the scene,
> That after-times will hardly know
> It ever was a green.

> (lines 45–8)

What Clare is regretting here is that the identity of the green – which consists in the simple fact of its *being* a green, and remaining one – will be effaced by the different use the same patch of land will be put to by the enclosure.

'The Lamentations of Round Oak Waters' is a much better poem than either 'Helpstone' or 'Helpstone Green', and indeed it seems to me the best thing Clare had written by the time his first collection appeared, although it was not included in that collection and was perhaps thought too radical for publication. But this poem too, for all its apparent unity of tone, remains as do the other two a meeting-ground of rather diverse themes and ideas which Clare cannot properly fuse together. It begins with Clare 'oppress'd with grief'[43] and sitting beside Round Oak Waters, the brook which had once led from Round Oak Spring. The genius of the brook hears his lamentations, and invites him to hear its own sorrows, those brought about by the enclosure. And once again the problem arises, exactly on what terms is the landscape being admitted into the poem? Are we to read the poem as an extreme use of the pathetic fallacy, and to understand the sorrows of the brook as an echo of Clare's own? The *genius loci*, before it begins properly to recount its own sorrows, talks at length of Clare's melancholy, of his loneliness in the village and of how 'different feelings thou possess'd/From any other boy'.[44] And yet, when it does finally come to describe its own misfortunes, the brook is particular about them in a way which extends the importance of the landscape far beyond the significance it seems first to have had for Clare, as an emblem of his own misfortune:

> Dire nakedness o'er all prevails;
> Yon fallows bare and brown

>
> Are all beset with posts and rails
>   And turnèd upside down;
> The gently curving, darksome balks,
>   That stript the cornfields o'er
> And prov'd the shepherd's daily walks,
>   Now prove his walks no more;
> The plough has had them under hand
>   And overturned them all,
> And now along the elting-land
>   Poor swains are forced to maul*.

(lines 77–88)

*Drag along wearily.

It is the landscape as itself, where it was, that is being regretted here; and from here onward the poem leaves Clare's melancholy behind, and becomes more like a direct political statement against the enclosure. And so the poem, as it gets better, falls in half; it could only be made whole again if we were made to feel that Clare's sadness is his personal share of a general sorrow at the enclosure; but this will hardly do. In the first half of the poem the genius of the brook has been emphasising Clare's apartness from the collectivity of the village, and although the cause of his sadness isn't explained, we are given good reason to think it is the result of his feeling unlike and indeed superior to the other villagers, and yet unable to rise above his social position and establish himself as a poet. These two related feelings are frequent in Clare's poetry until after his second collection, *The Village Minstrel*, appeared in 1821 (they occur after that only occasionally, for example in 'Valentine Eve');[45] in his early poems Clare often presents himself as being driven into the landscape away from the society of the village, and it is thus that he often puts the landscape in the position of sympathising with him in his solitude.

I want now to look at another of Clare's poems about the enclosure, 'The Lament of Swordy Well',[46] which was probably written at some time between 1821 and 1824. This poem is one of Clare's best; and the first thing, perhaps, to be said about it is that the language, and the tone, Clare employs in it are unusually free of the sort of dependence on eighteenth-century models which was so apparent in the earlier poems. Like 'The Lamentations of Round Oak Waters' 'The Lament of Swordy Well' is a dramatic monologue, although spoken this time not by the genius of the place but by the place itself; the language is direct and colloquial:

> I'm Swordy Well, a piece of land
> That's fell upon the town,
> Who worked me till I couldn't stand
> And crush me now I'm down...
>
> (lines 1–4)

> Alas, dependence, thou'rt a brute
> Want only understands;
> His feelings wither branch and root
> Who falls in parish hands.
>
> (lines 13–16)

The same connection is made in this poem, as was made at the end of 'The Lamentations of Round Oak Waters', between the sufferings of the land as it now is, enclosed, and of the labourers as they are after the enclosure; but here it is being made in a particularly witty way, by making what the place says correspond exactly to what the labourer, whose language the place is using, *might* say, about the enclosure – the identification is immediately established by the first stanza, in the line 'that's fell upon the town'; which applied to Swordy Well means (as we come to discover in the poem) that it has been given by the Award to the overseers for the roads in the parish, for mending-stone; applied to a labourer it means the same as that he 'falls in parish hands'. As the poem goes on, however, the place separates itself from the labourer and comes to concentrate more on its private suffering; and the same sense of the identity of a place, that we saw emerging briefly in the early poems, becomes the theme of this one. The identity of Swordy Well is seen to depend on its being left as it was before the enclosure; and the last four stanzas make this sense of place particularly immediate:

> And if I could but find a friend
> With no deceit to sham,
> Who'd send me some few sheep to tend,
> And leave me as I am,

> To keep my hills from cart and plough
> And strife of mongrel men,
> And as spring found me find me now,
> I should look up agen.

> And save his Lordship's woods, that past
> The day of danger dwell,
> Of all the fields I am the last
> That my own face can tell;

117

Yet what with stone-pits' delving holes,
And strife to buy and sell,
My name will quickly be the whole
That's left of Swordy Well.

(lines 61–76)

Partly the sense of locality I am trying to argue for here is the result of the poem being written so obviously about a particular place, about which we learn that some of it is being quarried and some of it being ploughed, although before it had been a sheep-pasture; the phrase 'his Lordship's woods' contributes to the same sense. But the sense of place resides most remarkably in the separation Clare makes between the place itself and its name: the enclosure will alter the face – and Clare's reinvigoration of that metaphor is striking – of the landscape so completely, that although the name of the place will survive the place itself will disappear: it depends for its identity not on its name, but on its being the same as it was, on being left as it is.

I want to look, finally in this section, at a piece of prose from the journal Clare was keeping in 1824:

Wed. 29 Sept. 1824. Took a walk in the fields saw an old wood stile taken away from a favourite spot which it had occupied all my life the posts were overgrown with Ivy & it seemd so akin to nature & the spot where it stood as tho it had taken it on lease for an undisturbd existance it hurt me to see it was gone for my affections claims a friendship with such things but nothing is lasting in this world last year Langley Bush was destroyd an old whitethorn that had stood for more than a century...[47]

The stile, says Clare, was 'akin to...the spot where it stood'; its identity depended, as did that of the trees and stones in 'Helpstone', on its being there where it was, and remaining there. He makes much the same point in a poem written perhaps some time after 1825, 'The Moorehen's Nest',[48] in which he describes a tree, its roots washed bare, growing on the bank of a river and apparently tumbling in, but

...every summer finds it green and gay
& winter leaves it safe as did the may

(lines 85–6)

It's worth pointing out, too, that where in the prose passage Clare introduces a conventionally philosophical note, 'nothing is lasting in this world', the effect is not at all what it would have been had he introduced the same sentiment, as he might well have done, into an early poem. The phrase is almost a form of shorthand, a

118

way of moving on to the next idea, and quite without the moralising content it would have in another context. Clare uses the phrase to mean little more than 'there have been other changes, too'; and 'in this world' means in fact 'in Helpston', and is followed by a note on the destruction of another local landmark.

It's clear that between the time when the first three poems we have discussed were being written, and the writing of 'The Lament of Swordy Well' and the *Journal*, Clare's poetry has changed direction – or perhaps it would be truer to say that it has settled decisively for one of the opposite directions the early poems were taking. The nature of the change can be shown from two comments Clare made on the long title-poem of his second collection, *The Village Minstrel*. Before this poem was published (in 1821), Clare was reading James Beattie's *The Minstrel*;[49] at this time the title of his own poem was 'The Peasant Boy'. He wrote: ' "The Minstrel" is a sweet poem & far as I have read a many thoughts occur which are in my 'Peasant Boy' I doubt the world will think them plagarisms, therefore I must alter or cut them out altogether, but nature is the same here at Helpstone as it is elsewhere.'[50] Soon after the poem was published, on the other hand, Clare was, according to his biographers, 'sorry he had not withheld the title poem much longer for revision',[51] and he wrote: 'The reason why I dislike it is that it does not describe the feelings of a rhyming peasant strongly or *locally* enough' (my italics).[52] It is this desire to write 'locally', to write his poems about nature as she did appear in Helpston and not elsewhere, that becomes around 1821 and 1822 Clare's main preoccupation; which informs almost all his poems while he is living in Helpston, and which encourages him to write, for example, the natural history letters that he thought of as a *Natural History of Helpston*,[53] and the catalogue of Northamptonshire birds.[54] I have been using the word 'local', and have spoken of Clare's 'sense of place', of the 'identity' of a place, rather freely, and in the next section of this chapter I shall explain more precisely what I mean by them: but first I should perhaps make it clear that I am not trying to argue that Clare's effort to write 'locally' can be *explained* in some simple fashion as the effect the enclosure of Helpston had upon him. It is certainly true, that his poetry becomes more concerned with the idea of the local at about the same time as the enclosure was being completed, and it may also be true that, as 'The Lament of Swordy Well' would suggest, to see the landscape of Helpston destroyed by the enclosure made him more conscious of the idea of the identity of that landscape. But one could equally well argue that his concern became more local as, for example, he became more able to emancipate himself from the influence of Goldsmith, and to discover a language of his own; and clearly there is nothing conclusive to be got out of the argument about causes and effects. The point I am trying to make, however, is that, for whatever reason, Clare's writing after 1821 or so is increasingly preoccupied with being 'local', and that he is concerned with one place, Helpston, not as it is typical of other places, but as it is individual; and individual not because it is different, but because it was the only place he knew: nature may well have been the same elsewhere as in Helpston, but Clare was only familiar with nature as it was in his own parish. This sort of concentration, this sense of place, was inevitably opposed to the ideology of enclosure, which sought to de-localise, to take away the individuality of a place, in ways which I described in the last chapter and in the first section of this. And his resentment at the changes in the use the land was put to – turning Swordy Well into a parish stone-pit, growing 'thick-cultur'd' crops on the green, and thus making both places no longer what they were – is similarly in opposition to the aims of the enclosers.

II

In the autobiography[55] that he was writing in the early 1820s, Clare describes an occasion when, as a child, he walked out of the parish and across Emmonsailes Heath, in search, he tells us, of 'the world's end'[56] – the tone of the passage may be a little arch. He soon got lost: 'So I eagerly wanderd on & rambled along the furze the whole day till I got out of my knowledge when the very wild flowers seemd to forget me & I imagind they were the inhabitants of new countrys the very sun seemd to be a new one & shining in a different quarter of the sky'.[57] What interests me particularly here is the phrase 'out of my knowledge', and the use Clare makes of it. The phrase itself is common enough in the early nineteenth century, although it is not listed in the *O.E.D.*; it is used for example by Robert Bloomfield in an anecdote he tells about Thomas Paine, published in his *Remains*.[58] When he was a boy, says Bloomfield, Paine went 'in company with his sister – I think it was – to Fakenham Wood, in search of nuts; and being by themselves, they wandered out of their knowledge, and knew not the way out again.'[59] As Bloomfield uses the phrase its meaning is clear enough: Paine and his sister went out of the place they knew; and for Clare, too, the primary sense of the phrase is 'out of the place I knew' – the place he was familiar with and knew his way about. But it is clear too that Clare is quite conscious of asking the phrase to mean more than that, to carry the full weight of its literal meaning – not just out of the place I knew, but out of *everything* I knew – 'the very wild flowers seemd to forget me'; and the sense of disorientation is recognised as precisely that, in the words that follow soon after: 'the very sun seemd to be a new one & shining in a different quarter of the sky'.[60]

In two other passages of the *Autobiography*, Clare describes his feelings on leaving Helpston as an adolescent and as a young man. When he was about fifteen, he travelled to Wisbech to be interviewed for the post of clerk in a lawyer's office:

I started for Wisbeach with a timid sort of pleasure & when I got to Glinton turnpike I turnd back to look on the old church as if I was going into another country Wisbeach was a foreign land to me for I had never been above eight miles from home in my life I coud not fancy England much larger than the part I knew.[61]

– and later, when he was about twenty or perhaps less, he walked to Grantham and on to Newark-on-Trent, again in search of work. At Grantham, he says, 'I thought to be sure I was out of the world';[62] and of Newark:

I felt quite lost when I was here though it was a very lively town but I had never been from home before scarcely further than out of sight of the steeples I became so ignorant in this far land that I coud not tell which quarter the wind blew from & I even was foolish enough to think the sun's course was alterd & that it rose in the west & set in the east I often puzzled at it to set myself right but I still thought so.[63]

These passages both contribute to the sense that Clare's 'knowledge', the place he knew, was to him a good deal more than that: as long as he was in Helpston, the knowledge he had was valid, was knowledge: the east was east and the west west as long as he could recognise them by the landmarks in the parish, and by the simple habit of knowing; the names he knew for the flowers were the right names as long as the flowers were in Helpston. But once out of the parish his knowledge ceased to be knowledge; what he knew as fact was only fact, only to be relied upon, within the parish or within 'sight of the steeples' of the parishes round. It is important to remember, when we read the poems about the enclosure, that when the old landscape was destroyed a part of Clare's knowledge was destroyed also, and it was no doubt to try and preserve what he *knew*, in Helpston, that he developed the idea of the identity of a place, that we discovered in the last section. And, finally, just how narrow the circle of Clare's knowledge was, is well suggested in the *Autobiography*, when he refers to Maxey, the next settlement to Helpston to the north, and less than three miles away, as 'a distant village'.[64] To walk to Burghley Park, a distance of less than five miles, was to travel in 'foreign ground', says Clare in his 'Narrative Verses'.[65]

The fragments of prose which make up the *Autobiography* were written, as I have said, in the early 1820s, when Clare had already published two collections of verse, one enormously successful, the other less so but still quite widely reviewed and well thought-of. Prose was at this time a new medium for Clare, and he approaches it in perhaps as self-consciously literary a spirit as he had first approached the writing of verse; and from time to time in these fragments Clare adopts the attitude, towards his early life, of a fairly well-travelled – he had by now been twice to London – and indeed almost metropolitan literary man, recalling with satisfaction but with nostalgia how far he has come from his days as a provincial *ingénu*. The occasionally knowing, affectionately condescending tone of his prose Clare had probably picked up from Lamb, and it seems to force him to assume a rather greater breadth of social and, so to speak, geographical experience than was really his. I think, in any case, that we are expected to understand a distance between the narrator of these recollections and the subject of them, and to understand that Clare is now far from the naive provincial, who 'coud not fancy England much larger' than the part he knew.

At the same time, however, and precisely as Clare was becoming more familiar with the literary tone of the metropolis, he was becoming also more tenacious in his desire to write exclusively about Helpston, to 'describe the feelings of a rhyming peasant... locally'. It seems that the more he came to know of what lay outside

the parish, the more he understood that his existence as a writer
depended on his remaining within the area that he knew, and
writing about that only; it is perhaps worth remembering here
what Clare said about the landscape of Helpston, that it 'made up'
his 'being'. The desire to write 'locally', to make the individuality
of Helpston the content of his poems, was not the product of an
unambiguous love which Clare felt for the place. He writes to his
publisher, John Taylor,

I wish I livd nearer you at least I wish London woud creep within 20 miles of
Helpstone I don't wish Helpstone to shift its station I live here among the
ignorant like a lost man in fact like one whom the rest seem careless of having
anything to do with – they hardly dare talk in my company for fear I shoud
mention them in my writings & I find more pleasure in wandering the fields
then in mixing among my silent neighbours who are insensible of everything
but toiling & talking of it & that to no purpose.[66]

Clare wasn't always so scornful of the other villagers, and was often
grateful enough for their company, although he frequently complains of his lack of literate companionship. But there is no desire
expressed here to leave Helpston, at the same time as Clare quite
clearly feels his confinement there is a limitation on him. It is a
limitation accepted reluctantly, but, once accepted it is, in his
poetry especially, insisted upon; we are continually made to feel
that his own identity, like that of the trees and flowers, depends
on his staying where he is. There is a poem by Clare about the sand-
martin, in which he describes that bird as a hermit, as preferring
the landscape of the heath to that where he might be more likely
to meet either men or other birds – we are entitled, I think, to
read the poem as one in which Clare to some extent at least is
identifying himself with the bird. The poem ends:

> Ive seen thee far away from all thy tribe
> Flirting* about the unfrequented sky
> And felt a feeling that I cant describe
> Of lone seclusion and a hermit joy
> To see thee circle round nor go beyond
> That lone heath and its melancholly pond.[67]
>
> ('Sand Martin', lines 9–14)

*Flitting.

The feeling that Clare can't describe includes within it precisely
those opposed attitudes that, in the letter to Taylor, he expresses
about Helpston: the bird cannot, perhaps, but certainly *does* not

go beyond the circle of the heath and pond, and yet this limitation is accepted by Clare as a perverse source of joy.

III

I want to look now at one of Clare's purely descriptive poems, to see in what way Clare's desire to write locally can be expressed in a poem which makes no attempt – as does, say, 'The Lament of Swordy Well' – explicitly to define the idea of place that is characteristically his. This poem, 'Winter Fields',[68] is a representative example of the large number of sonnets that Clare was writing between about 1824 and 1832:

> O for a pleasant book to cheat the sway
> Of winter – where rich mirth with hearty laugh
> Listens and rubs his legs on corner seat
> For fields are mire and sludge – and badly off
> Are those who on their pudgy* paths delay
> There striding shepherd seeking driest way
> Fearing nights wetshod feet and hacking cough
> That keeps him waken till the peep of day
> Goes shouldering onward and with ready hook
> Progs† oft to ford the sloughs that nearly meet
> Accross the lands – croodling‡ and thin to view
> His loath dog follows – stops and quakes and looks
> For better roads – till whistled to pursue
> Then on with frequent jump he hirkles§ through.

*Full of puddles; †pokes, or prods; ‡'shrinking from the cold'; §'to crouch, to set up the back, as cattle who shrink from cold' (*Selected Poems*, p. 207).

What is immediately striking about this poem is the richness of detail within it – a richness that seems to be in itself sufficient evidence of its accuracy. In the five-and-a-half lines about the shepherd, Clare tells us that he walks across the fields, resolutely and looking for the driest way; but the furrows between the raised lands are so full of water that the lands are almost submerged, and so the shepherd, unable to take the sloughs – the wet muddy furrows – in one stride, prods them with his crook to find out where the water is shallowest, and will allow him to ford the sloughs while getting his feet as little wet as possible. This sort of richness of detail can perhaps be taken, as I have said, as a guarantee of its own accuracy; but it isn't only in this 'local colour', or not in this local colour taken by itself, that the sense of place I discover in this poem resides. The details of the shepherd's walk, as I have paraphrased them, are not after all so extraordinarily particular that they could apply only in Helpston; and I want to suggest that it is especially in the language of his poems, and (as I shall argue in a later section) in the syntax of them, that Clare finds the specifically local quality that he is seeking.

Such attention as has been directed towards Clare's language in the past has been directed principally towards his use of dialect, of 'provincialisms' – there are examples in 'Winter Fields', 'pudgy', 'progs', 'croodling', 'hirkles' – and in this aspect of his poetry Clare was given plenty of advice from his literary friends and from the reviewers of his early volumes. Lamb's advice is perhaps particularly worth quoting:

In some of your story telling Ballads the provincial phrases sometimes startle me. I think you are too profuse with them. In poetry, *slang* of every kind is to be avoided. There is a rustic Cockneyism as little pleasing as ours of London. Transplant Arcadia to Helpstone. The true rustic style, the Arcadian English, I think is to be found in Shenstone. Would his 'Schoolmistress', the prettiest of poems, have been better if he had used quite the Goody's own language? Now and then a home rusticism is fresh and startling, but where nothing is gained in expression it is out of tenor.[69]

Taylor, who made himself responsible for editing Clare's poems as well as for publishing them, for a time defended Clare's use of dialect: 'His language, it is true, is provincial, and his choice of words in ordinary conversation is indifferent, because Clare is an unpretending man, and he speaks in the idiom of his neighbours, who would ridicule and despise him for using more or better terms than they are familiar with.'[70] But by the time *The Shepherd's Calendar*[71] was being prepared for publication, Taylor had come to find Clare's dialect as obnoxious as Lamb had found it; and although it was thought by Clare's biographers, J. W. and Anne Tibble, that on the evidence of the version of the poem published in 1827 Clare had almost entirely removed the provincialisms from his poetic vocabulary,[72] we now know that this was an impression caused mainly by Taylor's heavy editing. In their article, 'John Taylor's editing of Clare's *Shepherd's Calendar*',[73] Eric Robinson and Geoffrey Summerfield give a good number of examples of Taylor's alterations: thus 'douse' became 'plunge', and 'scratting' became 'scratching', 'burring' became 'buzzing', 'sild' became 'swoon'd':[74] 'I must have something to cut', said Taylor, in the first months of his friendship with Clare, 'or Othello's Occupation's Gone'.[75]

Clare's response was sometimes gracious, sometimes indeed grateful; but as often he found himself having to insist that no word was to be altered. He himself was quite clear why he used provincialisms; he had no choice but to use them. 'I think vulgar names to the flowers best', he wrote to Hessey, Taylor's partner, 'as I know no others'.[76] And while other 'peasant poets', Stephen Duck, Robert Bloomfield, had worked hard to learn the proper language of poetry, Clare had instead an Aristotelian idea of propriety, and thought that 'Putting the Correct Language of the Gentleman into the mouth of a Simple Shepherd or Vulgar Ploughman is far from Natural'[77] – and elsewhere, defending his use of the phrase 'eggs on' in his 'Address to a Lark',[78] he wrote: 'whether provincial or not I cannot tell; but it is common with the vulgar, (I am of that class,) and I heartily desire no word of mine to be altered'.[79] The connection between Clare's use of dialect words – 'I know no others' – and the sense in which the whole of his knowledge was only that, only knowledge, insofar as it was local, is too clear to need insisting upon; thus in 'Winter Fields' the phrase 'pudgy paths' means not simply paths full of puddles, but 'full of puddles in the way we know them to be in Helpston'; that the dog 'hirkles' means not simply that 'it moves with its hind quarters shrugged up against the cold', but that 'it moves in that attitude which, when we see it taken up by dogs round here, we describe as "hirkling" '.

But Lamb's and Taylor's concentration on Clare's provincial-isms has separated them off in criticism of his language from the rest of the words he uses – and Clare, by being forced to defend his dialect against his metropolitan critics, was forced to co-operate in this separation. For him, however, the words he used but which were not understood in London were not in the first place separate from those which (as it happened) Lamb and Taylor did understand, and did not think 'slang'; the difference between the two sets of words lay for Clare only in the idea his critics had of them, that they were parts of two different languages, English and provincial; and although as he read more Clare became, no doubt, more able to forecast what parts of his language would be understood, and acceptable, and what parts would not, he managed to prevent this knowledge affecting the language of his poems. This language was, for Clare, a unity, a vocabulary of provincialisms, some comprehensible outside Helpston, and others not. The point is well understood by Donald Davie, in what is by a long way the best comment that has yet appeared on Clare's language:[80] Davie quotes two lines from one of Clare's late poems:

> I love to see the shaking twig
> Dance till shut of eve;[81]

and he goes on:

even in a scrap like that one can isolate Clare's peculiar purity, in the prosaic word 'shaking', so honestly and unfussily Clare's name for what a twig does ...'shaking' stays stubbornly close to the thing it names, and won't let us look away or beyond to anything analogous.

And this is a virtue of the earlier Clare also. It is the reason behind his use of dialect, which is not for him a valuable resource, an artful freaking of language. He says that robins 'tutle' because this is his and his neighbours' name for what robins do, not a *mot juste* sought for and triumphantly found; not the one exquisitely right word, just the one right one. It is not so far from what Pound applauded in Johnson's *Vanity of Human Wishes*, 'the merits of the lexicographer', for whom one thing has one name, and only one name.[82]

It's clear enough that for Davie, at least, there is no separation between Clare's use of provincialisms and the rest of his dialect: the effort is always to find the one right word – as Clare says in his autobiography, of his early attempts at poetry: 'if an old pond with its pendant sallows fringing its mossy sides happend to be in the pleasant nook where I sat concealed among the blackthorns drawing its picture I calld it a pond'.[83] But we can perhaps go further than Davie, or suggest at least that his description of Clare's language leads in a different direction from the one he chooses to take: 'the merits of the lexicographer' seem to me quite absent from Clare's language. It is true that the words he uses are, on the one hand, prosaic, and pure in the sense that, as Davie says, they 'won't let us look away or beyond to anything analogous' – the language prescribes rigidly the limits of the poem's meaning. But the lexicographer is not only concerned with 'the one right word'; he is concerned also to distinguish the 'language of the centre' from the obsolete words and from the provincialisms that his dictionary may also list. His work is to define that language which Dante describes, in a passage Davie himself has quoted in another context: 'we declare that the Illustrious, Cardinal, Courtly, and Curial Vulgar Tongue in Italy is that which belongs to all the towns in Italy, but does not appear to belong to any one of them; and is that by which all the local dialects of the Italians are measured, weighed, and compared'.[84]

Clare's language is, on the contrary, purely local – a vocabulary of the names he and his neighbours use for what things are and what they do. It names things precisely, but as it does so it reminds us that this precision, the rightness of this or that word, is completely dependent on its being used of the things and actions in the place to which that language belongs. This isn't true only of the dialect-words, but of, as I say, the whole unity that is Clare's language. If we look again at 'Winter Fields' we will find plenty of words which are clearly not provincialisms, and yet which give the impression of existing in the same local context as do, say, 'pudgy' and 'hirkles' – 'peep', 'hook', 'roads' are examples of these; and the way in which these words, the provincialisms, and the words which are quite plainly used as they would be in London, coexist without tension in the poem, establishes the whole language of the poem as specifically of Clare's locality. And, finally, this sense of the local-ness of the language is reinforced by the peculiarity of Clare's grammar: in this poem he uses, for example, the dialect-form 'waken', and omits the definite article at least twice; in other poems he gives singular verbs to plural nouns; but in no case do we feel that these are simply mistakes, or expediencies adopted to help one line to scan and another to rhyme. Clare was, in fact, usually more amenable to Taylor's alterations of his grammar than he was to the omission of his provincialisms, and I think never defends his grammar on the grounds that it was as much a part of his dialect as was his vocabulary. There is one letter to Taylor, however, in which he does suggest that his irregular usages are the result not of an inability alone but also of an unwillingness to conform; he has been trying to alter a stanza in one of his poems, at Taylor's insistence: 'your verse is a devilish puzzle – I may alter but I cannot mend grammer in learning is like tyranny in government – confound the bitch I'll never be her slave & have a vast good mind not to alter the verse in question – by g—I've try'd an hour & cannot do a syllable so do your best & let it pass'.[85]

IV

Ever since the publication of Clare's first volume, the charge has been made against his poetry that it is *too* descriptive; that is, that it is descriptive at the expense of sentiment, of ideas, of (it is suggested) *content*. The early poems we have looked at so far were, as we have seen, very dependent on Clare's rather pious reading in eighteenth-century poetry, and are perhaps moralised enough, in Clare's anxiety to justify his descriptions by a counterpoise of explicit sentiment; but even these early poems, when they appeared in 1820 in *Poems Descriptive of Rural Life and Scenery*, were charged with being too preoccupied with 'true and minute delineations of external nature, drawn from *actual* observation'.[86] John Taylor was soon concerned that Clare should not 'let the Circumstances occupy so much of your Attention to the Exclusion of that which is more truly poetical. – I have not Time to-day to tell you exactly what I mean'[87] – but what Taylor did mean he made clear enough in another letter, written in 1826 when he was preparing *The Shepherd's Calendar* for the press: 'I have often remarked that your Poetry is much the best when you are not describing common things, and if you would raise your Views generally, & speak of the Appearances of Nature each Month more philosophically (if I may say so) or with more Excitement, you would greatly improve these little poems.'[88]

In addition to his own censures, Taylor was good enough to pass on also to Clare the opinions that Keats had formed of his work: and what Keats had to say was that, in Clare's poem 'Solitude',[89] 'the Description too much prevailed over the Sentiment';[90] and in another letter Taylor explained Keats's opinion more fully: 'I think he wishes to say to you that your Images from Nature are too much introduced without being called for by a particular Sentiment...his remark is applicable only now and then when he feels as if the Description overlaid and stifled that which ought to be the prevailing Idea.'[91]

This sort of advice was frequently offered to Clare, not by Taylor and Keats alone but also by, for example, Mrs Emmerson, a part-time poetess and of all Clare's literary friends perhaps the freest with her advice; of *The Shepherd's Calendar* she announced herself to be very pleased that Clare had at last proved himself 'capable of higher subjects than talking of Birds & Flowers'.[92] The pressure on Clare to think and feel properly about nature was very considerable, and it is not surprising that from time to time he took the advice of his friends, or allowed himself to be flattered into thinking of himself as potentially a philosophical poet; the quasi-Romantic poems he produced when he was thus persuaded have been highly regarded by some critics of his work – 'The Eternity of Nature'[93] is among them, and has been published in several selections of Clare's poems. I am bound to say that I find Clare's efforts in this genre without exception dull, and better than the album-verse they often take after only insofar as Clare was unable to imitate his models as exactly as he seems to have wished.

Since Clare was rediscovered, in 1920 or so, the charge of being too descriptive has again been brought forward against his poetry, in an excellent essay by John Middleton Murry about what he calls 'Clare's faculty of sheer vision';[94] 'it is hard to imagine', he writes,

that the poet...who could express what he saw with an ease and naturalness such that the expression strikes as part of the very act of seeing...should ever have thought, or should ever have had the impulse to think, about what he saw...Clare's faculty of vision is unique in English poetry, not only is it purer than Wordsworth's, it is purer even than Shakespeare's...And yet we feel that there is an intrinsic impossibility that vision of this kind, so effortless and unparading, should ever pass beyond itself; we feel it must demand so complete an engagement and submission of the whole man that it leaves no margin for other faculties. Clare's vision, we might say paradoxically, is too perfect.[95]

This seems to me both a very sensitive response to Clare, and a misguided one. It is true, as Middleton Murry says it is, that Clare's vision does not ever 'pass beyond itself', or at least it never did so successfully until the asylum-poems; it is true, too (and very well said), that we feel that this vision can leave 'no margin for other faculties'. At the same time we should be wary of the assumptions behind criticism of this kind; and particularly the assumption that for a descriptive poem to have content, it must pass beyond itself, into meditation or whatever. The poems of Wordsworth and of Keats, against whom Clare is here being measured, do obviously pass beyond themselves in this way; and although we are right to admire the 'organic unity' in their poems, the way in which image and idea coalesce, it is nevertheless true that there is always some part of their content which is separable from the images that have given rise to it. It isn't perhaps quite the point that for Middleton

Murry the detail, the description in a poem is in some way a bonus on top of the poem's real meaning, and finally separable from it; but if the description does not lead us to the more abstract content of the poem, then for Murry, and for Keats and no doubt for all of Clare's contemporaries, the description was either superfluous, or the poem somehow *purely* descriptive in a way that precluded its having *real* content.

But Clare's purely descriptive poems do have content, I want to suggest, which, although it is hardly at all separable from the description in which it inheres, is nevertheless perhaps evidence that Clare 'thought about' what he saw – if it is thus that content arises. The content of 'Winter Fields' is precisely the accuracy of the description, the richness and the completeness of it, understood in this particular way, that it is a body of knowledge, a set of details, that Clare has arrived at in this particular place, and not elsewhere. The content of the poem thus becomes the sense of place that the imagery and the language (and I shall argue later the syntax) together express, though they can none of them fully express it without the others. The sense of place that the poem expresses is that '*this* is how it is *here*'; and the poem thus contributes to the content that the larger part of Clare's poetry seeks to express, the particular individuality of Helpston. It is true that, as Middleton Murry says, the details of Clare's poetry – of 'Winter Fields' for example – is too rich and too accurate to allow the poem to pass beyond itself, and for the reason he gives, that Clare's descriptions are so complete that his poems are without any of the gaps through which they might have passed beyond themselves – and Davie's point is relevant here too, that Clare's language refuses to let us look beyond the things and actions he names, to anything analogous. But it is true too that it is hardly a question of the poem *failing* to pass beyond itself, and thus failing to offer us any content: the knowledge that Clare has in Helpston he has only there – it is by its very nature incapable of being abstracted, and it is in its incapacity for being abstracted that the knowledge consists.

Donald Davie is certainly right when he says, in the essay I referred to earlier, that Clare is not to be read primarily as a Romantic poet, but as writing 'in a tradition stemming from Thomson through Bloomfield, as competing therefore for the neo-classical laurels of "English Theocritus", stakes that Wordsworth and Coleridge, Keats and Shelley, were not entered for'.[96] I'd like finally in this section to compare Clare's versions of the conventional pastoral subjects of hay-making and the corn-harvest, with the versions of those subjects that appear in *The Farmer's Boy*,[97] by Robert Bloomfield, and in particular in *The Seasons*; and I hope the exercise will do something more to show how the content of Clare's poetry can be said to be his characteristic sense of place, and how his language can create the sense not only that his descriptions are precise, but that they are precise in a specifically local way. The English Theocritus who describes the hay-making and the harvest is engaged to tread a well-beaten path through the conventional imagery of the subjects: he must describe, for example, the village left empty because everyone is working in the fields, the rural and perhaps indelicate talk of the labourers, the relaxations and diversions of the lunch-hour. He must include a plea to the farmer to look kindly on the gleaners, and must permit himself the liberty of describing a village maiden in her work-day deshabille: the 'ruddy maid' in *The Seasons* is 'half naked, swelling on the sight';[98] in *The Farmer's Boy* she is 'divested of her gown', thereby revealing 'her full white bosom, exquisitely white';[99] while Clare's maidens have

> ...snow white bosoms nearly bare
> That charms ones sight amid the hay
> Like lingering blossoms of the may
> (*The Shepherd's Calendar*, 'July', lines 34–6)

Whatever conventions there are to be followed, Clare follows them no less meticulously or willingly than does Bloomfield; so that if, nevertheless, his own versions of hay-making and harvest seem peculiarly *local*, this isn't a matter of Clare's throwing off the conventions of the pastoral, and describing rural life as it really is: he is certainly not in competition with Crabbe, and if occasionally, like Crabbe, he upbraids the poets with whom he is competing for their failure to describe rural life properly, it is on account of the '*sweet* descriptions' they 'disdain to sing'.[100] But again the particularly 'local' feeling of Clare's poetry isn't simply the result of a greater wealth or accuracy of detail that he includes in his poems. Robert Bloomfield's description of the hay-harvest I won't quote from further, as it isn't among his best writing; but these lines from Thomson's 'Summer' are perfectly apt and precise:

> Wide flies the tedded grain; all in a row
> Advancing broad, or wheeling round the field,
> They spread their breathing harvest to the sun,
> That throws refreshful round a rural smell;
> Or, as they rake the green-appearing ground,
> And drive the dusky wave along the mead,
> The russet hay-cock rises thick behind
> In order gay: while heard from dale to dale,
> Waking the breeze, resounds the blended voice
> Of happy labour, love, and social glee.
>
> (*The Seasons*, 'Summer', lines 361–70)

This passage exemplifies all Thomson's characteristic and confident balance between what he has, as a pastoral poet, engaged himself to say, and his ability to keep the conventions of his theme alive by the originality and precision of his imagery – in particular here by the description of the mowers moving across the meadow, and by the phrase 'green-appearing ground' – the mown, 'russet' hay is raked off the meadow, revealing the new grass beneath. But still these images are faithful to an idea of 'general nature', as she is everywhere; and the point is that Thomson has no interest in describing the harvest as it is in a particular place; indeed, if he had discovered that any of the agricultural terms he had used were peculiar to one place or another, he would very probably have altered them. In Clare's poem 'The Harvest Morning',[101] on the other hand, we find these lines:

> The mower scythe now oer his shoulder leans
> And wetting* jars a sharp shill† tinkling sound
> Then swaps again mong corn and rustling beans
> And swath by swath flops lengthening oer the ground
>
> (lines 19–22)

*Whetting; †shrill.

– and in *The Shepherd's Calendar* we find:

> Some ted the puffing winnow down the land
> And others following roll them up in heaps
> While cleanly as a barn door beesome sweeps
> The hawling drag wi gathering weeds entwind
> And singing rakers end the toils behind
>
> ('August', lines 93–7)

– and:

> Hay makers still in grounds appear
> And some are thinning nearly clear

133

> Save oddly lingering shocks about
> Which the tithman counteth out
>
> ('July', lines 11–14)

– and:

> In hedge bound close and meadow plains
> Stript groups of busy bustling swains
> From all her hants* wi noises rude
> Drives to the woodlands solitude
>
> ('July', lines 19–22)

*Haunts.

– and:

> Some in the nooks about the ground
> Pile up the stacks swelld bellying round
>
> ('July', lines 41–2)

There is perhaps by now no need to argue the local-ness of these lines; but it is perhaps worth pointing out one particular aspect of Clare's language, the fine distinctions it makes between the different areas of the rural landscape. We have already come across, in the poems we have looked at in earlier sections, 'balks', 'fallows', 'furlongs', 'furrows', 'eddings', 'lands'; and in the lines quoted above we have, in addition, 'ground' – which Clare almost always uses of an enclosed piece of land, usually meadow-land; 'close', an enclosed field, usually for pasturing cattle and distinct from the 'plain', which refers almost always to open land, usually under grass; and finally 'nook', a particularly angular corner of a field. The distinct parts of the landscape that Clare describes are all subsumed by Thomson within the words 'mead' and 'field'; and he uses the latter word as Clare could never have used it, to denote a tract of meadow-land.

V

The set-piece descriptions of pastoral activity in *The Shepherd's Calendar* – of hay-making, harvesting, ploughing and the rest – show Clare quite at ease in the conventions of the pastoral tradition. He was able to include in those descriptions all that he was engaged to include, but in such a way that each activity h‹

describes is seen to be inseparable from the place in which it is being performed; he was able, that is, to grasp the way in which nature could be the same in Helpston as it was elsewhere, and yet different, too, in that it was in Helpston, and not elsewhere. *The Shepherd's Calendar*, although it was not published until 1827, was completed by Clare in 1823; so that by then he would seem to have worked himself quite free of the style that Lamb had advised him to perfect, the 'true rustic style', and to have decided that the themes and subjects of the pastoral tradition could be separated from the language in which they were traditionally expressed. How much the 'true rustic style' had kept the local sense out of Clare's earlier poems can be seen in these lines, from 'The Harvest Morning', a few lines of which I quoted in the previous section, and in which the language of the tradition, and the local language that Clare was learning to trust, exist awkwardly side by side; 'Emma' in these lines is a beautiful gleaner:

> O Poverty! how basely you demean
> The imprison'd worth your rigid fates confine;
> Not fancied charms of an Arcadian queen,
> So sweet as Emma's real beauties shine:
> Had Fortune blest, sweet girl, this lot had ne'er been thine.
>
> (lines 50–4)

These lines are merely conventional in the way that Bloomfield's verse so often is, and nowhere more so than in Clare's insistence that Emma is *not* a figure of Arcadian convention, but 'real'. This convention would not have seemed so over-familiar, of course, if Clare had been able to persuade us that Emma *was* real, which his language won't allow him to do. And yet, if the language he uses here is the language of the convention, or as near to it as Clare can manage, it isn't this fact alone that makes these lines seem so tired. James Thomson was able as we saw to use the most formal language, and yet still give life to the familiar subjects of the pastoral; but it seems that the original, local material that Clare had of his own to contribute could only exist for him in the local language he could not always bring himself to utter; his knowledge was knowledge for him only in Helpston, and only in the language of Helpston. Until 1822 or 1823, the poems keep passing between the style Clare's friends would often have preferred him to use, and his own, local language, and there are numerous early poems like 'The Harvest Morning', in which one line, strikingly local in its imagery and language, is followed by another written in Clare's attempt at what was, for him, the language of nowhere in particular.

The hold which the language of eighteenth-century poetry had on Clare, in his early poems, is nowhere more evident than in his attempts to describe landscape. Clare was familiar with the manner of landscape-description we examined in Chapter 1, and had encountered it in *The Seasons* mainly, but also in the poetry of John Cunningham, for example, and even of Bloomfield. But, as we saw in Chapter 1, the descriptive procedures that Thomson developed, and the compositional structure he took over from the Roman painters, demanded that the particular objects in a landscape be subdued to our impression of its total design; and this had the effect of making the language of landscape-description a very general one. Thus the words which have something of the same meaning as 'landscape' – 'scene', 'prospect' – suggest a particular visual relationship with the landscape – that it is over there – and thus also adjectives could be included in a passage of landscape-description only insofar as they reinforced the general idea of the design – the 'verdant field', the 'darkening heath' – and not to offer information which would focus our attention on this field, that heath, at the expense of the design. This language was clearly a good deal less easy to separate from the other conventions of the genre – the structure, the order of description – than the 'true rustic style' was from the conventional pastoral subjects to which it was applied. As long as Clare kept close to the language of the genre, he could give some sort of impression of observing its other conventions, too, of composition and procedure; but when he slips into something more like his own language, his descriptions lose all sense of design. The tendency of Clare's own language is to localise, to particularise; and the things he describes in this language are always becoming too salient, too striking, to take their place in an orderly, Claudian composition.

There are plenty of attempts among the early poems to describe landscape in the manner of Thomson: this sonnet, 'A Scene',[102] to which Tibble assigns the date 1810, is one of Clare's hardest tries:

> The landskip's stretching view, that opens wide,
>   With dribbling brooks, and river's wider floods,
>   And hills, and vales, and darksome lowering woods,
> With grains of varied hues and grasses pied;

> The low brown cottage in the shelter'd nook;
> The steeple, perking just above the trees
> Whose dangling leaves keep rustling in the breeze;
> And thoughtful shepherd bending o'er his hook:
> And maidens stript, haymaking too, appear;
> And Hodge a-whistling at his fallow plough;
> And herdsman hallooing to intruding cow:
> All these, with hundreds more, far off and near,
> Approach my sight; and please to such excess,
> That language fails the pleasure to express.

This could hardly begin more correctly: the general scope of the view is first described, as it was at the beginning of Thomson's description of the view from Hagley; and if Clare's first line has less of the excitement that Thomson's has, it conveys the depth and breadth of the terrain to be described no less accurately. And what is more the tension that arises in Thomson's syntax, but which so few of his imitators could achieve, arises in these opening lines too: 'the landskip's stretching view' must, we understand, be the subject of the main verb of the sentence; it is followed by a relative clause, that extends itself into the second, third, and fourth lines, full of images that we read through at some speed, anxious to find the verb that will make sense of the syntactical structure, and the visual structure too. But as we do hurry through those opening four lines, we begin to notice that the images aren't at all arranged in the proper order, and don't represent the successive planes of a Claudian landscape, as they would do in Thomson. The third line, which recalls Thomson's 'hill and dale...and darkening heath between', could certainly give us the impression of order, but not I think after the second, which would ask us to imagine a foreground of brooks, and in the second plane a river; while the colours in the fourth line do not suggest an arrangement of alternate dark and light tones across the landscape, but a much greater variety and confusion. It's clear that Clare has picked up from Thomson the tension that his syntax creates, but that he hasn't understood what that tension is for: these images have been stacked together according to some other idea of landscape than Thomson's, and have been pulled out of the landscape in a quite haphazard order.

As we read on into the fifth line, we realise also that the tension we experienced, of waiting for the verb, is not the same tension that we found in Thomson: the main verb does not come in the fifth line, or in the sixth – the 'low brown cottage' and 'the steeple' are clearly also the subjects of a main verb – but we know now exactly where that verb will come, and what the structure of the syntax will be in the remainder of the poem. We know, that is, that we are going to read through a list of subjects, all finally sharing the same main verb; but our impatience to find that verb has gone, and the list could extend well beyond the fourteen lines of the sonnet before we would lose our sense of the poem's struc- ture. By the eighth or ninth line any notion of composition has finally collapsed; we are presented with an assortment of particulars now, which are no longer even primarily visual: we can hear the landscape as well as we can see it; we can even *know* that the herdsman's cow is 'intruding'. The effect of all this is similar to that created by the passage from *The Task* we looked at in Chap- ter 1 (see p. 56), where Cowper, having positioned himself very deliberately on a commanding, 'speculative' height, immediately descended into the valley beneath him to describe a series of minute incidents and details.

It isn't so much that, as Clare says in the last line, the language has failed to express his pleasure in the landscape – it's done that very well, in the middle section of the poem at least – but it has suggested that whatever that pleasure is, it isn't Thomson's, which consisted in the ability to manipulate and control the bursting prospect he saw beneath him. Clare's pleasure is not in the idea of the design, and the active control he has over the landscape; but in the multiplicity and the particularity of images in the landscape, which he cannot control and before which he is passive – they approach his sight, his eye does not roam out over them, ordering them and placing them. And consequently, as the poem leaves the idea of design behind, and works its way out of Thomson's view of nature and into Clare's, the language becomes less and less formal: the four lines beginning 'and thoughtful shepherd' are far nearer to Clare's own language, the language of 'Winter Fields' and *The Shepherd's Calendar*, than are the first four lines; and in getting rid of the landscape of the tradition, Clare has got rid also of the other conventions that Thomson established – the order of descrip- tion, the concentration on the visual, and the fixed idea of the sort of objects that an ideal landscape contains.

But for all this the poem cannot be called a successful descrip- tion of landscape by Clare, one in which he manages to express a preference of his own, for multiplicity and particularity, over

Thomson's order and generality. Although by the end of the poem Clare is being quite explicit about what the pleasure is – that it consists in his idea of the disorder of the landscape – the structure of the poem, the syntax, are working under cover as it were to give the poem and the landscape a spurious sense of order, of unity. All these images, says Clare, and hundreds more, far off and near ...but the main verb, when it finally does come, gathers up these images, and reimposes the sense of order that, in the lines above, we had temporarily lost.

The pattern of this poem is the pattern of all the poems in which Clare apparently attempts to describe an extended landscape in the manner of Thomson: the composition is proposed deliberately enough, but immediately collapses into its component parts, each with an independent existence of its own; and sometimes at the end, not Clare so much as the syntax, the form he has adopted, will make an attempt to gather up the threads, to impose on the landscape a sort of retrospective design. It seems either that Clare did not understand the principles behind Thomson's procedure, or that he had no real desire to follow them, and that the conventional openings were there to provide a proper tone of voice, from which the enumeration of particulars could start:

> Upon a molehill oft he dropt him down,
> To take a prospect of the circling scene,
> Marking how much the cottage roof's-thatch brown
> Did add its beauty to the budding green
> Of sheltering trees it humbly peep'd between,
> The stone-rock'd wagon with its rumbling sound,
> The windmill's sweeping sails at distance seen,
> And every form that crowds the circling round,
> Where the sky stooping seems to kiss the meeting ground.
>
> (*The Village Minstrel*, stanza 16)[103]

In these lines Clare appears to be about to 'take a prospect'; but although the landscape he goes on to describe, in its content, in the images it contains, is not unlike a landscape from Thomson, there is no sense at all here of composition, except in the first two lines and in the last two, where once again we find a tension between Clare's sense, of the confusion, the multiplicity, of the 'forms' that 'crowd' the landscape, and the sense of finality and order which the form of the stanza, and the talk of the horizon, give to the description.

I don't want to go on too long producing examples of what is the same pattern in Clare's early attempts at the description of landscape, in which the structure he begins to establish collapses under the weight of particular images: I think it's fair to say that the pattern does occur, without exception, whenever Clare begins a passage of landscape-description in the tone of voice he has borrowed from eighteenth-century landscape-poets, and indeed whenever in the early poems he attempts to describe an extended view of landscape. There is a passage also in Clare's prose *Autobiography* which recalls that stanza from the *Village Minstrel*, in that it begins with Clare dropping down 'on the thymy molehill or mossy eminence to survey the summer landscape'.[104] He begins by describing large patches of colour, the different colours of the crops in the 'flat spreading fields'; he goes on to pick out the colours of individual trees in the landscape, and describes them with precise attention: 'the grey willow shining chilly in the sun as if the morning mist still lingered on its cool green'; until finally he is describing 'the shepherd hiding from the thunder shower in a hollow dotterel', and 'the dragonflys in spangled coats darting like winged arrows down the thin stream'.[105] Here the point isn't simply that Clare has described a multitude of particular objects at the expense of the structure, but that the desire to do so has made him get as close as possible to each object, no matter where it is imagined as being placed in the landscape as it appeared from Clare's viewpoint, the molehill or 'mossy eminence'. There is none of the scrupulously maintained focus we find in Thomson or in his imitators – for that was something that they could understand and reproduce without difficulty. There are times, in fact, when we begin to feel that Clare cannot compose his landscapes because he is unable to describe things in the distance; he keeps trying to bring the most distant objects into the sharpest possible focus – either because what he sees of them is inseparable for him from what he knows about them; or because he is, in some way, simply not happy looking at things in the distance. This second – and apparently improbable – explanation is I think as much part of the truth as the first:

> There lies a sultry lusciousness around
> The far stretched pomp of summer which the eye
> Views with a dazzled gaze – & gladly bounds
> Its prospects to some pastoral spots that lie
> Nestling among the hedge confining grounds.[106]

These lines are from a sonnet certainly written in the 1830s, when Clare had given up all attempt or desire to observe the procedures of Thomson, but we find the same sort of feeling in these lines, from a much earlier poem, 'Holywell':[107]

> The heath was left, and then at will
> A road swept gently round the hill,
> From whose high crown, as soodling by,
> A distant prospect cheer'd my eye,
> Of closes green and fallows brown,
> And distant glimpse of cot and town,
> And steeple beck'ning on the sight,
> By morning sunbeams painted white,
> And darksome woods with shadings sweet,
> To make the landscape round complete,
> And distant waters glist'ning by,
> As if the ground were patch'd with sky;
> While on the blue horizon's line
> The far-off things did dimly shine,
> Which wild conjecture only sees,
> And fancy moulds to clouds and trees,
> Thinking, if thither she could fly,
> She'd find the close of earth and sky;
> But as we turn to look again
> On nearest objects, wood and plain,
> (So truths than fiction lovelier seem),
> One warms as wak'ning from a dream.

(lines 31–52)

This starts off with all the proper ingredients of a Claudian landscape, and arranged in the proper order – green closes, brown fallows, the light falling on the distant steeple, and behind it, not blue hills but darksome woods that apparently close the prospect – they 'make the landscape round complete'. But Clare won't leave it there, and as he goes on he seems to be taking exactly that delight in a distant view that I have just said he often did not take. The distance is insisted upon, and it is the indistinctness of the far-off things – their not being in sharp focus – that particularly preoccupies Clare; he does not allow them, however, to remain indistinct, and has to imagine what precisely they are, converting his visual image of them into an image of something he knows – clouds and trees. And for all the insistence on the distance, Clare is very clearly relieved to get back to the home truths of the immediate foreground: the distance is indistinct, and unreal, and it is (by implication) cold: the foreground is lovelier, and *warm*.

141

There are poems, of course, in which Clare is able to look deep into a prospect and feel the delight of doing so quite unambiguously; but when he does so he makes very little attempt to describe what he sees in the distance. It is the simple fact of being able to look so far that intrigues him, but not in the same way as it intrigued earlier eighteenth-century poets, and Clare has an exact understanding of the particular significance of this experience for him. These lines are from 'Narrative Verses, written after an excursion from Helpstone to Burghley Park':[108]

> And sure it was a happy hour
>   That led me up to Barnack Hill;
> There uncontroll'd I knew no bounds,
>   But look'd o'er villages a crowd,
> And cots and spires to farthest rounds,
>   While far trees seem'd a misty cloud.

> (lines 107–12)

The word 'uncontroll'd' here can't be explained as a transferred epithet, and really attached to the prospect, which was boundless, bursting immense around: the word stays with the pronoun 'I', and by it Clare means that whereas normally he sees landscape in small parcels, and is controlled, limited by the area of his vision, he is on this one occasion subject to no such limitation. In the same way the word 'bounds' is part of the professional vocabulary of the landscape-painter and the landscape-gardener – 'he gains all points', says Pope in the 'Epistle to Burlington', who 'conceals the bounds',[109] and normally the word would be applied to the prospect itself; but here the phrase 'I knew no bounds', although it can be taken to mean that Clare saw no bounds in the prospect, can equally well, and perhaps more naturally, be taken to mean that Clare knew himself subject to no limitation: *he* was boundless. Some of Clare's most successful uses of the vocabulary of Thomson occur in this sort of context, when he introduces the idea of limitation into the wide and stretching landscape to which that vocabulary is usually applied. This stanza is from 'Summer Morning',[110] one of Clare's earliest poems:

> As slow the hazy mists retire,
>   Crampt circle's more distinctly seen;
> Thin scatter'd huts, and neighbouring spire,
>   Drop in to stretch the bounded scene.

> (lines 113–16)

The difference between Clare's feeling toward the distance in 'Holywell', and his feeling toward it in the 'Narrative Verses' and perhaps in this poem, is not unlike the ambiguity of his feelings to Helpston, that I discussed in an earlier section: he felt enormously restricted living there, but had no interest in leaving. The word 'uncontroll'd' is perhaps partly explained by saying that, of course, there aren't many hills about Helpston, so that this experience was an unusual one for Clare; but then that is part of the point – that Clare's attempt to use the language and procedure of Thomson is made without any of the experience that Thomson had, and his readers had, of mobility, and of the ability to compare one landscape and another that their mobility allowed them. In this way, precisely, Clare was controlled: what he knew was the foreground, in its particularity and local-ness; and it's interesting that in those lines, as I have said, when Clare is faced with the boundless prospect from Barnack Hill, he is able to say nothing about that, but only about himself: of the cots and spires we learn nothing, of the villages only that there were many of them.

In another of Clare's poems, 'The Mores',[111] the experience of being able to look into the distance is again related to the idea of freedom: the poem is about the enclosure of a tract of moorland to the east of Helpston, and the 'freedom' Clare speaks of must be understood, in the first place, in the context of the enclosure. The poem begins with a description of the old landscape of the moors, about which Clare says:

> Unbounded freedom ruled the wandering scene
> Nor fence of ownership crept in between
>
> (lines 7–8)

This trail of imagery, in which the idea of freedom is related to the openness of the old landscape, is followed throughout the poem; and later, when Clare speaks of the enclosure, it is a limiting and restricting influence on the men and livestock on the moors:

> Fence now meets fence in owners little bounds
> Of field and meadow large as garden grounds
> In little parcels little minds to please
> With men and flocks imprisoned ill at ease
>
> (lines 47–50)

But at the same time the idea of freedom has to be understood in another context than that of the enclosure; it has to be understood, in fact, in the same terms as we took the word 'uncontroll'd' earlier, to refer to the particular associations Clare had with the idea not of openness so much as of *distance*. Thus if the moorland was 'boundless', this wasn't simply a matter of its being without fences: the moors were free because they expressed the idea of distance without limitation, without end:

> One mighty flat undwarfed by bush and tree
> Spread its faint shadow of immensity
> And lost itself which seemed to eke its bounds
> In the blue mist the orisons edge surrounds

(lines 11–14)

On the one hand, then, the moors are free because open; on the other they are free because limitless. These ideas are, for Clare, one and the same – in this poem; but in fact the complexity of the poem is precisely the result of Clare's managing to identify here what more often appear in his work as opposed attitudes to Helpston. Thus when the moors are thought of as open, they are emblematic of the freedom of the villagers before the enclosure; when they are thought of as boundless, they express the possibility of a movement *towards* freedom, and out of the 'crampt circle' of life in Helpston, whether before the enclosure or after it.

This is a long poem, and one of Clare's best, and it deserves to be discussed at much greater length than I can discuss it here: but the particular point I do want to make here is that, if Clare is able in this poem to describe the distance, and to take a delight in a landscape

> That seemed to lengthen with the following eye
> Moors loosing from the sight far smooth and blea*

(lines 37–8)

*Bleak.

it is because, in the first place, he is not describing any particular *thing* in the distance – the moors are free not only of fences, but of trees and bushes as well; the eye moving to the horizon is engaged by nothing. This sort of empty prospect is precisely the one which more mobile writers, James Tyley and James Thomson, could not look into: it hurt Tyley's eyes to do so, and when Thomson imagined the vast emptiness of the tropical savannahs, it 'unfixed' his eye, too. But Clare is describing not the distance so much as the idea of distance, and its significance; and if he is particularly at home there, it is because the idea of an escape from limitation is, in this

144

poem, conveniently confused with the idea of what the escape is from – confused, that is, with the landscape of Clare's 'knowledge', with the knowledge that is, at times, a reassurance to him, but which, by its very nature, by its purely local truth and its incapacity for being abstracted, is always a limitation on him.

On one of his visits to London in the early 1820s, Clare met, among other painters, Peter De Wint; and soon after this meeting he wrote an essay on De Wint.[112] It begins by attacking the method of landscape-painting we examined in Chapter 1, the method established by the Roman painters and adopted in England most notably by Richard Wilson; and the terms of Clare's attack show that, by this time at least, he had a good grasp of the procedures of the Claudian method, although he had by now stopped trying to reproduce Thomson's version of them in his own poems: 'There is no worse trickery of disposal of lights & shadows to catch the eye from object to object with excessive fractions of diminishings untill the eye rest upon that last pinspoint effect that makes a tree appear a mile high & the neighbouring background a mile off.'[113] 'De Wint', says Clare, 'is none of these Artists'; in his pictures: 'there is no harsh stoppage no bounds to space or any outline further then there is in nature – if we could possibly walk into the picture we fancy we might pursue the landscape beyond those mysterys (not bounds) assigned to it so as we can in the fields'.[114] What Clare says in favour of De Wint is ironically enough reminiscent of what Richard Wilson said of Claude, that 'you may walk in Claude's pictures and count the miles' (see above, p. 8). The trouble is that the techniques of the Claudian method invite recognition, indeed they insist on being recognised; but Clare recognises them only as tricks, and thus they destroy for him the illusion of space they are meant to create. De Wint, on the other hand, can maintain for Clare the illusion of spaciousness; and he can do so because his pictures are without 'bounds' – without any hills, for example, to close the prospect at the horizon – and it is characteristic that Clare finds the horizon in his pictures invitingly mysterious. Clare admires also the 'undiversified plains' of De Wint – the flat, empty tracts of grass seen from a low viewpoint. It is once again as though Clare, unlike Tyley and unlike Thomson, is happy to look into the distance only if it is empty, if there is nothing there; and if there is a thing there, it destroys for Clare the illusion of space and depth, because it makes him want to examine it, in its particularity and detail, and thus he focuses on it too sharply. It seems at times that the objects in a landscape aren't properly part of it for Clare, but the objects of a quite different interest he has, in the truth and accuracy of detail. De Wint satisfies this interest of Clare's too: his pictures are 'as true as if nature had just left them',[115] and without any of the 'ridiculous situations oft to be found in modern fancy Landscapes where we often meet a group of cattle indiscrimatly intermixed just as they fancied not as they found them thus cows horses & sheep are scened cooling themselves in a pool which is out of nature for sheep were never seen in that situation since Noahs flood'.[116] Clare replies elsewhere to Keats's criticism of his own poems, that the description prevailed too much over the sentiment, by saying that Keats 'often described nature as she appeared to his fancies & not as he would have described her had he witnessed the things he describes'.[117] Robert Bloomfield was also preoccupied by accuracy of detail in landscape-painting: of Westall's picture *A Storm in Harvest* he says: 'The sheaves, whether meant for barley or wheat, are a bad crop; more straw than corn, or rather the straw is not defined. It appears in the stem as a bundle of fine grass, and there are not ears enough (reckoning a stem to each and no more) to make a sheaf of a quarter the size.'[118]

Clare was, of course, in his own poems, a stickler for fullness and accuracy of detail; and Robert Bloomfield was thought by Hazlitt to excel in the 'minute and often interesting description of individual objects in nature',[119] although which passages of Bloomfield he has in mind he does not say. But beyond all this there is I think something defensive about the tone of these last three prose quotations. Both Clare and Bloomfield were introduced to landscape-painting in the sophisticated literary and artistic circles of London: they were taken to exhibitions, put in front of paintings of rural subjects, and asked to comment. It is not surprising if, in that situation, both men were careful to say only what they, as farmer's boys, could be allowed to know better than anyone else.

VI

The poems we looked at in the last section revealed fairly clearly the difference between Clare's idea of landscape and Thomson's, even though Clare was doing his best to adopt, in some of them at least, the characteristic tone of Thomson's descriptions, if not also his attitude to nature; and they indicate as well why Clare was unable to express his own idea of landscape and still keep within the Claudian conventions. The pattern of the poems in which Clare did begin to use Thomson's structure was, I said, invariable: the structure broke down under the weight of the particular things that Clare asked it to carry; he had none of the resources that Thomson had, to maintain the structure against the intrusion of its particular components. In his description of the view from Shene, Thomson discovered a syntax which brilliantly kept the idea of the design in front of our eyes, and led us progressively into the landscape; while at the same time it made room for a remarkable amount of particular information about the view: and the design of the landscape, as it finally emerged in the pattern of syntax, was a synthesis between the idea of the Claudian design, in its immediate form, and the particular details of the landscape which resisted the imposition of the design.

There was no such dialectic possible for Clare, or no such synthesis: the idea of the design resided, for him, not in any desire such as Thomson had, to impose order on landscape, but simply in the memory of Thomson's procedure which was contained in some parts of Clare's language. And so we have in Clare a simple and irresoluble opposition: between the tradition, on the one hand, and his own sense of landscape – which I hope to define in this and the following sections – on the other. In the sonnet we looked at earlier, 'A Scene', or in the stanza from *The Village Minstrel* (see above, p. 139), the particular objects Clare brings into his description don't exist for him at all as the parts of a composition – they are brought in for their intrinsic interest alone. Such an image as this, for example,

> The stone-rock'd wagon with its rumbling sound,

is presented as part of the 'prospect' taken of the 'circling scene'; but we are given no idea of where in the composition this wagon is to be found, whether in the foreground or background. What is more, we can hear as well as see this wagon, and we *know* what it contains (it is possible, I suppose, that the wagon is being rocked by a stone it is passing over, and not by a load of stones); as in 'A Scene' we knew that the herdsman's cow was intruding.

A writer who could use the method of Thomson with more conviction would describe what he saw only, and not what he knew, and this insistence on the primacy of the visual impression would make the things he described properly remote from him – a remoteness reinforced by the actual physical distance he imagined between his viewpoint and the landscape. There's none of this remoteness about Clare's wagon; and, as I have said, no information about where it is in the design: it is simply there, a manifold of impressions, which has rumbled into the landscape for no reason at all – and because it has no reason to be there, has spoiled the design which, up to that point in the stanza, Clare had more or less been able to maintain.

It might seem that Clare, instead of trying to follow Thomson, might have done better to have tried to write himself into the tradition of picturesque poetry, as Robert Bloomfield had tried to do in *The Banks of Wye*:[120] if the theory of the Picturesque did not abandon the idea of composition, it did at least invite a greater concentration on the particular image. Until Clare went to London in the early 1820s, he seems to have had no knowledge at all of the Picturesque, beyond an awareness that the fashionable landscape to describe was now rocky, difficult, and sublime. He several times apologises for the lack of mountains in his own landscapes, and perhaps the earliest way in which his concern for the local manifests itself is in his understanding that the flat landscape he knew was the proper subject of his poetry:

> Swamps of wild rush-beds, and sloughs' squashy traces,
> Grounds of rough fallows with thistle and weed,
> Flats and low valleys of kingcups and daisies,
> Sweetest of subjects are ye for my reed.
>
> ('Song', lines 1–4)[121]

In London, Clare came to know not only Peter De Wint, but William Hilton also, and E. V. Rippingille, whom he described as, yes, the 'Theocritus of English painting';[122] and from then on Clare took as much interest in landscape-painting as his exile in Helpston would allow him to take. We find the word 'picturesque' quite often in the poems that Clare was writing in the 1820s and 1830s, and we find also the occasional image quite clearly written out of a knowledge of what was thought to be of picturesque interest:

> The sunshine threading through these broken rails
> In mellow shades no pencil e'er conveys;
>
> ('Wood Pictures in Spring', lines 12–13)[123]

and

> The autumn morning waked by many a gun
> Throws oer the fields her many coloured light
> Wood wildly touched close tanned and stubbles dun
>
> ('A Autumn Morning', lines 1–3)[124]

– where the phrase 'wildly touched' comes directly from the vocabulary of the connoisseur of the Picturesque. And yet these images never occur more than occasionally, and when they do they seem strangely separate from the rest of the poem and the images around them; these lines are from 'Evening school boys':[125]

> Harken that happy shout – the school house door
> Is open thrown and out the younkers* teem
> Some run to leap frog on the rushy moor
> And others dabble in the shallow stream
> Catching young fish and turning pebbles oer
> For muscle clams – Look in that mellow gleam
> Where the retiring sun that rests the while
> Streams through the broken hedge – How happy seem
> Those schoolboy friendships leaning oer the stile
> Both reading in one book...
>
> (lines 1–10)

*Youngsters.

When we are looking at the things in a room, for example, that we know very well, it is sometimes possible, by an effort of the imagination, to see them suddenly in a very remote and objective light; and in this passage, which begins by describing a scene in which everything is familiar and known, the sudden introduction of the picturesque image has something of the same effect. The familiar landscape is made to seem, suddenly, very strange; and this suggests that the sort of concentration on particulars that the picturesque allowed was completely different to the sort that Clare was usually after: the picturesque poet can understand an image as particular only by isolating it from its familiar context, and by looking at it across the distance created by his insistence on the primacy of the visual, and in the abstract light of its relation to the 'picturesque rules'.

Nor do I think that the example of Cowper – a poet who, like Clare, was less interested in scenes than in scenery, in what the scenes contained – would have been especially helpful to Clare, in his desire to render the particularity of objects in landscape. It may seem from what I have so far said about Clare, that in breaking up the structure of Thomson, or in his inability to reproduce it, he was doing what I said in the first chapter Cowper was doing: appearing to use the method of Thomson, and then abandoning it and his viewpoint in search of particular incidents and details. Clare was doing this, of course, but not at all in the same way as Cowper. In the first place, Cowper is able to describe the particular in very much the same, formal language as he describes the general; whereas for Clare the description of the particular involves also a reversion into his own language, for the particular to him was not simply that, but local as well. There is nothing in the language of Cowper's description of the valley of the Ouse which makes us certain that he must have been describing that valley, and no other. But beyond that, the sense of design is never lost from Cowper's descriptions, however particular his imagery may become. In the passage we looked at in Chapter 1, the particular images were carefully located in the landscape as a whole:

> The sheep-fold here
> Pours out its fleecy tenants o'er the glebe...
>
> ('The Task', book I, lines 290–1)

> There from the sun-burnt hay-field, homeward creeps
> The loaded wain...
>
> (lines 295–6)

> Here the gray smooth trunks
> Of ash, or lime, or beech, distinctly shine...
>
> (lines 302–3)

> There, lost behind a rising ground, the wood
> Seems sunk...
>
> (lines 305–6)

> O'er these, but far beyond (a spacious map
> Of hill and valley interpos'd between),
> The Ouse, dividing the well-water'd land,
> Now glitters in the sun, and now retires...
>
> (lines 321–4)

These excerpts are taken from a passage of nearly fifty lines; and obviously the design here is much more relaxed than it is in Thomson: it seems able easily to contain everything that is in the landscape, and yet at the same time allows each thing to be described in considerable detail: the detailed descriptions of the wain, the forest-trees, and the rest, occur between the lines I have quoted. And the design is able to be, apparently, so inclusive, and yet also so liberal in its treatment of its component parts, because, in fact, there is hardly anything in the landscape at all. The adverbs 'here', 'there', 'here', 'there', give the impression that the whole ground has been covered; instead, in nearly fifty lines, Cowper has described only a flock of sheep, the meeting of two wagons, 'the woodland scene', and the River Ouse. What he does include is thus able to extend itself, to discover its identity, its particularity, over a space of a number of lines.

Cowper's way of revealing the particularity of a thing is to heap it with details, and he gives himself time and room in which to do this. The objects in Clare's landscape become particular objects in a very different way: if we compare the line about the wagon, with the long description of the wagons by Cowper (it will be found on page 56), it becomes obvious that the particularity of an object isn't necessarily a matter of the abundance of detail attached to it. Clare's way is to fix the object with one or two striking images – 'the stone-rock'd wagon' – which separate it from its background because they are *too* striking to be contained in a properly composed landscape; and also to make us feel, as he often does by the resources of his language, that the object he is describing is familiar to him, and that its original will be found in the actual landscape of Helpston.

It is important to stress that Clare does not give himself anything like the same amount of time to describe an object as does Cowper; and I want to suggest now that this is because his poems are concerned to express not only his sense of the particularity of things in a landscape, but his sense also of the multiplicity of them. The objects Clare introduces into his descriptions of landscape obliterate by their particularity whatever traces remain in his poems of correct eighteenth-century descriptive procedure; and when they do so, we might expect them to take as much time to discover their identity, their particularity, as they would do in a passage of Cowper. But in fact no sooner does one object enter the poem than it is pushed aside by the next; so that we have the sense always that outside the poem are hundreds of images hammering to be admitted: 'all these', says Clare, at the end of 'A Scene', 'and hundreds more, approach my sight'. In the prospect from Barnack

Hill he 'look'd o'er villages a *crowd*'; in the stanza from *The Village Minstrel* he speaks of 'every form that *crowds* the circling round'.

Clare understood his own idea of landscape very much in eighteenth-century terms – as a descriptive poet no less than as a pastoral poet he thought of himself primarily as continuing an eighteenth-century tradition. At the same time he realised that his idea of landscape did not satisfy any of the principles of eighteenth-century taste. The desire to describe things as particular, therefore, he understood as a tendency towards disorder, because a thing could make itself felt to be particular in an eighteenth-century landscape only at the expense of the composition, or the rule of order. The desire to represent the multiplicity of things in a landscape he understood also as a tendency towards disorder; and out of these two desires he developed a whole aesthetic of disorder, in which landscape was praised on account of its formlessness, its failure to accommodate itself to correct taste:

> Some spruce and delicate ideas feed
> With them disorder is an ugly weed
> And wood and heath a wilderness of thorns
> Which gardeners shears nor fashions nor adorns
>
> ('Shadows of Taste', lines 153–6)[126]

The phrases 'sweet disorder', 'rich disorder', occur frequently in the poems; and of course the idea of disorder was related in Clare's mind (as I shall suggest, briefly, later (see below, p. 169) to the enclosure and reorganisation of land in Helpston.

It seems that Clare felt that if his sense of the particularity of things in a landscape was a disorderly one, and if his sense of their multiplicity was the same, then the two of them, added together, must have tended twice as much towards an idea of landscape as formless and unruly. I want to suggest, however, that these two senses are not two complementary parts of one idea of landscape. Each object, I said above, no sooner enters a description of Clare's than it is pushed aside by the next:

> And thoughtful shepherd bending o'er his hook;
> And maidens stript, haymaking too, appear;
> And Hodge a-whistling at his fallow plough;
> And herdsman hallooing to intruding cow...
>
> ('A Scene', lines 8–11)

– the sense of these images being crammed together is more sharply felt if the poem is imagined in the form in which it was originally written, without punctuation. And if there is this sense of urgency in Clare's descriptions, it's clear that the desire to express the particularity of things, and the desire to express their multiplicity, are not complementary but in fact opposed to each other; perhaps I can give an idea of the opposition between them by saying that, if an eighteenth-century poet felt overwhelmed by the sheer number of objects that confronted him in a prospect, the threat they represented was (as he understood it) to the composition, to his ability to organise what he saw; if Clare felt similarly overwhelmed, the threat was to his desire to express the particularity of each object. The sense of particularity, I want further to suggest, and the sense of multiplicity, are in the same sort of dialectical relationships as were, in Thomson's description of the view from Shene, the idea of the Claudian structure, on the one hand, and, on the other, the particularity of the objects in the view; and this dialectic in Clare is capable of the same sort of synthesis as was the dialectic in Thomson, in the form of the landscape as it is to be discovered in the structure and momentum of his syntax.

VII

It is clear, I think, that if Clare was going to be able to express his own idea of landscape, and not a hybrid of his own and Thomson's, it was necessary for him to abandon Thomson's method. It is true that, in so far as he understood his own idea of landscape in eighteenth-century terms, as an aesthetic disorder, it could express itself, so to speak, negatively, in Clare's repeated failure to observe the principles of Thomson, after embracing them so deliberately at the beginning of each passage of description. But these principles were, finally, stronger than Clare's ability to deviate from them; and at the end of 'A Scene', and at the end of the stanza we examined from *The Village Minstrel*, the composition reasserted itself over the particulars which had earlier managed to suppress it. The pattern of these poems, then, was not simply that the structure was stated, and ignored; the structure reappeared at the end, and the impression we were left with was not that Clare had arrived at his own aesthetic of disorder, but that he had, simply, been unable to reveal his landscape as an orderly composition.

Clare discovered the new form that he needed, expressive of his own idea of landscape, in the poems that he was writing between about 1822 and the middle of the 1830s; this sonnet, 'Emmonsails Heath in winter',[127] is one in which I think this new form has emerged:

> I love to see the old heaths withered brake
> Mingle its crimpled* leaves with furze and ling
> While the old heron from the lonely lake
> Starts slow and flaps his melancholly wing
> And oddling† crow in idle motion swing
> On the half rotten ash trees topmost twig
> Beside whose trunk the gipsey makes his bed
> Up flies the bouncing woodcock from the brig‡
> Where a black quagmire quakes beneath the tread
> The field fare chatter in the whistling thorn
> And for the awe§ round fields and closen‖ rove
> And coy bumbarrels¶ twenty in a drove
> Flit down the hedge rows in the frozen plain
> And hang on little twigs and start again

*Wrinkled, crumpled; †'one differing from the rest of a family, brood, or litter; generally applied to the smallest, or to one with a peculiarity' (*Selected Poems*, p. 208); ‡bridge; §haw; ‖closes; ¶long-tailed tits.

The language of this poem is much more Clare's own, much more 'local', than was the language of 'A Scene', and I shall have something more to say about that at the end of this section. But what I especially want to direct attention to in this poem is Clare's syntax, and I want to begin by comparing it with the syntactical patterns we saw developed by Thomson in *The Seasons*, when he was describing landscape. The syntax of, say, the description of the view from Hagley was fairly complex; there was only one main verb in eleven lines, so that all the other clauses in those eleven lines were subordinate to the one main clause; and the movement of Thomson's eye, placing the objects in the landscape and seeking to make them, precisely, *subordinate* to the design and to the action of the main verb, was acted out, as we say, by the pattern of this syntax.

The syntax of this poem by Clare, as it emerges from a formal grammatical analysis, is no less complex: in the first seven lines there are six clauses, of which only one is a main clause, on which the remaining five are all in one or another relation of dependence.

But the images in this poem are not *organised* by the structure of the syntax in at all the same way as were the images in that passage from Thomson: the words at the beginning of the poem, 'I love to see', although they mean what they say, are there mainly to provide the simplest possible framework, the least intrusive one, to contain the images in the poem, so that we may read the poem as, simply, a succession of images all of equal weight. In the first four lines it might be hard to grasp, from a formal analysis of the syntax, why Clare should love to see the leaves of the brake mingle with the furze, as he says he does, *particularly* when the heron starts up and flies – why should that add to the pleasure? – but as we read the poem, of course, the difficulties inherent in the syntax do not really register, and we understand well enough that Clare's meaning is that he loves to see the leaves of the brake do this, and he loves to see the heron do that. In the same way, the function of the clause beginning 'and oddling crow' is unclear – it could be the object of 'to see', or – Clare does occasionally omit the final 's' from the third person singular form – it could be another adverbial clause, after 'while'. But whatever it is, the problem remains a theoretical one only, which doesn't much affect our understanding of the poem; the image of the crow fits easily into the succession of images already established: I love to see the leaves do this, the heron do this, and the crow do that; and the images in their particularity seem to insist on being treated equally, however much one of them may be contained in a clause technically subordinate to another.

The syntax of this poem is apparently, then, the 'syntax as music' that Donald Davie describes in his book *Articulate Energy;*[128] the grammatical connections it makes between one image and the next purport to be logical connections also, but in fact are not: the syntax is there to provide only a loose sense of connectedness, so that each image appears to be part of what John Wilson, reviewing Clare's final volume, *The Rural Muse,*[129] in *Blackwood's,* described as 'a series of images all naturally arising, as it were, out of each other'.[130] The poem is a continuum of related impressions; we understand that we are not to enquire too closely into the particular nature of the relations between them.

But this account of the syntax of the poem isn't after all quite adequate, because it is hard to see how the particular forms of the connections between the images and between the clauses can be ignored so completely. It's one thing to say, for example, that the word 'while' doesn't really mean *while*; but the fact remains that Clare has used the word when he could perfectly well have used 'and', and it makes a difference. In the same way, it is one thing to say that a subordinate clause in this poem isn't, in any meaningful sense, *subordinate*; its status must still be different in some way, nevertheless, from that of a main clause, and the difference must affect our reading of the clause. In lines six and seven –

> On the half rotten ash trees topmost twig
> Beside whose trunk the gipsey makes his bed

– the connection is certainly not there to be ignored; it is insisted upon. The gipsy seems to have come into the poem as an after-thought: if Clare had known as he wrote line six that he was going to speak of the gipsy, in the next line, he would no doubt have constructed the line in such a way – I'm not suggesting he would have done so deliberately – that the ash-tree came at the end of the line, as the natural antecedent of 'whose'; he would have written something like (something better than)

> On topmost twig of the half rotten ash.

As it is, the surprisingly formal style of the connection is at odds with the ungrammatical way it is introduced; we have to shuffle the images in our mind to make the connection work; and whereas before the grammatical connections were as unobtrusive as they could be, the connection between the images here becomes more striking than the images themselves.

I said earlier that this poem was apparently a 'continuum' of related impressions, but the word does not quite express the sense I think the syntax of this poem communicates. I was trying to make the point that to remove the sense in which one clause was felt to be subordinate to another was to remove also the sense that the images were to be apprehended as the parts of an orderly, composed landscape. But although a 'continuum' of images will not coalesce into a composition as Thomson would have understood it, it still dictates the order in which we apprehend the images in a landscape as surely as does the complex syntax of Thomson. Obviously this order is going to be present in any linguistic structure – we cannot say 'heath' and 'heron' at the same time, as we can see a heath and a heron together. But I want to suggest that the syntax in this poem is not content to go along with the order which the language must inevitably impose, and that it attempts instead to conceal it. I want to suggest, that is, that while Clare has suppressed as far as he can the sense that one clause is subordinate to another, one image more important than another, he makes, nevertheless, the particular connections he does make between the images, to reveal them all as parts not so much of a continuum of successive impressions as of one complex manifold of simultaneous impressions. The only way we can reconcile, in the first four lines for example, the notion that the images there are all of equal importance, and the notion that the two clauses introduced by 'while' are nevertheless in some sense subordinate, is to understand that for Clare the experience of seeing the leaves of the brake is somehow inseparable from the experience of seeing the heron: they are both parts of the same complex impression, not just this *and* that, but this *while* that. And in the same way the experience of seeing the crow is inseparable from these two experiences, and inseparable also, for Clare, from his knowledge that, beside the ash-tree on which the crow is perched, the gipsy makes his bed. This syntax cannot obviously remove the fact that we do apprehend these images in a certain order; but it can suggest that the experience of seeing one thing is simultaneous with, and so cannot be disentangled from, the experience of seeing another.

I can perhaps best demonstrate that this *is* the effect of the syntax in the first seven lines of this poem by comparing them with the last five, which try perhaps to achieve by parataxis – main clauses loosely connected – what Clare achieves earlier by hypotaxis; and it's clear, I think, that there isn't the same sense in these lines that the various images are the inseparable parts of what I have called a manifold of impressions. To a degree, of course, the syntax of the first part of the poem, in its desire to do away with the sense of subordination, aspires to the condition of parataxis; but the trouble with parataxis, for Clare's purpose, is exactly this, that it cannot express the idea that a group of impressions are being apprehended simultaneously; it cannot help but co-operate with the order which language itself imposes on those impressions, because it cannot make connections *across* that order. What is more, the insistent connections Clare makes between the various images in the first seven lines oblige us to read those lines at a run; we keep finding new momentum in each connecting word or phrase. This momentum is a crucial part of our reading the poem as a manifold of simultaneous impressions, or at least of impressions somehow pressed up against each other in time, and inseparable. If the second half of the poem has anything of the same pace, it is borrowed from the first half, and there is nothing in the nature of parataxis itself to prevent us from choosing, as we certainly could choose if these lines were at the beginning of a poem, the pace to read them at. We have no choice with the first half – we have to take it at a run, and submit to the experience of apprehending these images not one by one, but simultaneously: no sooner the heath than the heron, no sooner the heron than the crow. It's not that the last half of the poem is any worse for using parataxis, or for having within it no new sources of syntactical momentum – there's enough energy in the first seven lines to push us through the last seven at some speed – but such a passage, placed at the beginning of a poem, would certainly not have established the same impression of simultaneity that is in fact established at the beginning of this poem.

Before I go any further in this discussion of Clare's syntax, I should perhaps meet the objection that the effects of simultaneousness and of momentum that I have been describing are the inevitable, and not especially remarkable, results of Clare's failure to punctuate. It seems to me, on the contrary, that the syntax of such a poem as 'Emmonsails Heath in winter' was something that Clare had to work for: if we look at one of the earlier poems – if we imagine 'A Scene', for example, without punctuation – I think it will be clear that the syntax there is meant to be a good deal more formal, and orderly; it organises the images in the poem in such a way that they become the separate parts of a disorderly composition, not entangled with others in a complex manifold of impressions. It is true, of course, that the effect of Clare's syntax has been easier to recognise since editors have begun to publish the poems as Clare wrote them, without punctuation; the free articulation of the clauses becomes more obvious when the relationships defined by punctuation are removed. But the poems were, after all, without punctuation in the first place, and that Clare's editors have felt obliged in the past to change the words Clare wrote in order to make orthodox syntactical sense of his poems is enough to suggest that the lack of defined relationships between clauses is intrinsic to Clare's way of writing. Although Clare was happy enough for others to punctuate his poems for the press, he had no great respect for the discipline of punctuation:

I am genneraly understood tho I do not use that awkward squad of pointings called commas colons semicolons etc and for the very reason that altho they are drilled hourly daily and weekly by every boarding school Miss who pretends to gossip in correspondence they do not know their proper exercise for they even set gramarians at loggerheads and no one can assign them the proper places for give each a sentence to point and both shall differ[131]

This idea that the art of punctuation is a military and artificial discipline, to which even the punctuation-marks themselves cannot properly be subdued, suggests clearly enough how the lack of punctuation allowed Clare to use a more free-running, a more freely articulated language; and as we can see from this passage of a letter to John Taylor, which I quoted earlier, he felt much the same about orthodox grammar, which threatened to take away the freedom he derived from his habit of using dialect as well as orthodox grammatical forms: 'grammer in learning is like tyranny in government – confound the bitch I'll never be her slave & have a vast good mind not to alter the verse in question' (see above, p. 128).

The syntax that Clare developed to express his idea of landscape – I shall be giving other examples in this section and the next – is, I want to argue now, a form as precisely developed to express that idea as Thomson's was to express his. The form of Thomson's landscape was arrived at as a synthesis of the idea of landscape he found in Claude, but abstract and immediate – not yet applied to any particular landscape – and the particular imagery of the place he was describing; a synthesis which, ideally, preserved in the poem's syntax the idea of the design no more and no less than it preserved the particulars of the place; the form of the syntax was the form of the place as he perceived it. That Thomson's descriptions of landscape are thus formal, that they do have form, is clear enough; but Clare's descriptive poems have often been denied any virtue in this respect, even by his warmest admirers. According to Edmund Blunden, Clare 'lacked form a little'; but, he asks, 'what poet ever made up for that with greater riches of material?'[132] And according to Murry, 'Though comparatively few of his poems achieve the beauty of form which is the evidence of completely mastered and related perceptions, scarce one of them is without a strange intrinsic beauty of the perception itself.'[133] The terms of these judgements are revealing: the implication is there somewhere in Blunden's, that Clare lacked form perhaps *because* his material was so rich – how could he have had form, with all that to describe? – and Murry makes the charge still clearer; the perceptions are not 'mastered', not 'related'; the poems therefore lack form; and what is more (as a passage quoted earlier, on page 130 suggests) this lack of form is the unfortunate but inevitable result of Clare's greatest virtue, the sharpness of his eye. The word *mastered* shows that Murry's idea of form, in writing about nature, is based finally on the same assumptions as Thomson's: the landscape is something to be controlled, the form something to be imposed.

I said earlier that there is an opposition in Clare's descriptive poems, between his sense, on the one hand, of the multiplicity of images that make up a landscape, and on the other of the particularity of each of these images. It's clear that thus far Clare understood his own idea of landscape consciously enough, and that the aesthetic of disorder he developed was to some extent a response to this opposition: in the terms of his eighteenth-century inheritance, particularity – the individual images predominating over the sense of the design – meant disorder, and multiplicity – the images in the landscape not selected so as to reveal its structure – also meant disorder; and so the two together could add up only to more disorder. But in fact of course Clare's ability to express one aspect of this opposition, particularity or multiplicity, is always limited by his desire to suggest the other: a poem such as 'Emmonsails Heath in winter' offers us, as I have said, a manifold of impressions, each of them particular but immediately suggesting another; the images are each as detailed as they can become in whatever time they have before the next image is introduced; the syntax moves as rapidly as it can, encumbered by the descriptive phrases that impede it. The syntactical shape of the poem which emerges is, just as much as Thomson's, a synthesis of two contradictory ways of experiencing the landscape; it is the shape of the landscape as Clare perceives it, no less than the form of the description of the view from Shene is the form of that view perceived by Thomson.

It is clear by now that the syntax of such a poem as 'Emmonsails Heath in winter' is as much an expression of Clare's sense of place as I argued earlier his language is; and we can now understand Clare's attempt to write 'locally' as a more complex undertaking; as an attempt to describe the landscape of Helpston as a manifold of particular impressions, in a language which is his own and Helpston's, and in a syntax which, apart from being the perfectly achieved form of Clare's idea of landscape, is no doubt a good deal nearer to the syntactical shapes his own dialect adopted, than his versions of eighteenth-century poetic syntax could have been. I have been speaking of Clare's 'idea of landscape', and I have said that I was using this phrase only provisionally, to compare Clare's manner of describing a landscape, a tract of land or whatever – I am looking for that word which does not exist – with Thomson's; but it's clear I think that in fact Clare has no such 'idea', except when he borrows Thomson's own. The opposition in Clare's descriptive poems is not between – as it is in *The Seasons* – an idea, an *a priori* conception of the structure of landscape, on the one hand, and the particular landscape, the place itself, on the other; it is between two ways of perceiving the place which seem to emerge out of the place itself as soon as Clare attempts to describe it. I shall have more to say about this distinction between an eighteenth-century idea of landscape and what should be called simply Clare's sense of place; but meanwhile other distinctions suggest themselves. In Clare's attempts to write properly Thomsonian landscape-poetry, the sounds of the landscape were continually intruding into what should, ideally, have been a purely visual image; but although there are sounds, too, in 'Emmonsails Heath in winter' – the fieldfare chattering, the wind whistling – they are now not at all obtrusive. The place now appears as a complex of impressions which may equally well be visual or not; and the place would become less a 'complex manifold', less a group of images apprehended as it were simultaneously, if by some arbitrary criterion of propriety non-visual images were still definitely excluded from the poem. What Clare is intending to describe now is what he calls, in 'Shadows of Taste', 'a landscape heard and felt and seen'. (It might seem an odd procedure to compare descriptive passages by Clare in which non-visual imagery may properly be included with passages by Thomson from which such imagery is firmly excluded; especially when there are several passages in *The Seasons* – the description of animals drinking at a pool, for example, in 'Summer' (lines 480 ff.) – in which there is no shortage of sounds. But my purpose is to compare descriptions of places: and it is only in his purely visual set-piece descriptions of landscape – and only in some of them – that Thomson claims to be describing particular places. The description in 'Summer' referred to above, and others like it, are meant to be characteristic, and could take place anywhere. See below, p. 171).

The final distinction I want to make in this section is also one which I will consider later in this chapter perhaps at greater length, but it is convenient to notice it here, in the context of 'Emmonsails Heath in winter'. I wrote in the previous chapter of the difference between the linear idea of space of the agricultural reformer, and the circular sense which I suggested might be characteristic of an unimproved, open-field imagination. The way that Thomson conceives of a landscape in linear terms will be clear enough by now: his eye moves in a straight line from foreground to horizon, across the parallel lines of the composition; only after it has reached the horizon does it circle back on itself, to take in the details of the landscape at greater leisure; and the eyes of his imitators rarely if at all pass beyond that initial straight progress across the straight bands of landscape. In 'Emmonsails Heath in winter', although the spatial relationships between the separate images are sometimes quite explicitly stated, there is no sense of the images being disposed in any linear relationship one to another, or of them being displayed within a square space-box. The movement of Thomson's eye was also a movement from point to point in time; and we have already seen how Clare's syntax in this poem works against a linear notion of time, so that impressions are meant to be understood as being perceived by Clare simultaneously. He can of course do no more than give us the temporary illusion that we perceive them thus simultaneously, but he does, at the end of the poem, offer to replace the linear notion of time, which seems to be the inevitable product of using language at all, with a circular one. The last words of the poem, 'start again', are attached in the first place of course to the 'bumbarrels' which, as soon as they have settled start up again; but the phrase directs our attention back, too, to the start of the poem, so that the images in the poem become like beads on a necklace: they cannot change places with each other, but can be told in a circle in such a way that we lose the sense of a beginning and end, and so of one sort of order. This circular sense of time in the poem makes the sense of space circular too, as our attention is led away from each image and back again to it.

I'm not suggesting that this is an invariable technique of Clare's, inseparable from the sense of place expressed in this and other poems; the poem I will begin by discussing in the next section, for example, 'Beans in Blossom'[134] although it shares many qualities with this sonnet, does come to a definite end, a closure. But the sense of circular activity occurs often enough to be characteristic; in this poem, for example, 'The Sky Lark':[135]

> The rolls and harrows lies at rest beside
> The battered road and spreading far and wide
> Above the russet clods the corn is seen
> Sprouting its spirey points of tender green
> Where squats the hare to terrors wide awake
> Like some brown clod the harrows failed to break
> While neath the warm hedge boys stray far from home
> To crop the early blossoms as they come
> Where buttercups will make them eager run
> Opening their golden caskets to the sun
> To see who shall be first to pluck the prize
> And from their hurry up the sky lark flies
> And oer her half formed nest with happy wings
> Winnows the air till in the clouds she sings
> Then hangs a dust spot in the sunny skies
> And drops and drops till in her nest she lies
> Where boys unheeding past – neer dreaming then
> That birds which flew so high would drop agen
> To nests upon the ground...
>
> (lines 1–19)

The sentence doesn't end here, but continues for the same number of lines until the poem ends. There's no need to analyse in any detail the syntax of this, which works in much the same way as does that of 'Emmonsails Heath in winter'; but it is worth pointing out how the circular movement is working, referring us back to images earlier in the sentence and thus making the poem less a continuum than a manifold in which everything is kept before our eyes. Thus we return, in the sixth line, to the harrows we met in the first – Clare isn't at all embarrassed to use the same word twice in such a short space of lines; the boys pass the lark's nest; we follow the bird as it flies up, and down, back to the nest which the boys have now passed; and as the bird settles, our attention is led back to the boys, with whom it stays for what remains of the poem.

VIII

The sort of syntax that Clare uses in 'Emmonsails Heath in winter' is not found only in that poem, or in that and a few others: it is the characteristic form of the poems, and particularly of the sonnets, that he wrote in Helpston between about 1823 and 1832, when he moved to Northborough. It occurs, for example, in this poem, 'Beans in Blossom':

> The south west wind how pleasant in the face
> It breathes while sauntering in a musing pace
> I roam these new ploughed fields and by the side
> Of this old wood where happy birds abide
> And the rich blackbird through his golden bill
> Litters wild music when the rest are still
> Now luscious comes the scent of blossomed beans
> That oer the path in rich disorder leans
> Mid which the bees in busy songs and toils
> Load home luxuriantly their yellow spoils
> The herd cows toss the molehills in their play
> And often stand the strangers steps at bay
> Mid clover blossoms red and tawney white
> Strong scented with the summers warm delight

In the first six lines of this poem an apparently very complex pattern of syntax is built up; so that the last clause, 'when the rest are still', is dependent on the clause, 'and the rich blackbird ...litters wild music', which is itself dependent on the clause, 'while...I roam...by the side of this old wood', which is in turn dependent on the main verb. But this chain of dependence doesn't make one clause, one image, in any meaningful sense *subordinate* to any other, and we feel with these lines too that the syntax is trying to suggest that the images we apprehend as parts of a continuum were apprehended by Clare as a manifold of simultaneous impressions: 'the south-west wind breathes *while* I roam by this wood *where* birds abide and where the blackbird sings *when* the rest are silent'. A similar sort of paraphrase could be made of

164

the next four lines, where the phrase 'mid which' makes the same insistent connection, against the movement of the language which seeks to present the images in a continuum, that the phrase 'beside whose trunk' did, in 'Emmonsails Heath in winter'. And something like the same thing happens in the last four lines, where the phrase 'mid clover blossoms', etc., is in theory an adverbial phrase to tell us where the cows are standing, but in fact introduces a new impression in its own right, too precise and too extended to remain content with its position of dependence on the verb 'stand'.

The poem describes a walk; and whereas the whole of 'Emmonsails Heath in winter' was one manifold of impressions of that heath, this poem offers us three such manifolds, corresponding to three separate parts of the rural landscape that Clare encountered on his walk. It's worth comparing the poem with these lines from *The Task*:

> I saw the woods and fields, at close of day,
> A variegated show; the meadows green,
> Though faded; and the lands, where lately wav'd
> The golden harvest, of a mellow brown,
> Upturn'd so lately by the forceful share.
> I saw far off the weedy fallows smile
> With verdure not unprofitable, graz'd
> By flocks, fast feeding, and selecting each
> His fav'rite herb; while all the leafless groves,
> That skirt th'horizon, wore a sable hue,
> Scarce notic'd in the kindred dusk of eve.
>
> (Book IV, lines 311–21)

This is one of Cowper's most formal, most Claudian descriptions of landscape, and one of his most successful, not least in the way he has made the four planes of the landscape, alternately light and dark, correspond with the four main areas of different land-use of a type of eighteenth-century agricultural landscape: the green meadows, the brown arable 'lands', the fallows 'with verdure not unprofitable' – Cowper has a kind word for everything – and finally the sable woodland merging with 'the kindred dusk of eve'. There are no more than four planes in the composition, presumably because the resources of a rather primitive system of rotation have been exhausted – and yet this description of an extended prospect, remarkable as it is, is no more complete than is Clare's poem, in its representation of the variety of rural landscape. The first manifold of images in Clare's poem, the first six lines, represent the arable fields and woodland; the next four lines, the bean-fields; the last four, the pasture. Each place exists as a manifold of things seen, heard, smelled, and for Clare each thing exists only as foreground; he does not detach himself from the landscape as Cowper does, or post himself on a 'commanding height', but describes only what is immediately around him. The attempt, then, is not so much to describe a landscape, or even to *describe* each place, as to suggest what it is like to be in each place.

Clare made the decision – if it was as conscious a thing as that – to write 'locally', after he had finished *The Village Minstrel*; at about that time, too, he had the idea of writing a sequence of 100 sonnets, which eventually became the manuscript-collection 'The Midsummer Cushion'.[136] It is particularly in the sonnets in this collection, many of which were published in Clare's final two volumes, *The Rural Muse*, that the sort of syntax we have been looking at in this section and the last, and the sense of place of which it is an expression, are to be found. Clare's idea of the sonnet, I should perhaps add, is not necessarily ours – it may have twelve or sixteen lines, and may be in couplets.

That Clare was particularly conscious in his sonnets of writing 'locally' is very clearly suggested by this 'Sonnet to * * *':[137]

> I walked with poesy in the sonnets bounds
> With little hopes yet many a wild delight
> As timid childern take their summer rounds
> & scarce dare leave their cottage out of sight
> Till field & meadow & the summer light
> Tempteth them farther with their fears to roam
> So from the sonnets little garden home
> I went sweet natures wilderness to trace
> A stretching landscape where the [word illegible] sight
> Skimmed like a bird and found no resting place
> Heaths flats & sky its undivided blue
> A timid minstrel through their varied maze
> I strayd oft cheered in bringing up to view
> The little spots that won thy early praise

This poem is very obviously written out of Clare's frustration at the limitations imposed on him by living in Helpston: the form of the sonnet is identified with the 'bounds' of a landscape, and it restricts him – Clare's understanding of his situation is invariably so precise – to his 'knowledge', as children are restricted to the area around their cottage; the phrase 'summer rounds', by the way, again evokes a circular notion of space. This restriction is a source of 'wild delight' to Clare, as was the closed circle of the sand-martin's flight, in the poem quoted on page 123; but to break out of the sonnet-form is, precisely, to go out of his knowledge into the freedom of the wilderness. The poem reminds us again of how opposed are foreground and distance in Clare's poetry: the delight he takes in describing the things around him, and the sharpness of his descriptions, are the product of his inability to move outside his knowledge; and on the other hand, when he contemplates the sense of freedom which the idea of travelling towards the horizon affords him, in this poem as in 'The Mores', he is as much attracted as frightened by the lack of *things* in the distance, by the emptiness in which the eye finds no resting-place.

The sense of place, then, that Clare's sonnets express is closely related to his consciousness of their form: the alternative possibility, the long poem, has the same attractions and arouses the same apprehensions as does the thought of leaving the 'crampt circle' of his knowledge. And it must be said that the sense of place communicated by Clare's language and syntax is much better communicated in his sonnets than in his longer poems, with a few exceptions, notably, as I shall argue, *The Shepherd's Calendar*.

The poems which are perhaps most often praised by Clare's critics are the long odes, 'Autumn'[138] and 'Summer Images'.[139] The first is written in the unrhymed stanza of Collins's 'Ode to Evening'; Murry quotes among other images this one:

> Ploughed lands thin travelled with half hungry sheep
>
> (line 46)

This is certainly a remarkable image, 'precise', as Murry says, 'not merely to a fact, but to an emotion'.[140] And yet somehow this poem exists only to display the wealth of such images, it creates out of them no complex manifold. The syntax is continually pulled up in its stride at the end of each stanza, whose falling cadence brings each set of images regularly to a halt, and isolates it from the next set. This is not, it is worth pointing out, a fault that Clare took over along with his stanza-form from Collins; who, in the opening twenty lines of the 'Ode to Evening', constructs one of the longest and most complex sentences in English lyric poetry, which yet lifts its own increasing weight across the breaks between stanzas in a way that Clare finds impossible.

This stanza from 'Summer Images' is singled out by the Tibbles for particular praise:[141]

> And note on hedgerow baulks in moisture sprent*
> The jetty snail creep from the mossy thorn
>   In earnest heed and tremolous intent
>   Frail brother of the morn
>   That from the tiney bents† and misted leaves
>   Withdraws his timid horn
>   And fearful vision weaves

(lines 106–12)

*Sprinkled; †coarse grass.

and it was with particular reference to this stanza that Murry made his remark about the 'purity' of Clare's vision, quoted on page 130. It certainly is an astonishing piece of writing; but in insisting that Clare's main strength lies in his inexhaustible ability to create images as precise and as detailed as this, Clare's critics have inevitably been led to argue that he 'lacked form a little'; a long poem which is simply a succession of images as expansive as this one – and 'Summer Images' is such a poem – certainly invites the charge. The form of the sonnet is short enough to create the opposition I have spoken of as being a crucial part of Clare's sense of place; but this stanza, and the poem of which it is a part, were clearly not written by a man in a hurry, who as he puts one image into his poem hears the next one hammering to be admitted. There is both multiplicity and particularity in 'Summer Images', but no opposition between them; the poem simply grows to accommodate every image as it occurs to Clare, and the snail may proceed as slowly as it chooses.

The same sort of expansiveness occurs in many of Clare's long poems in couplets; but only in 'The Mores', which we have already had occasion to examine, does this expansiveness become a virtue, which corresponds to the enthusiasm Clare feels in the poem for a freedom without 'bounds':

> Cows went and came with evening morn and night
> To the wild pasture as their common right
> And sheep unfolded with the rising sun
> Heard the swains shout and felt their freedom won
> Tracked the red fallow field and heath and plain
> Then met the brook and drank and roamed again

> The brook that dribbled on as clear as glass
> Beneath the roots they hid among the grass
> While the glad shepherd traced their tracks along
> Free as the lark and happy as her song
>
> (lines 25–34)

It's clear that the freedom of the cows, who come and go when they please, and of the sheep, wandering in no particular direction across land which has since been closed to them, is related to the freedom Clare assumes in his syntax and in his use of the couplet: the poem knows no bounds because before the enclosure the sheep knew none; it is as free to wander as they were. 'The Mores' is probably the most successful of Clare's long poems in couplets, with the exception of some of those in *The Shepherd's Calendar*, and it is of course no accident that it is in this poem that Clare is most attracted out of his 'knowledge', and that the sense of 'localness' is most felt to be oppressive.

It is *The Shepherd's Calendar* which seems to me to express, better than any other of Clare's long poems, the sense of place I have been trying to define in this chapter. The poem describes the village in each month of the year; and especially in those months the dominant image of which is of communal rural activity – ploughing in 'March', hay-making in 'June' and 'July', harvesting in 'August' – the sense of the landscape as a manifold of simultaneous impressions is as striking as it is in any of Clare's sonnets. In this passage, for example, from 'March', the freedom of the couplet-form does not tempt Clare to look up from the villagers he describes as working in the foreground, towards the attractive emptiness of the distance:

> The stooping ditcher in the water stands
> Letting the furrowd lakes from off the lands
> Or splashing cleans the pasture brooks of mud
> Where many a wild weed freshens into bud
> And sprouting from the bottom purply green
> The water cresses neath the wave is seen
> Which the old woman gladly drags to land
> Wi reaching long rake in her tottering hand
> The ploughman mawls along the doughy sloughs
> And often stop their songs to clean their ploughs
> From teazing twitch that in the spongy soil
> Clings round the colter terryfying toil
> The sower striding oer his dirty way
> Sinks anckle deep in pudgy sloughs and clay

And oer his heavy hopper stoutly leans
Strewing wi swinging arms the pattering beans
Which soon as aprils milder weather gleams
Will shoot up green between the furroed seams
The driving boy glad when his steps can trace
The swelling edding as a resting place
Slings from his clotted shoes the dirt around
And feign would rest him on the solid ground
And sings when he can meet the parting green
Of rushy balks that bend the lands between
While close behind em struts the nauntling cow
And daws whose heads seem powderd oer wi snow
To seek the worms – and rooks a noisey guest
That on the wind rockd elms prepares her nest
On the fresh furrow often drops to pull
The twitching roots and gathering sticks and wool
Neath trees whose dead twigs litter to the wind
And gaps where stray sheep left their coats behind
While ground larks on a sweeing clump of rushes
Or on the top twigs of the oddling bushes
Chirp their 'cree creeing' note that sounds of spring
And sky larks meet the sun wi flittering wing

('March', lines 53–88)

The language of this has the same peculiarities we noted earlier in
'Winter Fields': the frequent dialect words, 'mawls' (= drags
wearily along), 'nauntling' (= holding itself upright), 'oddling',
'sweeing' (= swaying), which take their places among the words
more familiar to us without any sense of intruding; the presence
of other words, 'sloughs', 'hopper', 'edding' (for 'heading', or
'headland'), 'balks', 'colter' (for 'coulter'), which, though not
perhaps especially local to Clare's region, were more common in
the conversation of farmers and farm-labourers than in rural
poetry; the confusion, real or apparent, between singular and
plural forms, evidence of an attempt by Clare to marry the grammar
of his own dialect with that of his public. The syntax, too, has the
same momentum we found in 'Emmonsails Heath in winter', and
the directions it takes, if they cannot be shown here to be actually
circular, are clearly following no linear movement of Clare's eye:
the long sentence of eighteen lines, beginning 'the driving boy',
is able to give, by the same use of subordinate connections that we
noticed in Clare's sonnets, an image of a 'landscape' which 'reels
with life' – the phrase comes from one of the versions of 'July'[142] in
The Shepherd's Calendar. The activity of the driving boy is pre-

sented as simultaneous not only with that of the ditcher, cress-gatherer, ploughmen, sower, but also with that of the crows, the jackdaws, the rooks, the wind and the elms moving in it, the dead twigs, the ground-larks, the swaying rushes and the sky-larks. The impression is very much like that which William Marshall, and the writer quoted by Marc Bloch, described as characteristic of open-field landscape, and which I referred to in the first section of this chapter: that of being able to see the whole field, and the whole of what was being done in it, at one *coup d'œil*. The landscape of Helpston was fairly well enclosed by the time Clare was writing this poem, but it seems likely that he is describing, even after the enclosure has taken place, an open-field landscape, in which most of the work being done at any one time is being done in the same part of the parish; and it may perhaps be that this habit of understanding a place as a manifold of impressions, not organised by perspective and thus all as it were in the foreground, is a habit formed by an up-bringing in open-field landscape. That this might be so is suggested to me not only by Clare's poems, but also by the illustrations of the labours of the months that we find in *Books of Hours*[143] and by illustrations such as Plate 6. This was made in France around 1755, and comes from the collection of plates illustrative of agriculture in the *Encyclopédie* of Diderot and D'Alembert:[144] in the use it makes of space it is quite unlike anything that could have been produced in England at that date, and the connection we noticed in the last chapter, between the increasing sophistication of agriculture and an increasingly linear sense of space, may be operating here as well. There is a certain knowledge evident in this picture of how to use Claudian planes and masks; but the space in it is so displayed, and the rules of diminishing perspective so completely ignored, that the man working in the distant field below the village is quite as visible to us – is in one sense as *near* to us – as is the plough-team in the foreground; so that in fact the whole field becomes the foreground, in some such way perhaps as it does in the passage from 'March'.

It might seem that in offering the descriptions of rural activity in *The Shepherd's Calendar* as examples of Clare's sense of place, and in comparing them not with the descriptions by Thomson of similar activities in *The Seasons*, but, by implication, with the set-piece descriptions of landscape in that poem. I am making my argument a little too easy. But the comparison is fair, I think:

Thomson, as I argued earlier, does not attempt to express any sense of locality in his descriptions of rural activity – they are as generalised from that point of view as they can be. If Thomson does try to describe a particular place, or to give us the sense that he is writing about one place and not another, it is only in his descriptions of landscape, and it is the topography of a place that fixes its identity for him, if anything does. But for Clare a place is a good deal more than a landscape: a place is a manifold of images, not of visual images only, and not only of topography but of the people and living things that work and live in the place. We have to understand how for Clare the identity of a place is more than its topography, to understand how Clare, despite his exposure to London and to *The Seasons*, could still at times feel that his 'knowledge' was at once the place he knew, and *everything* he knew.

Finally, in the context of *The Shepherd's Calendar*, I'd like to try to answer one more of the charges quite frequently made against Clare's poetry: that if the poems have content, they still have no human content – the people we meet in Clare's poems have no character, no reality. There is a certain undeniable truth about this charge: in *The Shepherd's Calendar* Clare certainly makes no attempt to present ploughmen or threshers or shepherds as individuals, with strongly marked character-traits of their own. But we should be careful to notice what sort of assumptions are behind this charge, about the society Clare was describing. I imagine there's no need to argue that the notion of 'character' as we understand it in our literature is in essence a post-feudal one: we hardly look for the presence of strong individual characters before the Elizabethan drama, and we are right to relate their appearance in that period, as also the importance of the individual, of 'character', in Romantic writing from say Crabbe onwards, to the ascendancy in literature of a bourgeois social philosophy over an aristocratic one. This philosophy has nothing to do with the society Clare describes, which he presents as in some sense still feudal, a society in which 'character', if it exists at all, is primarily a function of what people do. Thus, shepherds in Clare's poems are remote and lonely, because it is the nature of what they do to make them so; while threshers take some of their 'character' from the pallor of their faces, the result of working indoors all day in barns, and seldom seeing daylight; and when the labourers of the

172

village engage in communal activity, say reaping, they also take such character as they have from the nature of that activity, that it is, say, hard work, but pleasantly social.

The people Clare writes about are what they do: if they were anything else – if they had, somehow, *more* character – then the sense of place they help create in Clare's poems would change, and would have engaged in some compromise with what it is designed to exclude – the spirit and values of agrarian capitalism. We should instead be grateful, I think, that Clare has not entered the half-way house that the early Hardy inhabited, and created 'characters' out of the villagers, each with one dominant characteristic – say, idiocy – in terms of which they respond to all occurrences, as do the rustics in *Far From the Madding Crowd*. But to ask him to go beyond that, and to offer us the sort of human content we find in Crabbe's or in Wordsworth's poems about the rural poor, is to ask him to change utterly the nature of his poetic enterprise, and to accept the assumptions about character and society of a class he didn't belong to, and distrusted.

What Clare can perhaps with more justice be accused of, is that he chose deliberately to arrest the development of his villagers, and that their lack of individuality is appropriate only to a period long before Clare was writing, and before the growth of agrarian capitalism. But this charge may well be based on an over-sophisticated historical hindsight, a refusal to believe that the English peasantry in the early nineteenth century could possibly have been as uncorrupted as Clare suggests it was by any notion of the importance or the value of the individual. Certainly the experience Clare describes, in 'The Lamentations of Round Oak Waters', in his autobiographical poem *The Village Minstrel*, and elsewhere, of being an outsider in the village, crippled by his own sensibility and individuality, is credible enough; and it would hardly have encouraged him to see the, for him, apparently monolithic class of peasants and labourers in Helpston as in fact made up of so many other self-conscious individuals. (For a further discussion of Clare's attitudes to, and descriptions of, the rural poor, see the appendix.)

IX

In the spring of 1832 Clare moved with his family to a cottage at Northborough, a fenland village some three miles north-east of Helpston. His feelings about the move were mixed: the new cottage had enough land attached to it to make him independent, but to be independent and out of Helpston was to exchange his 'knowledge' for a way of life quite unknown. In his letter to John Taylor, dated October 1831, Clare suggests that the move will be less of a dislocation than he might have anticipated, because Helpston is now changing so fast that it has almost ceased to be the place he knew:

> I shall have fewer regrets to leave this old corner where I now write this letter the place of all my hopes & ambitions for they have insulted my feelings latterly very much & cut down the last Elm next the Street & the old Plumb tree at the corner is blown down & all the old associations are going before me[145]

But in another letter to Taylor, written some three months later but never sent, Clare is anticipating a greater sense of disorientation:

> I have had some difficulties to leave the woods & heaths & favourite spots that have known me so long for the very molehills on the heath & the old trees in the hedges seem bidding me farewell – other associations of friendships I have few or none to regret – for my father & mother will be often with me – & altho my flitting is not above three miles off – there is neither wood nor heath furze bush molehill or oak tree about it[146]

This letter recalls the passage of Clare's *Autobiography*, in which he writes that, outside Helpston, 'the very wild flowers seemd to forget me' (see above, p. 120), and he is clearly concerned at leaving the landscape of limestone heath that 'made up' his 'being'. We may expect that this move, although of three miles only, will have had a considerable effect on Clare's sense of place, and on his ability to write 'locally'.

At about the time of his removal to Northborough Clare wrote three remarkable poems, which between them reflect the ambiguous feelings towards the move that are expressed in the letters to Taylor, and also suggest the way in which Clare's poetry was to change during the next few years at Northborough. The first of these poems, 'Remembrances',[147] is concerned with Clare's changing attitude to Helpston, and the sense that the associations he has with it are with a place that disappeared with the enclosure. There's something of the same confusion about this poem that we noticed in the early poems about the enclosure, in which it's hard to grasp quite what Clare's nostalgia is for: whether it is for a vision of Helpston which has inevitably left him as he has grown older, or for a Helpston which has undergone the concrete change of being enclosed. But these two themes are confused, it might be possible to say, more knowingly now: so that if it is not stated, it is still perhaps understood that the enclosure has now become for Clare in some way an emblem for whatever it is that takes away the joys of childhood and so takes away too the pleasant associations we used to have with places. Thus at the end of the second stanza Clare writes of when he used 'to cut a straw at the brook to have a soak', and goes on:

> O I never dreamed of parting or that trouble had a sting
> Or that pleasures like a flock of birds would ever take to wing
> Leaving nothing but a little naked spring
>
> (lines 18–20)

– where it seems that the spring is now naked of its associations with Clare's childhood; at the end of the seventh stanza, however, he writes:

> Inclosure like a buonaparte let not a thing remain
> It levelled every bush and tree and levelled every hill
> And hung the moles for traitors – though the brook is running still
> It runs a naked stream cold and chill
>
> (lines 67–70)

– in which the spring is now to be understood as naked of the trees which once clothed its banks. The effect is to make the enclosure seem to have been as inevitable as is the loss of childhood and the pleasures of childhood; and the bare landscape of Helpston after the enclosure becomes also a landscape now stripped by time of its pleasant associations, and now no more than a collection of impersonal things.

The longest of the three poems, 'The Flitting',[148] describes Clare's sense of disorientation in Northborough in terms by now familiar to us:

> Ive left my own old home of homes
> Green fields and every pleasant place

175

> The summer like a stranger comes
> I pause and hardly know her face
>
> (lines 1–4)

– and there is another echo here too of the passage in the *Autobiography* referred to above, in which Clare writes, 'the very sun seemd to be a new one & shining in a different quarter of the sky'. In 'The Flitting' this becomes:

> The sun een seems to lose its way
> Nor knows the quarter it is in
>
> (lines 55–6)

The poem describes Clare's feelings in a landscape in which nature is apparently no less benevolent than in Helpston – the trees are no less green, the birds still sing – but in which the scenes are strange, 'mere shadows', 'vague unpersonifying things',[149] compared with his 'old hants'[150] rich in associations:

> Here every tree is strange to me
> All foreign things where ere I go
> Theres none where boyhood made a swee
> Or clambered up to rob a crow
> No hollow tree or woodland bower
> Well known when joy was beating high
> Where beauty ran to shun a shower
> And love took pains to keep her dry
>
> (lines 97–104)

Towards the end of the poem Clare begins to argue himself out of this nostalgia, and to accept his new situation; and he does so by trying to attach his associations of Helpston to the trees and flowers he sees around him in Northborough. This idea brings another with it, however, and Clare seems to understand that what he is attempting to do is to replace his old love of nature as it was in Helpston and not elsewhere, with a love for nature as it is everywhere; so that the triumphant end of the poem –

> And still the grass eternal springs
> Where castles stood and grandeur died
>
> (lines 222–4)

can offer Clare comfort only on condition that he accepts, instead of his earlier notion of the uniqueness of Helpston, a notion of abstract nature very similar to the one he experienced in 'Remembrances', and recoiled from: a notion of things as they are, naked of associations. In 'Decay',[151] the third poem, the fact that things are now thus naked is recognised again by Clare, but without any attempt at cheerfulness; and his belief, that 'there is nothing of poetry about manhood but the reflection and remembrance of what has been',[152] leads him to believe also that the nakedness of things has left him with nothing to write about:

> The stream it is a naked stream
> Where we on sundays used to ramble
> The sky hangs oer a broken dream
> The brambles dwindled to a bramble
> O poesy is on its wane
> I cannot find her haunts again

(lines 45–50)

There's something in this poem of that inversion of the pathetic fallacy we often find, for example, in Wordsworth; whereby the attempt to see nature as nature-in-itself, impersonal – 'the brambles dwindled to a bramble' – leads quickly to a re-personification of nature as cruel and without *feeling*.

In the more specifically descriptive poems that Clare began to write in Northborough there is an acceptance that his task is now to write about nature as abstract and not as local; and as a result his poetry changes very considerably. This poem, 'Quail's Nest',[153] is a case in point:

> I wandered out one rainy day
> And heard a bird with merry joys
> Cry 'wet my foot' for half the way;
> I stood and wondered at the noise,
>
> When from my foot a bird did flee –
> The rain flew bouncing from her breast –
> I wondered what the bird could be,
> And almost trampled on her nest.
>
> The nest was full of eggs and round;
> I met a shepherd in the vales,
> And stood to tell him what I found.
> He knew and said it was a quail's,
>
> For he himself the nest had found,
> Among the wheat and on the green,
> When going on his daily round,
> With eggs as many as fifteen.

177

> Among the stranger birds they feed,
>   Their summer flight is short and low;
> There's very few know where they breed,
>   And scarcely any where they go.

This is an excellent poem, and I find it a very moving one: and yet in tone, language, syntax, it could hardly be more different from the sonnets by Clare we have looked at so far. The narrative plainness of the description is quite unlike that rapid and exhilarated record of impressions we found in the sonnets; the language is free of dialect-words; and – at least as far as one can judge from this text – the syntactical connections are made here in a much more orthodox way than before, and subordinate clauses are what they seem. There is, in fact, none of the sense of place we found in the earlier poems: the objectivity is that of a natural historian, but isn't that, on the other hand, of the natural history journal that Clare kept in Helpston – in which hardly a bird or a flower is noticed without particulars of just where in the parish or outside Clare saw it. In this poem we learn, simply, that the nest was 'among the wheat and on the green', which means, perhaps, that it was on an unploughed strip of turf, a 'balk', in a field of wheat; but there is no longer the sense that this was one particular field, and could have been no other.

What I find moving about this poem is finally, I suppose, a matter of the tone Clare adopts to offer us the knowledge he has about the quail, a knowledge which is now precisely 'abstract' in that it is no longer felt to be valid only, only knowledge, in the particular context of Helpston. It is perhaps for this reason that this poem is now more obviously influenced by Wordsworth than anything Clare had written before; the form and tone is like that of the Lucy poems, and the last stanza is a very clear echo of the first stanza of 'She dwelt among the untrodden ways': it is as though Clare, having moved out of Helpston to a place where nature is the same as it is everwhere else, can only now find in Wordsworth anything that he needs. But the sense of dislocation is present only in the tone, and makes no open appeal to be recognised: as a man who feels, Clare enters the poem hardly at all, but does so obliquely, perhaps, in the line,

> Among the stranger birds they feed

– an idea that occurs so often in Clare's poems of every period (see for example 'The Sand Martin' (above, p. 123); and note the choice of '*lone* heron', '*oddling* crow', in 'Emmonsails Heath in winter'), that we are I think entitled to connect it with his sense of isolation, whether, as earlier, alienated from the other villagers in Helpston, or, as now, exiled from the place he knew.

The characteristics of 'Quail's Nest' are shared by many of the large number of sonnets Clare wrote in Northborough: they have none of the idiosyncratic syntax of the earlier sonnets, and they too are almost empty of dialect-words, although I don't intend to suggest that the purification of Clare's diction was the result of some conscious acceptance that his language had now to be de-localised along with his knowledge. The new objective attitude to nature emerges in two main types of sonnets: some, such as 'Winter Weather'[154] or 'Autumn Birds',[155] are written in couplets so lacking in connection that they could be arranged in any order in the poem, or exchanged with couplets from other poems on similar subjects without any serious loss:

> The crows drive onward through the storm of snow
> And play about, naught caring where they go.
> The young colt breaks the fences in his play
> And spreads his tail and gallops all the way.
> The hunkèd ploughman...
>
> ('Winter Weather', lines 1–5)

There is just as much knowledge here as in 'Emmonsails Heath in winter'; what is lacking is any sense of a relationship between the images; so that we have no idea of whether these are images all taken from the same place, as in an earlier sonnet we would know they were by the syntactical connections made between them, or whether these are meant to be what they appear, isolated fragments of Clare's knowledge about winter, which come together in the poem only, and not in any specific place. Other sonnets, such as 'Blackberrying',[156] or 'Sheep in Winter',[157] which restrict them-selves to the description of one particular scene or activity, are constructed in the loosest possible parataxis. The imagery remains as precise as ever, but the sense that each scene, and the activity performed within it, are a complex manifold of simultaneous im-pressions has quite disappeared, and we are left instead with a strange continuum of impressions, image following image with an automatic regularity:

> The sheep get up and make their many tracks
> And bear a load of snow upon their backs,
> And gnaw the frozen turnip to the ground
> With sharp quick bite, and then go noising round
> The boy that pecks the turnips all the day
> And knocks his hands to keep the cold away
> And laps his legs in straw to keep them warm
> And hides behind the hedges from the storm.
> The sheep, as tame as dogs, go where he goes
> And try to shake their fleeces from the snows,
> Then leave their frozen meal and wander round
> The stubble stack that stands beside the ground,
> And lie all night and face the drizzling storm
> And shun the hovel where they might be warm.
>
> ('Sheep in Winter')

The language of this is still recognisably Clare's – it still has affinities with the language he used in Helpston – but it is not therefore still recognisably local; in no sense does Clare now seem inseparable from the places he describes.

In 1837 Clare was taken to the asylum at High Beech, Epping Forest; in 1841 he escaped and walked home to Northborough; at the end of that year he was taken to Northampton General Asylum, where in 1864 he died. The poems he wrote in the last twenty-seven years of his life, which include a large number of love songs to Mary Joyce, and a group of poems written in the spirit – I mean the phrase to be taken as literally as possible – of Byron, have been admired as much and more than the poems he wrote when he was, apparently, sane. My own preference is for the earlier poems, but in any case there is no need for me, for the purposes of this book, to discuss the asylum-poems, few if any of which attempt, understandably enough, to evoke or to describe places or landscape. The nature of Clare's insanity – he sometimes imagined that he was Byron, the prize-fighter Jack Randall, or Queen Victoria's father, and insisted for many years after her death in 1838 that Mary Joyce was still living – has often been the subject of conjecture by Clare's biographers and critics.[158] I want to appear, myself, to be entering this discussion with some diffidence; but it is worth repeating here, in the light of what has emerged as Clare's very great dependence on the notion of Helpston as his 'knowledge', the suggestion that other writers have made, that the losses of identity Clare suffered can perhaps be connected with his sense of dislocation at the enclosure and at his removal from Helpston. It's worth remembering that a characteristic idiom of Clare's to express that notion of his knowledge is, for example, that 'the woods & heaths...have known me so long', as though he is the object of their knowledge, and not they of his: so that for 'the very wild flowers' to 'forget' him is certainly for him to lose, in some sense, his identity. And in a fragment of prose written in 1841, and published as *Self-Identity*,[159] Clare speaks several times of the possibility that the 'world' might 'forget' him – not as a poet, but as a man of any sort – and so leave him to become 'a living-dead man dwelling among shadows'.[160]

EPILOGUE

I want to begin this final section by comparing, briefly, the sense of place in Clare's poetry, with the sense of place we find in the works of two writers whom we think of as having been more than usually attached to the places they wrote about. At the end of Chapter 1 I referred to this passage of *The Prelude*, in which Words-worth distinguishes his own way of apprehending a landscape, from that of the picturesque connoisseur, 'disliking here, and there,

> Liking, by rules of mimic art transferr'd
> To things above all art. But more, for this,
> Although a strong infection of the age,
> Was never much my habit, giving way
> To a comparison of scene with scene,
> Bent overmuch on superficial things,
> Pampering myself with meagre novelties
> Of colour and proportion, to the moods
> Of time or season, to the moral power
> The affections, and the spirit of the place,
> Less sensible.
> (*The Prelude* (1805–6), book XI, lines 154–64)

The scorn for picturesque rules, and the concern instead with 'the spirit of the place', could invite us to believe that Wordsworth, in his attachment to the landscape of the Lake District, might have had more to offer Clare than Clare realised, and might have been a useful model for him, in his attempts to describe, if not the 'spirit' of a place, at least its identity. But of course, in making that very distinction between what it was the two men were trying to discover about a place, we open a gap between them as wide as that between Clare and Thomson, for Wordsworth's idea of nature was always more or less platonic, and the 'spirit' of a place was something, for him, to be found by looking *through* the place itself. The theory of the influence of natural objects need not be rehearsed here; but it is to the point, of course, that for Wordsworth it is a gift of maturity to be able thus to see through a landscape, as we learn for example in 'Tintern Abbey' and in a number of passages of *The Prelude* too familiar to need quotation. The idea that Clare entertained of his 'knowledge', on the other hand, at once the place he knew and everything he knew, means that the sense of place he communicates in his poems becomes their entire content, from which no other more abstract knowledge could be deduced. And for Clare of course Wordsworth's very determination *not* to compare one place with another would have been a luxury: the opportunity of making such comparisons, and the possibility of choosing not to do so, were both equally beyond his reach.

In one poem by Wordsworth, however, we discover some such notion of place as Clare's, the idea that one particular landscape might be inseparable from the whole of man's knowledge. I am thinking of these lines from 'Michael':

> And grossly that man errs, who should suppose
> That the green valleys, and the streams and rocks,
> Were things indifferent to the Shepherd's thoughts.
> Fields, where with cheerful spirits he had breathed
> The common air; hills, which with vigorous step
> He had so often climbed; which had impressed
> So many incidents upon his mind
> Of hardship, skill or courage, joy or fear;
> Which, like a book, preserved the memory
> Of the dumb animals, whom he had saved,
> Had fed or sheltered, linking to such acts
> The certainty of honourable gain;
> Those fields, those hills – what could they less – had laid
> Strong hold on his affections, were to him
> A pleasurable feeling of blind love,
> The pleasure which there is in life itself.

(lines 62–77)

The idea here is different from that in 'Tintern Abbey', in which the knowledge Wordsworth has arrived at by the influence of natural objects can finally be discussed as separate from those objects; and in which we are entitled to feel that another landscape carefully enough chosen, might have served Wordsworth as well in helping him to see 'into the life of things'.[161] The sense that the landscape is for Michael 'like a book', preserving the memories of his life; the idea that the landscape was therefore to him 'the pleasure which there is in life itself' – the similarity between what Wordsworth describes as Michael's sense of place, and Clare's own, is undeniable, and I think unique in Wordsworth – I can think of no other passage which suggests as much. But it is of course Michael's sense of place that Wordsworth is describing, with however remarkable an insight; he would not have claimed that his own knowledge was as directly linked as Michael's to one particular landscape; and in the rest of the poem adopts an attitude to place so opposed to Michael's that it becomes the authentic and unabashed tone of the returning tourist, or of the guide-book:

> If from the public way you turn your steps,

the poem begins. If you do thus turn your steps, you arrive at 'a hidden valley', which Wordsworth is nevertheless willing to reveal to his curious readers; 'nor should I', he goes on,

> have made mention of this Dell
> But for one object which you might pass by,
> Might see and notice not.
>
> (lines 14–16)

We are now reminded how close, in this respect at least, was Wordsworth to the picturesque travellers whom he despised: in this passage he opens up the landscape, and explains its mysteries, in a way not substantially different from the way William Gilpin or Arthur Young might have reclaimed a similarly rough, secluded landscape for the metropolitan imagination.

It seems to me, indeed, that Wordsworth's sense of place is no more and no less remote from Clare's than was Young's, or Marshall's, or James Thomson's. I don't want to labour this point, but a number of people who have read the typescript of this book have suggested to me that there is more to be gained by the comparison with Wordsworth; and that Wordsworth's attempts, especially in his inscriptions, to incorporate into 'a particular scene the very process of inscribing it or interpreting it' are somehow analogous to what, I have argued, Clare was doing in Helpston. That quotation is from Geoffrey Hartman's essay,'Wordsworth, Inscriptions, and Romantic Nature Poetry',[162] which continues: 'The setting is understood to contain the writer in the act of writing: the poet in the grip of what he feels and sees...' This sounds, perhaps, something like what I have been saying about Clare; but if it does, that is the fault of my language, which cannot represent the concreteness of Clare's experience and its incapacity for being abstracted; it can only describe that experience in general terms which apparently invite comparisons. Thus, in speaking of Clare's 'sense of place', I should perhaps have spoken of his 'sense of Helpston': the word 'place', is a modish term in current literary criticism, and to say that a writer's subject is 'place' is to say that he has a general predisposition to write about places as particular experiences, isolated for the moment from the general movement of life. Clare's enforced concentration on one place, Helpston, is quite different from this, and different in kind: it has nothing in common with the 'sense of place' of any number of writers from Wordsworth to, say, Charles Olson, who attend to one place, and then perhaps another, with care and in detail, but who are, wherever they are, at the end of the turnpike or the freeway to somewhere else, and can choose to be in this place, or that one.

Thomas Hardy often situates himself in the landscape of Wessex quite explicitly as tourist or guide; a case in point would be this passage – I apologise for its length – from *Tess of the D'Urbervilles*: the vale of Blackmoor, writes Hardy,

is a vale whose acquaintance is best made by viewing it from the summits of the hills that surround it – except perhaps during the droughts of summer. An unguided ramble into its recesses in bad weather is apt to engender dissatisfaction with its narrow, tortuous, and miry ways.

This fertile and sheltered tract of country, in which the fields are never brown and the springs never dry, is bounded on the south by the bold chalk ridge that embraces the prominences of Hambledon Hill, Bulbarrow, Nettlecombe-Tout, Dogbury, High Stoy, and Bubb Down. The traveller from the coast, who, after plodding northward for a score of miles over calcareous downs and corn-lands, suddenly reaches the verge of one of these escarpments, is surprised and delighted to behold, extended like a map beneath him, a country differing absolutely from that which he has passed through. Behind him the hills are open, the sun blazes down upon fields so large as to give an unenclosed character to the landscape, the lanes are white, the hedges low and plashed, the atmosphere colourless. Here, in the valley, the world seems to be constructed upon a smaller and more delicate scale; the fields are mere paddocks, so reduced that from this height their hedgerows appear a network of dark green threads overspreading the paler green of the grass. The atmosphere beneath is languorous, and is so tinged with azure that what artists call the middle distance partakes also of that hue, while the horizon beyond is of the deepest ultramarine.[163]

The recommendation of where the 'acquaintance' of the vale may best be made; the advice to the 'unguided' rambler, whose good opinion of the landscape Hardy is keen to elicit; the attempt to put himself in the shoes of the traveller, and to describe the view as he would first encounter it; the appeal to a knowledge of landscape-painting, which will certainly be among the acquisitions of the picturesque traveller of the nineteenth century – the tone of all this is the tone of a well-written Victorian guide-book; I intend that as a comment only, not as a judgement. The high viewpoint is insisted on by Hardy no less than it might be by an eighteenth-century connoisseur: the vale is to be seen all at one glance, 'extended like a map', and then described by means of a comparison with the landscape the traveller has just traversed. The vale is thus seen as a geographical region contained within the bounds of the landscape, but also situated in the wider region of Dorset as a whole: we learn at once how it differs from, and how it is related to, the landscape of the rest of the county. To remind ourselves how much greater than Clare's is Hardy's breadth of reference here, we may look, for example, at these two stanzas by Clare:

> What is there in the distant hills
> My fancy longs to see
> That many a mood of joy instills
> Say what can fancy be
>
> Do old oaks thicken all the woods
> With weeds and brakes as here
> Does common water make the floods
> Thats common every where
>
> (untitled, lines 1–8)[164]

The tone of this is a little over-ingenuous; but is perhaps so only as a result of Clare's embarrassment at confessing what was probably true, that he had never been as far as the hills on the horizon.

We are meant to remember the passage from *Tess of the D'Urbervilles* when, later in the book, Tess leaves the Vale of Blackmoor for Froom Vale, which Hardy describes thus:

It was intrinsically different from the Vale of Little Dairies, Blackmoor Vale, which, save during her disastrous sojourn at Trantbridge, she had exclusively known till now. The world was drawn to a larger pattern here. The enclosures numbered fifty acres instead of ten, the farmsteads were more extended, the groups of cattle formed tribes hereabout; there only families. These myriads of cattle stretching under her eyes from the far east to the far west outnumbered any she had ever seen at one glance before. The green lea was speckled as thickly with them as a canvas by Van Alsloot or Sallaert with burghers. The ripe hue of the red and dun kine absorbed the evening sunlight, which the white-coated animals returned to the eye in rays almost dazzling, even at the distant elevation on which she stood.

The bird's-eye perspective before her was not so luxuriantly beautiful, perhaps, as that other one which she knew so well; yet it was more cheering. It lacked the intensely blue atmosphere of the rival vale, and its heavy soils and scents; the new air was clear, bracing, ethereal. The river itself, which nourished the grass and cows of these renowned dairies, flowed not like the streams in Blackmoor. Those were slow, silent, often turbid; flowing over beds of mud into which the incautious wader might sink and vanish unawares. The Froom waters were clear as the pure River of Life shown to the Evangelist, rapid as the shadow of a cloud, with pebbly shallows that prattled to the sky all day long. There the water-flower was the lily; the crowfoot here.[165]

This vale too is described as being perceived from a 'commanding' summit, but this time it is meant to be Tess who is perceiving it, and not an imagined traveller. It seems at first that Hardy is trying to suggest how Tess might have been struck by seeing, virtually for the first time, any landscape different from her own. But he is soon overcome by the impossibility of the undertaking: the cows, he says, stretching under *her* eyes, were as numerous as the burghers in a Flemish painting – the impression we have is of a guide or an experienced tourist, standing beside Tess and prompting her to false comparisons. We feel the same about the other implied appeal to a knowledge of painting, the impossibly sophisticated (for Tess) description of the colours of the cattle, which Hardy nevertheless attempts to present as a picturesque observation of Tess's own, 'at the distant elevation on which she stood'. By the second paragraph, Hardy has fairly clearly lost sight of his original intention; it is by now emphatically the experience of a tourist that we are being offered, and not Tess's. The landscape of Froom Vale, we are told, was 'more cheering' than that of Blackmoor, a comparison more likely to be made by a man on a walking tour than by Tess, who, however much her spirits were lifted by this new landscape, was unlikely to have been responding to any intrinsically cheering property of the view. By the end of the passage, Hardy has abandoned even Tess's viewpoint, and is stooping beside a river, to listen to its prattling, and examine its water-flowers.

It seems to me that there is something deliberately factitious about the tone of this passage and of other descriptive passages in Hardy's novels. It is as if he is *determined* that it should be understood that his own place in the landscape is that of guide, and ours that of tourists: and these two roles, as we have seen, are not very different, for the successful guide will adopt the point of view of the tourist, and emulate his detachment from the landscapes he examines. Thus in *The Woodlanders*, for example, he directs us to Little Hintock in his capacity as a guide: 'the rambler who', he begins, 'for old association's sake, should trace the forsaken coachroad running almost in a meridional line from Bristol to the south shore of England, would find himself...'[166] This is the tone of the opening, too, of 'Michael'. But now Hardy becomes a tourist himself: we enter the village in company with a stranger to it, Barber Percomb, and are allowed to know no more about it than he can deduce from observation. Thus Hardy moves continually from the role of guide to that of tourist: he opens up, he *explains* a landscape in the most literal sense of that word, but in doing so becomes as detached from the places he writes about as we are, and comes to see them as we might, as new acquisitions for our experience.

This self-conscious detachment from places is something I admire in Hardy, and particularly for this reason, that it seems to have arisen from something other than an awareness of the difference between his own sense of place, as a mobile and a literate man, and that of the rural class to which, for example, Tess belonged. It seems instead to have arisen out of a surprised recognition on his part that, at the time he was writing, that difference had almost ceased to exist. In his fine essay 'The Dorsetshire Labourer',[167] Hardy describes the effect of a much greater mobility among the rural population of Dorset, which has come about by the practice of hiring labourers by the year only: 'it is only natural that, now different districts of them are shaken together once a year and redistributed, like a shuffled pack of cards, they have ceased to be so local in feeling or manner as formerly, and have entered on the condition of inter-social citizens, "whose city stretches the whole country over"'.[168] We are all tourists in Dorset now, is Hardy's point, which he finds it impossible to regret: 'change is also a certain sort of education'.[169] The conditions of employment he is describing – and to which he refers also in *Far From the Madding Crowd*[170] – were part, of course, of the same historical process as was responsible for the enclosure of Helpston: a long process of de-localisation inseparable from the progressive capitalisation of agriculture, and which operated indifferently by opening up a village to the world outside, or by opening up the world outside to the villagers.

It is in the context of this process as a whole that we should, finally, understand Clare's poetry and his sense of place. At the beginning of this chapter I described the enclosure of Helpston in sufficient detail, I hope, to show that the intentions behind the enclosure, and its effects on the landscape, were those which, I argued in Chapter 2, were characteristic of the enclosure movement in general. I have suggested that it was in response to the enclosure that Clare became conscious of the sense of place I have been trying to define, and which, having once become articulate in Clare's writing, had to be insisted upon tenaciously: for of course it became explicit only as a response to that historical process which was attempting to destroy it, and the condition of its becoming thus explicit was precisely Clare's awareness of other perspectives being made available to him. The movement to de-localise operated in him, perhaps more than most, as a desire to leave his 'knowledge', and to submit to the attractions of the world outside.

The diffusion of literacy and the availability to Clare of works of literature, which enabled him in the first place to conceive of becoming a poet, were also themselves of course part of the process of delocalisation. We have seen that the descriptive poetry of the eighteenth century appeared to offer Clare a medium through which, in describing Helpston, he could express a sense of its identity; but of course what it offered him was what he wrote to oppose – a detachment from the places it described, and a habit of looking at landscape with reference to an *a priori* notion of its design. The eighteenth-century poets, compared with Clare, moved as tourists through the places they wrote about – but we are all tourists now, so that insofar as Clare was successful in expressing his own sense of place, he was writing himself out of the main stream of European literature.

APPENDIX

John Clare and the enclosure of Helpston

=============

Almost every critic who has written about John Clare has seen the importance of relating the enclosure of Helpston to Clare's development as a writer and to the content of his work, and Clare himself makes constant reference to the enclosure in the poems apparently composed between about 1812 and 1825. The difficulty, however, has been to escape from the stereotyped notions of 'the effects of enclosure', and to establish exactly what sort of significance the enclosure might have had for Helpston and for Clare. In this, his critics have not been helped by the sort of historiography that has, throughout this century, especially recommended itself to literary people. Particularly unhelpful has been the absolute reliance on *The Village Labourer*, by J. L. and Barbara Hammond,[1] a book which, for all its virtues, does offer an unusually one-sided account of the economic effects of parliamentary enclosure, and has a habit of presenting the exceptional case as the general one; and the conclusions the Hammonds come to in that book have been a little too eagerly endorsed by critics who stress that side of English rural literature which seems to be a continuous lament for the passing of the 'organic' rural community. I don't want to seem, here, to be joining in that still fashionable game of abusing the Hammonds, as sentimentalists who were yet cunning enough to gain acceptance for a wilfully distorted view of history, and I had better say here what I shall repeat later, that a good deal of what they say about the condition of the lowest classes in rural society – about Clare's class, indeed, labourers without land and without a legally constituted right of common – is extremely important and in great danger of being forgotten by orthodox historians. But still their account of the effects of enclosure *is* one-sided; and that they are virtually the only historians referred to by Clare's best biographers, J. W. and Anne Tibble,[2] by the most perceptive critic of his writing, J. Middleton Murry,[3] and by his most professional editors, Eric Robinson and Geoffrey Summerfield,[4] has placed Clare's poetry in a context in which it is difficult for the reader of his work not to make several large but quite unjustified assumptions about its content and about the social and economic situation in which Clare found himself after the enclosure.

The brand of writing about the countryside which in this century has particularly found favour with literary critics – the brand produced by George Sturt,[5] for example, and apparently vindicated by the historical enquiry of the Hammonds – has established a stock notion of the nature and effects of enclosure, and critics who hold on to this notion repeat it automatically when they meet the word 'enclosure' in Clare's writing. It is assumed that when he writes about enclosure, about rural poverty, he is making the same sorts of connections between them as the Hammonds made; and when he writes about rural poverty without mentioning enclosure, it is nevertheless assumed that what he is describing is the effects of enclosure on Helpston. Thus, according to Clare's most recent editors, Clare's 'long satiric poem, *The Parish*',[6] is take up with 'the evil social effects of enclosure', and the 'inflationary agriculture of the Napoleonic Wars'[7] – although, if we look at the poem more closely, we will see that enclosure is referred to in it only once, and that more than three-quarters of the way through a poem of over 2,000 lines. James Reeves, in the introduction to his excellent selection of Clare's poems,[8] tells us that Clare's father was a 'cottage farmer' (which he was not), and goes on to say that 'during the period of the Industrial Revolution and the Napoleonic Wars this class was obliged to struggle hopelessly against rising prices and the stranglehold of enclosure, by which means the open fields and commons where smallholders grazed their animals were legally stolen in the interest of the large landowners'.[9] J. Middleton Murry, who does however admit that the directly socio-economic effects of enclosure are not what concern Clare most about it, asserts that in Clare's picture of enclosure 'we see the pathetic figures of the villagers who suffer as their little margin of subsistence is torn from them'.[10] Kenneth MacLean is clearly disappointed at the *lack* of a connection in Clare's work between the enclosure and the poverty of the agricultural labourer, and writes that Clare 'has chosen to mourn the plumage [the changed landscape] and forget the dying bird'[11] – that the bird *was* dying is taken for granted.

The Tibbles are unwisely more precise in their account of the effects of the enclosure, and claim to be interpolating them not only from Clare's writing but from primary historical sources. 'What the Clares lost', they say in the first version of their biography, 'was the chance of near and permanent work for father and son';[12] 'many farm labourers lost their strips of land';[13] 'farmers bought up land from those who could not afford to keep it';[14] 'while the labourer lost his independence and his cow, at the same time he frequently lost his work as well'.[15] In the revised version, the Tibbles become still more explicit:

The Helpston Enclosure Award of 1820,[16] typical of its kind, betrays to any modern disinterested scrutiny that the Commissioners saw themselves paid; the larger landowners and the Church did not suffer. Those who could make a claim were not without redress even if it was not always to their liking as to commonable rights. But those who could not afford, or did not know how, to write a claim, naturally stood to lose any recompense that was going. The practical, energetic, and shrewd, as ever, did not fare badly; the thriftless, the illiterate, or the peace-loving rustic who detested the haggle of voices, often received less than his clearest dues.[17]

The Tibbles go as far as to suggest that some villagers with claims to land or rights of common legitimate even in the reduced terms of the commissioners were unable to submit paper claims and thus lost everything, and that the 'peace-loving rustic' often received less than his clearest dues. How these suggestions can be made using the enclosure-award as evidence is hard to understand: it is, taken by itself, the last document to apply to, to substantiate such charges. It would be good to know, too, from what sources the Tibbles arrived at their determinations of the characters of those villagers who (allegedly) profited, and those who (allegedly again) lost by the Award. The work of the Tibbles, in presenting Clare to the twentieth century, has been of enormous value, but the spurious historical content of their biographies has considerably distorted our view of Clare's account of rural life in the early nineteenth century.

I do not want to suggest that the enclosure of open field by Act of Parliament did not have the crucial effect that the Hammonds argued that it had, of reducing the labourer whose customary right of common went unrecognised by the commissioners from the status of 'a labourer with land', to that of 'a labourer without land';[18] and certainly in this way enclosure could have disastrous effects on the social structure of the open-field village community. But it is by no means clear that in every case, or even in the majority of cases, the labourer in a parish newly enclosed was *poorer* than he had been before the enclosure. More recently the orthodox historical view of the Agricultural Revolution and the history of parliamentary enclosure has become more optimistic, as the work of Sir John Clapham has become more influential. J. D. Chambers and G. E. Mingay, for example, have argued that during the peak period of parliamentary enclosure, at the end of the eighteenth century, the number of small owner-occupiers of land increased rather than diminished, and that there is no evidence that parliamentary enclosure was generally followed by any de-population of the parish enclosed. They argue also that, if the standard of living of the agricultural labourer did fall between 1780 and about 1830, this was not a result of the local effects of enclosures, depriving the labourer of his commons and cutting back on the demand for labour, but of the large increase in the rural population.[19] This view is essentially that of *economic* historians: it does not take great account of the sort of effects enclosure might have had on the labourer but which cannot be measured statistically, and in this area even the Hammonds are more trustworthy. As far as it goes, however, the modern orthodox optimism has at least as much claim to be believed as the Hammonds' view of enclosure. What *is* unpleasant about it is, say, Mingay's single-minded concern to praise the spirit of expansion above everything else, so that the disappearance of the small landowner, for example, becomes for him a process of 'the weeding out' of 'the unsuitable and inefficient'[20] – too slow a process, clearly, for Mingay. As one critic has remarked, 'it is proper that such a hard-faced, unromantic capitalist enterprise as the Agricultural Revolution should have found in [Chambers and Mingay] its historians'.[21]

When I first began this research, faced with the sort of assump-tions that have been made by Clare's critics about the enclosure of Helpston, and which now provide the context in which his poems and his life are usually read, and with the challenge made to the Hammonds by more recent historians, it seemed necessary to undertake some historical research on my own account, to see if

192

anything could be established about the economic effect of the
enclosure of Helpston. In the second section of this appendix I have
summarised, as best I can, the available evidence about the effects
of the enclosure, in economic terms, on the small owner-occupiers,
on the large landowners, the large tenant-farmers, and the agricultural labourers of Helpston, in the period from 1807, two years
before the Act of Enclosure was passed, until 1825, by which time
the enclosure was no longer one of Clare's major preoccupations,
or not, at least, one of the main themes of his poetry. The evidence
is not conclusive, but several things emerge fairly clearly: by 1825,
the number of peasant-farmers – small owner-occupiers – was the
same as it had been two years before the Act was passed: there is no
evidence that some of them 'lost their strips of land'. The large
landowners seem unlikely to have seen, by 1825, any substantial
return on the capital they had invested in the enclosure; nor were
they able to buy up more land 'from those who could not afford
to keep it'. The large tenant-farmers may have been unable to
pay the rents on their new farms – rents had doubled and in some
cases trebled after the enclosure, and thereafter had to be reduced
as the tenants reported heavy losses. The agricultural labourers, on
the other hand, may well have been marginally better off in 1825
than they were in 1807; though still not anything but very badly
off. Before the enclosure there had been a drift of population away
from Helpston; after the enclosure there was in fact a drift into it,
work seems to have been fairly generally available in the parish,
and the expenditure on poor-relief was considerably lower than
that in the neighbouring parishes, and lower than the average for
the county. I have found no evidence, by the way, that any owners
of land or common rights were unable to submit claims to the
commissioners.

I should perhaps apologise for taking the reader, as I do in the
second section of this appendix, so laboriously through the land-
tax assessments and census returns, only to arrive at a set of conclusions which do not differ at all significantly from the picture
offered by the Clapham school of the effects of enclosure generally.
It might have been quicker, certainly, to have taken the modern
historical view on trust, at least as far as the economic effects of
enclosure are concerned. But we should remember here what E. P.
Thompson has pointed out about the work of Clapham, because it
is true also of his followers: that their overall conclusions are often

arrived at by taking an average of statistical information which cannot properly be averaged.[22] Thus, when E. Davies, in his article 'The small landowner...in the light of the land tax assessments',[23] says that, 'though there were marked diminutions of [small landowners] in Leicester and Nottingham, the increases in Lincoln and Derby more than preserved the balance',[24] we must remember that it can have been less comforting to the small landowners of Leicester than clearly it is to Davies to know that their neighbours in Derbyshire were doing so well. The need in the case of Helpston – as in every case – is for a severely local study: simply to replace the pessimistic general view of the Hammonds with the current orthodox view, and without offering supporting local evidence, would be, obviously enough, to make unjustified assumptions about the effects of the enclosure in the same sort of way as, for example, the Tibbles have made them.

It might, on the other hand, seem possible to have disposed of the traditional assumptions without doing any local historical research at all, but simply by referring to Clare's poems, and seeing whether or not he does say what he is alleged to say about the effects of the enclosure: this method would be the properly literary one, but not, I think, the right one in this case. In fact, in the poems in which he writes of the enclosure or of the poverty of the agricultural labourer, Clare does not go out of his way to connect the one with the other: he is concerned with the new *social* situation of the poor after the enclosure, and not with how much better or worse off they have become. But the assumptions we want to question are not, after all, based on a reading of Clare's poems so much as on a reaction to the word 'enclosure'; and since the argument would have to be based, not on what Clare does but on what he does not say about the effects of the enclosure, it would be unlikely to persuade the followers of the Hammonds to forget their old associations with the word. And we should, anyway, be more wary than Clare's critics have been in the past of extracting particular historical information out of his poems. *The Parish* is the poem by Clare which is most directly about the social situation of Helpston, and which, he tells us, he 'forebore to publish'. This poem, he says,

was begun and finished under the pressure of heavy distress, with embittered feelings under a state of anxiety and oppression almost amounting to slavery, when the prosperity of one class was founded on the adversity and distress of

the other. The haughty demand by the master to his labourer was 'Work for
the little I choose to allow you and go the parish for the rest – or starve'. To
decline working under such 'advantages' was next to offending a magistrate,
and no opportunity was lost in marking the insult by some unqualified oppression.[25]

This note perhaps invites us to expect a rather different poem from
the one Clare wrote, and *The Parish* has been read, both by the
Tibbles and by Clare's most recent editors, as an account of the
effects of the enclosure on the social structure of Helpston, and on
the standard of living of the rich and poor. 'The fullest picture of
the new order which had succeeded the old [after the enclosure] is
to be found in Clare's long satirical poem *The Parish*,'[26] say the
Tibbles, and Robinson's and Summerfield's description of the
poem as 'taken up with the evil social effects of enclosure', among
other things, I have already quoted. But in the first place *The
Parish* is not much concerned with enclosure at all – which is
referred to only once, as we have seen, towards the end of the
poem – and in the second place it does not give us anything like a
full or reliable picture of social change in Helpston. What Clare
does say, for example, about enclosure in the poem is ambiguous.
In these lines –

> ... mockd improvments plans enclosed the moor
> And farmers built a workhouse for the poor
>
> (*The Parish*, lines 1,642–3)[27]

– he clearly associates the workhouse and the effects of the enclosure, as he does also in these lines from another poem, 'The
Fallen Elm':[28]

> Thus came enclosure – ruin was its guide,
> But freedom's clapping hands enjoyed the sight
> Though comfort's cottage soon was thrust aside
> And workhouse prisons raised upon the site.
>
> (lines 55–8)

It looks as though what we have here is a clear connection between
the enclosure and poverty, and that Clare has given us a piece of
historical information to cement the connection: after the enclosure
a new workhouse was built in Helpston. But later in the poem,
Clare describes the workhouse as a 'mouldering shed',[29] which
doesn't suggest a new building; and anyway a few lines earlier he
has referred to the 'parish huts'[30] in Helpston before the enclosure,

so that if a new workhouse was built, it was not necessarily to meet a new need, but to meet an old one more efficiently.

The point is that if we try to read *The Parish* as a direct account of the social and economic changes that enclosure, or the high prices of the wartime years, or whatever, brought to Helpston, we will certainly misread it. The confusion about the workhouse is only important to us if we insist on reading the poem as the Tibbles, or Robinson and Summerfield, seem to want to read it – as a useful source of historical and thus of biographical information. The couplet I quoted from the poem comes in the middle of a passage which, in its content and the movement of the verse, is reminiscent of *The Deserted Village*, and Clare has just been re-calling the old vicar of the parish in much the same terms as Goldsmith had described the 'village preacher' of Auburn;[31] in the passage which describes the workhouse as a 'mouldering shed', on the other hand, Clare is writing in the vein of George Crabbe. Neither passage borrows directly, from Goldsmith or from Crabbe, but that Clare is writing to a degree in the manner first of one, and then of the other, is immediately clear, and is sufficient explanation of the difference in content between the two passages. The work-house is being seen through the conventions of eighteenth-century rural poetry: and accordingly it is new when it is to be seen as a symbol of the recent degradation of the old-style labourer; it is old when it is to be seen as particularly squalid. The interesting ques-tion is how Clare manages to marry the vision of Goldsmith and that of Crabbe in the same poem; and he does so, of course, partly because he had found a way to make Crabbe's deliberately anti-conventional imagery acceptably conventional. Clare was offended by Crabbe's brutal image of the rural poor,[32] and clearly valued the ideal image that Goldsmith or, for example, Morland offered him, as a reassurance of the dignity of the labourer. He seems to have thought, however, that his own imagery in the style of Crabbe could keep Crabbe's persuasive force, but lose his tendency to degrade (as Clare felt) what he described, if he surrounded it with verse using the tone and imagery of Goldsmith; but he succeeded more often in burying the realistic images so that they became a part of the convention Crabbe had written to attack. The most angrily satirical of Clare's paragraphs in *The Parish* must often seem diluted to us because, against his conventionally over-reaching image of the 'modern farmer', he sets an ideal image of the rustic which, in his more private statements, he often seems to attack himself.

The real subject of *The Parish* is the increasing gap between the large farmers – converting themselves into a middle class, into professional men, literate, preferring plate to pewter – and the agricultural labourers. Clare does not suggest why the gap was widening, but he does, in the note to the poem quoted earlier, claim to be writing about events of the very recent past. 'Each character is a true one and as little coloured as possible', he wrote also,[33] and after acquainting myself as far as I have with the history of Helpston after the enclosure, I continually find myself making tentative identifications, of the farmers the poem satirises, with actual farmers in Helpston when Clare was writing. But when we look at what Clare does say about the changed times in the parish, the sense of 'real history',[34] as Raymond Williams calls it in the context of rural poetry, does not really come through, at least not in the details Clare gives us about how the changes are occurring. Here are the lines in the poem which first announce its subject:

> That good old fame that farmers earned of yore
> That made as equals not as slaves the poor
> That good old fame did in two sparks expire
> A shooting coxcomb and a hunting Squire
> And their old mansions that was dignified
> With things far better than the pomp of pride
> At whose oak table that was plainly spread
> Each guest was welcomd and the poor was fed
> Were* master son and serving men and clown
> Without distinction daily sat them down
> Were the bright rows of pewter by the wall
> Served all the pomp of kitchen or of hall
> These all have vanished like a dream of good
> And the slim things that rises were they stood
> Are built by those whose clownish taste aspires
> To hate their farms and ape the country squires

> (*The Parish*, lines 105–20)

*Where.

These couplets are good but not especially so; the wit in the third and fourth lines for example depends too heavily for its success on our willingness to think 'flame' when we read 'fame'; certainly next to, say, *The Village*[35] on one side, and Clare's own poems about the landscape of Helpston on the other, this passage is not very remarkable. The problem is again one of the way Clare uses literary conventions – here particularly those established by Goldsmith – and I think we are justified in feeling that the conventions of the nostalgic pastoral, and the conventional language of early nineteenth-century nostalgic radicalism, are coexisting here rather too harmoniously. The word 'slaves', for example, is too submerged in the pattern of the first couplet to allow us to pick it out and consider whether to take the sense of it literally – *slaves*, or just underpaid? And if the 'poor' in the eighth line are the same people as those who were once the 'equals' of the farmers, it is fair to ask why these equals agree to think of themselves as being 'fed' by the farmers, when they themselves were no doubt the producers of what they were eating – the point is the same as that made by Raymond Williams, in his article 'Literature and rural society',[36] about Jonson's use of the conventional myth of the Golden Age in his poem 'To Penshurst'. In fact, the first thing to point out about these lines is not a correspondence between the charges made against the new farmers and the way the farmers in Helpston did actually behave after the enclosure, but that the charges made are conventional ones in the tradition of rural literature of protest, and find their counterparts in Cobbett[37] and in Ebenezer Elliott[38] while Clare was writing, and in say Massinger (as Williams has pointed out)[39] and Jonson earlier. However much of a present evil the modern farmer was for Clare, when he came to write about him he wrote according to the conventions of a long tradition; and when he looked back to the old village community, he used the other side of the same conventions.

The Parish, then, may certainly speak to us about the 'new order which had succeeded the old', but it does not speak about it very directly. In some of Clare's other poems – in 'The Fallen Elm', for example – he does have a good deal to say about the social situation of the labourer after the enclosure, but even when he does thus try to locate his protest more precisely, he still describes, for example, the changed relations between employer and employed in terms of political if not also of literary conventions. In 1821, Cobbett wrote: 'When *master* and *man* were the terms, every one was in his place, and all were free. Now, in fact, it is an affair of masters and slaves...'[40] – and we find the same terms used by Elliott, by other radical writers of the period, and often at the end of the eighteenth century, for example by Crabbe.

Clare uses the same terms in another of his poems more specifically
to do with enclosure, 'The Mores',[41] and indeed in that poem seems
to suggest (as far as I can understand the second couplet here) that
the proud nostalgia for a lost independence – master and *man* – is
all the property of the labourer now: and that in fact that nostalgia
is the myth by which the labourer is able to hang on to some of his
lost dignity – as Clare himself preferred Goldsmith's image of the
rural poor to Crabbe's:

> Inclosure came and trampled on the grave
> Of labours rights and left the poor a slave
> And memorys pride ere want to wealth did bow
> Is both the shadow and the substance now

(lines 19–22)

At this point I should say that, although the article by Williams
that I have been referring to seems to me the most illuminating
discussion of English rural literature that I have read, I am not
sure that I follow the argument of the article, which seems finally
to put *more* weight than necessary on the importance of the sort
of convention we have been examining. Williams is quite right to
point out that the same complaints and the same nostalgia appear
in rural literature for at least 400 years if not from the time of
William Langland; but he does not try to explain *why* the same
complaints re-emerge from time to time *when* they do, and we are
invited to think that, well, they simply *do* re-emerge, as part of the
long history of resistance to the long development of rural capitalism. Outside the tradition of conventional protest, Williams places
the poetry of Crabbe, in which 'real history' enters, because
Crabbe sees the situation of the agricultural labourer in terms not
of a dignified past and a degraded present, but of the relations
between employer and employed as they are inevitably and always,
independent of the sort of recent or local historical changes which
Cobbett or Clare often claim to be writing about.

It must be so that, whether or not the conventions that Cobbett
and Clare use are adequate to describe the situations they are
being used to describe, their need to use those conventions is itself
a part of the history of resistance, and Williams should perhaps
make clearer than he does that the Golden Age, located by Cobbett
and Clare not in pre-history but a generation or two before they
were writing, the myth they set against the world of the modern
farmer, is used by them to interpret – the passage quoted from

'The Mores' suggests that for Clare the process was a quite conscious one – the particular local changes they seem to see. That the myth is a conventional one is important to remember, but it does not mean that when the myth is invoked it is not therefore a response to such particular, local changes: even Goldsmith, as we now know, had a particular enclosure in mind,[42] And in Cobbett's and Clare's case, the myth may not have been used quite as conventionally, or quite as unhistorically, as Williams suggests: it is after all possible that the gap between employer and employed had increased during the Napoleonic Wars, a time of high profits and high poor-rates, more rapidly than before; and of course if Clare *felt* the gulf between employer and employed had become wider during his lifetime, that feeling must itself have become a factor in his social relations with the employers, and in that way done something to justify itself.

I think, too, that Williams should distinguish more carefully than he does between the conventional and the *merely* conventional. The word Clare uses so tamely – so conventionally – in *The Parish*, to describe the agricultural labourer in his new condition – 'slaves' – he uses elsewhere so deliberately that the word insists on being taken at its face value – *slaves*, and not simply underpaid. This is very clear, for example, in a poem I quoted from earlier, 'The Fallen Elm', in which Clare plays on the sense of the word 'freedom' as it was used by those who advocated enclosure, the theorists of economic individualism and Whig liberty, and the freedom arguably enjoyed by the labourer before the enclosure; and the passion behind the poem, and the old-fashioned Tory but still quite sophisticated handling of the concept of freedom, points behind the otherwise conventional language to a more than conventional response:

> I see a picture which thy fate displays
> And learn a lesson from thy destiny;
> Self-interest saw thee stand in freedom's ways –
> So thy old shadow must a tyrant be.
> Thou'st heard the knave, abusing those in power,
> Bawl freedom loud and then oppress the free;
> Thou'st sheltered hypocrites in many a shower,
> That when in power would never shelter thee...
> – Such was thy ruin, music-making elm;
> The right of freedom was to injure thine:
> As thou wert served, so would they overwhelm

In freedom's name the little that is mine.

And there are knaves that bawl for better laws
And cant of tyranny in stronger power,
Who glut their vile unsatiated maws
And freedom's birthright from the weak devour.

(lines 35–42, 65–72)

It is true, of course, as Williams says, that the process of creating
an efficient capitalist agriculture – which involved also the creation
of a rural middle class, and a rural proletariat – was an immensely
long and slow process; and the protests that have come down to
us over 400 years are written in the same sort of terms because
they are, fundamentally, protests about the same sort of thing.
But – and this seems to me important – the process did advance
at different speeds in different areas; and these lines from 'The
Fallen Elm' are a reminder that an enclosure, for example, coming
as one stage in the process as it took shape in any particular parish,
could represent a totally disorienting advance in the creation of
the rural proletariat in the particular parish being enclosed.[43]

I said earlier that if we read *The Parish* as a fairly direct account
of particular social changes taking place in Helpston as Clare was
writing, we will be in danger of reading the poem too literally, and
fail to notice the conventions behind the writing; but it is true, too,
that if we want to regard Clare's complaints primarily in the light
of a long tradition of rural complaint, we are equally in danger of
forgetting that he was writing out of a situation in which, clearly
enough, he did feel the poor to have been unusually oppressed. I
don't think I have ended up by saying nothing at all: it *is* true that
The Parish will not tell us at all directly how social change in
Helpston manifested itself, or what the actual condition of rich
and poor was once, and is now: when Clare does offer to be specific,
the only language he can find is the language of tradition. At the
same time, however, it is also true that this language as Clare uses
it is not always merely conventional, and is capable of saying
very forcefully, for example, that the gap between two classes is
getting wider, without being able to offer us any historical explanation of why this is happening.

There is no way of deciding whether the enclosure of the commons
in Helpston did destroy the independence of the agricultural
labourers there. Clare had access to literary and political conventions which said that it did so, and so, for him, it clearly did: the

measurable effects of the enclosure were far less important to Clare than those which the tradition of rural protest told him to expect and recognise, and that helps to explain why he is so much less interested in the effects of the enclosure on the standard of living of the labourer than in its effect on his social position. The point is, however, that it was the enclosure – and not a generalised, long-drawn-out creation of a capitalist agriculture – which was the occasion for the tradition and its conventions to re-emerge in Clare's poetry, and which provided the context in which the conventional language of the tradition of rural protest was sometimes capable of being charged with the force of Clare's own response to a particular moment of history, which nevertheless it could not adequately describe.

II

The complaint most often repeated by Clare's biographers and editors, and so perhaps the one to discuss first, is that by the enclosure smallholders in Helpston were dispossessed – presumably because they could not afford to pay the high costs of fencing their allotments, or their share of the cost of the execution of the Act[44] – and that large farms were thus created by engrossing the small. We can check the substance of this complaint most readily by reference to the land-tax assessments for Helpston[45] – the tax was levied on land, on houses with land, and in some cases on houses without land, and the assessment forms usually tell us the names of all the proprietors and occupiers of land in a parish, together with the assessment on the land. I should say first, however, that recently G. E. Mingay has pointed out a large number of difficulties which arise in using the land-tax assessments to chart the decline of the small landowner, and it is important to mention some of them here.[46] In the first place, after 1798 the very smallest proprietors – those whose land was of an annual value of less than 20s. a year – were exempted from the tax and cease to appear on the forms of assessment; thus if there were any owners of land or houses reckoned to be of an annual value lower than that amount in Helpston – which as I shall soon suggest is unlikely – the assessments will not tell us anything about their fortunes during the enclosure. Secondly, there is no standard correlation between the amount of the tax levied on a piece of land and its acreage: Mingay quotes an example from Nottinghamshire, of an estate in which, of two assessments of 4s., one represented a piece of land less than two-thirds of an acre in size, and the other a piece of land more than four acres.[47] Thus it is not possible to discover from the assessments exactly who was richer than whom, or precisely where each piece of property is to be placed in the scale of property values. Another difficulty raised by Mingay is that after an enclosure it was usual for the assessments – which normally went unaltered for long periods of time – to be changed, according to the new distribution of land within the parish, and the improvements made after the enclosure; and this change has the effect of making it impossible to tell whether, for example, a farmer paying £1 before the enclosure and 30s. after has in fact increased the size of his holding, has bought a holding assessed at 10s. from another farmer, or has simply had his new allotment assessed differently from his pre-enclosure holding. Fortunately, no such large-scale reassessment took place in Helpston: the total assessment for the parish increased by half a crown, from £98. 14s. 1d. to £98. 16s. 7d., in 1816, and had risen only another two shillings by 1825; and this means that the assessments give us a very clear picture (within their limitations) of the degree to which property changed hands immediately before and after the enclosure.

But perhaps the most important difficulty Mingay points out is that the attempt to distinguish between large and small owners of land according to the tax they paid in one particular parish is unlikely to be very accurate, since in practice of course a man might own land in more parishes than one, and though according to the assessments for one parish he might appear to be a very small smallholder indeed, he might well be discovered by reference to another set of returns to own half the neighbouring parish. This last problem seems a good deal more awkward to me than it does to Mingay, who immediately after raising it concludes his article by saying that, nevertheless, 'the relative paucity or plenty of small owners is one fact that the returns can indubitably establish';[48] which I would have thought he had satisfactorily proved they could not do. One wonders if the problems Mingay raises would seem more substantial to him if, in the end, the evidence of the assessments did not endorse so fully (as we shall see) the optimistic view he takes of the decline of the small landowner between 1780 and 1832. But in any case a correlation of the assessments for Helpston with those of the neighbouring parishes show that, although a number of landlords, and a number of tenant-farmers, were much more substantial men than they appear to be from the Helpston assessments alone, the small owner-occupiers – the class that particularly concerns us here, of peasant-farmers – were not much in the habit of renting land outside the parish: of sixteen owner-occupiers who paid an annual tax of less than £1 in 1816, only three of them rented land outside, and none of them enough to raise their total tax assessment above £2.

As far as can be established from the land-tax assessments for Helpston, the enclosure had had no catastrophic effect on small owner-occupiers by 1825, the date by which the enclosure has ceased to be one of Clare's major preoccupations. Table A shows the number of owner-occupiers at various dates between 1807, two years before the enclosure, and 1825. The date 1807 was chosen partly to counteract the effect of any hasty selling of land immediately before the Act was passed, and partly because the assessment forms for the years 1808, 1809 – the year of the Act – and 1810 are too damp to be opened. The table shows no decrease at all in the number of the owner-occupiers of the smallest class; those paying less than 5s. tax maintained the same numbers throughout the eighteen years; those paying between 5s. and 10s. increase their numbers considerably; the one who pays between 10s. and £1 has disappeared from the table by 1825, but in fact this is explained by his ceasing to occupy his land, which he still owns and lets to another farmer. The total of all owner-occupiers paying less than £5 tax per annum – and those who paid more than that were certainly fairly substantial farmers, employing labour – remains quite stable throughout the period. Nor do the assessments show land changing hands a great deal among the small owner-occupiers, which might have been an indication of a volatile traffic in small pieces of land which the table conceals.

Certainly the evidence does not suggest that 'many labourers lost their strips of land', or that 'farmers bought up land from those who could not afford to keep it' (see above, p. 197). Of the four largest landowners, three acquired no new land at all between 1807 and 1825, and the fourth acquired only one additional holding, taxed at £2. 15s. 6d., and purchased before the Act was passed,

TABLE A. *Numbers of small owner-occupiers of land in Helpston at various dates from 1807 to 1825*

	Land tax paid				Total under £1	Total under £2	Total under £5
	Under 5s.	5s. – 10s.	10s. – £1	£1 – £2			
1807	9	2	1	3	12	15	16
1812	9	3	1	2	13	15	17
1816	10	3	3	2	16	18	18
1820	9	4	1	2	14	16	16
1825	9	6	0	1	15	16	17

apparently from a pair of absentee landowners. Whatever evil effects the enclosure did bring to Helpston, the small owner-occupier seems to have weathered them. According to Clare, one smallholder, John Billings, had mortgaged his land at the time of the enclosure, and by 1821 or so was finding it difficult to meet the payments on this mortgage;[49] still, he did survive with his property intact until 1825. It is, of course, impossible to know to what extent there were hidden mortgages among the smallholders of the parish; but if Billings's case was typical, one would have expected the number of owner-occupiers to have decreased to some extent at least between 1807 and 1825.

We must remember, of course, Mingay's warning that the land-tax assessments after 1798 may not include the name of every small landowner, if some of them owned property of less than £1 annual value. But the evidence of the enclosure claims,[50] submitted to the commissioners shortly after the Act was passed, suggests that it is unlikely that there were any such very small landowners in Helpston. The claims contain, or should contain, the claim of every landowner in Helpston on the land in the parish, and even those with only a cottage and garden seemed to have submitted a statement of their property to the commissioners. All the names that appear on the land-tax assessments appear in the claims, and vice versa, and so it seems simplest to conclude that the assessments contain the names of all the proprietors of land in Helpston, and also that all the proprietors were able to submit claims – unless the Tibbles, as they seem to want to suggest, found evidence to the contrary.

The conclusion, then, to be drawn from the assessments, that the enclosure of Helpston did not diminish the number of small owner-occupiers, is in line with that of E. Davies, in his article 'The small landowner, 1780–1832, in the light of the land-tax assessments', and with that of Mingay, in his *English Landed Society in the Eighteenth Century*.[51] Both Davies and Mingay argue that the numbers of owner-occupiers in England probably increased from 1780 to 1832, even in areas affected by enclosure; the important periods for the decline of the small landowner, they suggest, are the first half of the eighteenth century, when agricultural prices remained critically low for decades, and the middle of the nineteenth century, when farm machinery began to make large units of land very much more economical to farm than smallholdings. The point is, that by the time of the enclosure of Helpston the number of small owner-occupiers all over England had already considerably declined, and that, although the enclosure of Helpston made the largest farms there much more compact, it did not thereby make them very much more efficient and cheap to run during the period we are concerned with. It is possible that the Tibbles imagined the distribution of land among the villagers under the open-field system was a good deal more egalitarian in Helpston than in fact it was, or indeed than it normally was even in open-field parishes by 1800. By then, large estates were nearly as common in unenclosed as in enclosed areas, and in 1807 30 proprietors out of 41 paid less than one-fifth of the total land-tax assessment for Helpston, and thus perhaps owned less than one-fifth of the total acreage; while 6 out of 41 paid more than two-thirds of the total assessment. The important period of engrossing and consolidation had clearly come before the enclosure.

Another substantial body of evidence about the economic effects of the enclosure – and particularly about its effects on the small landowner – is offered by the enclosure-award;[52] and it is important to point out that the evidence the Award offers, while it does not upset the evidence of the assessments, does suggest that the small landowner was not quite in such an advantageous position as the assessments suggest. It is clear from the Award that if it is true that it needs three or four acres to keep a cow, then three or four of the smallest landowners with rights of common were not sufficiently recompensed by the commissioners for the loss of their common rights, and if they had kept a cow or geese before the enclosure were probably unable to do so after it. As we have seen, this did not mean that, by 1825 at least, they had had to give up their allotments; and they may have done as well by growing potatoes and garden vegetables on their two or three acres as they had done earlier by their right of common – but to keep a cow was worth more within the village community than the value of its milk. Furthermore, the Award, unlike many other enclosure-awards, makes no provision for the establishment of allotments for the poor – those who, without rights of common before the enclosure, or without the proof to convince the commissioners of their rights, were certainly without any land after it. The most obvious devices, however, for dispossessing the small landowners – making their plots excessively long and thin, and thus expensive to fence; siting the new holdings at a great distance from the village – these do not seem to have been practised at Helpston.

If the owner-occupiers do not seem to have lost everything if anything by the enclosure, the large landowners, by 1825, do not seem to have gained much by it. According to F. M. L. Thompson, the largest landowner, Earl Fitzwilliam, obtained a return of 30 per cent on an outlay of £10,364 on the enclosure of Maxey and Helpston;[53] but how this profit was calculated, and, more important, when, he does not say. Certainly it was usually possible after an enclosure to double rents, or even to treble or quadruple them: the per-acre rent of the land owned by Christ's College, Cambridge, in Helpston was more than doubled from 1808 to 1816, from 12s. to about 29s.[54] But by 1816 the long period of low prices for agricultural commodities had begun; the price of corn fell from 126s. 6d. in 1812 to 75s. in 1814, and remained low until 1825; and for several years from 1816 rents were continually being lowered all over the country. According to the Board of Agriculture Report on *The Agricultural State of the Kingdom* (1816),[55] rents were abated in Northamptonshire by anything between 10 and 60 per cent for that year, and were even then being paid out of capital. The per-acre rent of 29s. 6d. on Christ's College farm in Helpston had fallen to about 25s. 6d. by 1819, and by 1833 it had fallen again to about 21s.[56] According to Chambers and Mingay, 'in the early 1820s, some landlords, but not all, were obliged to make considerable permanent reductions in rentals';[57] in

Northamptonshire in 1820 rents were reduced by an average of 20 per cent.[58] The financial crisis of the period after 1815, and the notorious failure of the country banks, made it extremely difficult for farmers to obtain credit, and as a new enclosure demanded an immediate and fairly extensive outlay of capital to be properly successful, the enclosure of Helpston, first conceived at a time of high wartime prices, but paid for at a time of poor credit facilities and low prices, must have made large inroads into the capital of the Helpston landowners. The only detailed evidence I have come across, of the state of the finances of tenant-farmers and landlords in the Helpston area during the financial crisis, is the account book of one of Fitzwilliam's tenants in Etton, the next parish to Helpston, who claimed to have made a loss of £456 in 1820–1, on a farm of 332 acres.[59]

The situation of the landless labourers – the class that Clare was born into – is more difficult to determine. There is no doubt, of course, that they were appallingly badly off – very few agricultural labourers in the Midlands can have stayed off poor-relief in the years after 1815; the questions are whether they were worse off after the enclosure than before it, and whether, if they were worse off, this can be said to have been a result of the enclosure. There is very little evidence by which these questions can be answered: the crucial document – the records kept by the overseer for the poor of how much relief he gave out, to how many people, and according to what system – is missing: we have to make do with the simple totals of expenditure on poor-relief each year.[60] Apart from the information about poor-relief, we have the evidence offered by the census returns[61] and the parish registers,[62] and the knowledge that the Award, as I have already noted, made no allotments for the poor. Finally, Clare's own two autobiographical sketches – *Sketches in the Life of John Clare* and *Autobiography* – give us some idea of the availability of work in Helpston after the enclosure.

The population of Helpston in 1801 was 301; in the ten years until the census of 1811 – the ten years, roughly speaking, before the enclosure, or before it could have had much effect – it fell to 276. In the ten years until 1821 the population increased to 372, or by 35 per cent on the figure for 1811; and between 1821 and 1831 it increased again, by 30 per cent to 485. The rural population of the whole county – Northamptonshire – rose by 62 per cent between 1801 and 1811; by 14 per cent between 1811 and 1821; and by 7 per cent between 1821 and 1831 (see notes to Table B, p. 211); so that, in the period after the enclosure, the population of Helpston increased at about twice the rate of increase of the rural population of the whole county. If we calculate from the parish registers the surplus of births over deaths for each year between 1801 and 1831 (using the figures for 1831 as a base), we can make a guess at how the population fell and rose when it did – whether a decrease is to be accounted for by a surplus of deaths over births, or by depopulation; whether an increase is the result of a surplus of births over deaths, or by a drift of population into the village, or by both. And the evidence suggests that, though the number of deaths for the first decade was unusually high – 74 as against 75 births – there was also some depopulation of the parish in the years before the enclosure; whereas there is a fairly clear indication that after the enclosure – not necessarily, of course, as a direct result of it – the natural increase in population was supplemented by a movement of population into the parish. Such a movement seems to have occurred in about the same proportions between 1811 and 1821 and between 1821 and 1831; and that it did occur is suggested also by the fact that the percentage increase in the population of Helpston during those years is so much higher than the average for the rural population of Northamptonshire as a whole. The traditional notion of the effects of enclosure on the population of open-field villages is reversed in the case of Helpston: instead of being followed by a drift of population away, the enclosure seems to have been followed by a drift into the village.

That a newly-enclosed parish was able to keep its indigenous population in the years after the Napoleonic Wars is not in itself at all surprising, and not necessarily a cause for optimism. Northamptonshire was a Speenhamland county – one in which, in most parishes, a labourer's wages were made up out of the poor-rates, but only if he had a legal settlement in the parish he worked in; under such a system it was difficult for the poor to move around in search of employment. However, the fact that Helpston was able to attract population from *outside* does suggest that work was fairly available in the parish after the enclosure. The only other possible explanation is that there were 'closed' parishes nearby – parishes in which the landlords combined to pull down cottages as they fell vacant, to reduce the population and thus the amount of the poor-rates; and that Helpston was an 'open' parish – in which the poor were able to obtain settlements without too much difficulty. If this were the case, we would expect it to be reflected in the figures for the poor-rates for Helpston and the surrounding parishes.

Table B shows the population of Helpston, and of four of the other five parishes involved in the same enclosure (Peakirk, the most distant from Helpston of the six parishes enclosed, has been omitted), in 1816, 1821, and 1827, with the total expenditure on poor-relief for those years, and with the average expenditure on poor-relief per head of the population of each parish. The population-figures for 1816 were estimated by averaging the population of each parish in 1811 and 1821, as shown in the census returns; the population-figures for 1827 were calculated from the returns for 1821 and 1831. The first date, 1816, was chosen because by then the work of enclosure, in Helpston at least, seems to have been largely completed; 1827 was chosen because by about that time, as I have said, Clare had ceased to write much about the enclosure. Between these two dates the table shows the corresponding figures for 1821: we have accurate population-figures for that year, and in that year the post-war agricultural depression was probably at its worst.

It will be seen at once that the average expenditure on poor-relief per head was a good deal lower in Helpston, until 1821 at least, and somewhat lower in 1827, than it was in any of the other parishes except Northborough, where the population remained stable from 1811 to 1831, and where the expenditure on relief was so unusually low that we may suspect it of having been a 'closed' parish. It is unlikely, however, that because the population of Helpston increased so quickly, it was itself an 'open' parish: its expenditure was a good deal lower not only than the expenditure of the remaining three parishes, but a good deal lower, too, than the average for the county, in 1821 at least; and all this while the population increased at twice the county rate, and generally speaking at a greater rate than that of the other parishes being enclosed. It does seem that for some reason or another – there was no new industry, for example, established in the parish – it was marginally easier to find work in Helpston than in the country round, after the enclosure, and certainly much easier than, say, in Etton, where the decline in population between 1821 and 1831

APPENDIX

Table B. *Expenditure per head on poor-relief in Helpston and four other parishes in 1816, 1821, and 1827*

	1816	1821	1827
Helpston			
Population	324	372	442
Total expenditure on relief	£129*	£166. 15s.	£286. 11s.
Average per head of population	7s. 11d.	9s.	13s.
Population increase: 1811–21, 35%; 1821–31, 30·5%.			
Etton			
Population	111	125	121
Total expenditure on relief	£112. 6s.	£169. 15s.	£200. 5s.
Average per head of population	£1. 0s. 3d.	£1. 7s.	£1. 13s. 1d.
Population increase: 1811–21, 29%; decrease: 1821–31, 5%.			
Maxey			
Population	340	374	402
Total expenditure on relief	£162. 10s.	£185. 1s.	£317. 2s.
Average per head of population	9s. 9d.	10s. 1d.	15s. 9d.
Population increase: 1811–21, 22%; 1821–31, 13%.			
Glinton			
Population	342	372	397
Total expenditure on relief	£209. 10s.	£265. 4s.	£291. 1s.
Average per head of population	12s. 5d.	14s. 4d.	14s. 8d.
Population increase: 1811–21, 19%; 1821–31, 11%.			
Northborough			
Population	227	232	229
Total expenditure on relief	£32. 17s.	£66. 14s.	£127. 10s.
Average per head of population	2s. 9d.	6s. 3d.	11s. 2d.
Population increase: 1811–21, 4·5%; decrease: 1821–31, 2%.			

The increase in the population of the rural districts of Northamptonshire, 1811–21, was 14·7%; 1821–31, 7·07%. The average per head expenditure on poor-relief in Northamptonshire in 1821 was 19s. 2d. (See J. D. Marshall, *The Old Poor Law 1795–1834* (London, 1968), pp. 40–1.)

*No return submitted for this year. This figure appears in the official statistics (see below, p. 233, note 60), and is the average of the returns for the years immediately before 1816.

211

was accompanied by a considerable increase in the expenditure on relief. The figures, however, may not be conclusive: it is impossible to discover what system of relief the overseers employed in Helpston and in the neighbouring parishes – not all overseers, for example, gave child-allowances, and the varieties of the Speenhamland system were numerous – and so it is impossible to be sure that the comparison of *per capita* expenditure on relief is of any significance at all.

The assumption that employment was more available in Helpston than in the nearby parishes – and perhaps more available than in the county as a whole – is supported, however, by the impression that Clare gives, in his *Autobiography* and in his *Sketches in the Life of John Clare*, that work was usually available to him in Helpston after the enclosure; and this *is* the impression he gives, in spite of the odd construction put on what he says on the subject by the Tibbles. Clare was sixteen in 1809 when the Act of Enclosure was passed, and that year he went to work in the gardens at Burghley,[63] between Helpston and Stamford. By the beginning of 1810 he was back in Helpston, and says of this period: 'I now followd gardening for a while in the Farmers Gardens about the village & workd in the fields when I had no other employment to go to'[64] – which suggests that field-labour – which Clare did not like, and which he was not strong enough to perform – was usually available as a stand-by, when other employment was short. The Tibbles, however, gloss this sentence of Clare's by saying that 'at either gardening or field-work, there was hardly sufficient employ to keep two, let alone four'[65] (Clare's father was becoming increasingly disabled, and could earn only 5s. a week mending the roads; so that Clare was required to help support his parents and sister as well as himself.) In 1811 Clare joined the Northamptonshire Militia; not apparently because 'there was little present hope of permanent employ for the rough gangs of labourers',[66] but because, he says, 'we had a cross-graind sort of choice left us which was to be forced to be drawn & go for nothing or take on as volunteers for a bounty of two guineas I accepted the latter'.[67] Clare served a month in the militia in 1812, and again in 1813; meanwhile the work of enclosing was beginning: 'mixing among a motley set of labourers that always follow the news of such employments I usd to work at setting down fencing & planting quick-lines'[68] – the work of enclosing seems to have kept Clare, and probably his partners from outside the parish, in employment until 1817, and this while (according to the Tibbles) 'employment became more and more difficult'.[69] In fact, there was probably more work involved in enclosing Helpston than in the enclosure of any of the other five parishes except Northborough. About one-sixth only of the acreage of Helpston was old-enclosed land, and the whole of the remainder had to be divided and fenced; in addition to the remaking of roads and the execution of very considerable drainage projects. Etton, by comparison, was as much as two-thirds already enclosed by 1809; Maxey one-third; and Glinton a quarter enclosed. It may not be a coincidence that the amount of expenditure on poor-relief in each parish in 1816 is in very roughly the same proportion, between one parish and another, as was the amount of land in each parish still waiting in 1809 to be enclosed.

In the spring of 1817, say the Tibbles, 'acute lack of employment'[70] sent Clare to look for work in Casterton, in Rutland. In this they receive some support from Clare's text. In the *Sketches* he tells us that he left Helpston in the company of an out-town labourer, who 'got me from home with the promise of many advantages from working with him';[71] but in the *Autobiography* he explains that it was because he could not help his parents sufficiently to keep them from the parish that he left Helpston.[72] The suggestion may be that he could find no work in Helpston; but just as likely an explanation is that his wages even as a full-time labourer were not now sufficient to support his family – his father was by now completely disabled – and that he left to take up lime-burning in Casterton because that job offered higher wages. Certainly his wages there were (comparatively) high: he was able to *save* 50s. in six weeks;[73] and when he left Rutland, after working for a while as a gardener, it was because his new employer wanted to reduce his wages by 2s. to 7s., at a time when 7s. per week was probably as much as an agricultural labourer could hope to earn in the fields.[74] We know, finally, from the records kept by the Fitzwilliam estate,[75] that Clare worked regularly in the fields in Helpston from May 1820 on through the following winter; although the Tibbles suggest that he worked only in the harvest months of 1821.[76] Certainly Clare seems to have been able to find fairly regular employment in Helpston at least from the time of the enclosure through to 1821.

I am not trying to argue here that the agricultural labourer in

Helpston was anything but appallingly badly off: even if he was able to stay off parish relief, he was unlikely at this period to be earning much more than 7s. per week, at a time when a 4 lb loaf could cost 1s. But, as far as the evidence of the totals for expenditure on poor-relief can be assumed to be reliable, and as far as Clare's experience was typical, it does seem that there were probably fewer families on the edge of starvation in Helpston than there were in the neighbouring parishes, or indeed than there were in any number of parishes in the Midlands which had *not* recently undergone enclosure. It is certainly unlikely that the enclosure of Helpston cut back on the demand for labour there. It has often been assumed in the past that immediately after an enclosure the techniques of farming were rapidly improved and made more economical, farm machinery was introduced, and one way and another the demand for labour greatly reduced. In fact, machinery was not at all generally used on farms until the last half of the nineteenth century; and where enclosure was followed by the introduction of more sophisticated systems of rotation, the demand for labour was likely to be increased rather than diminished: turnips are the most labour-consuming of crops. It seems that in Helpston, in point of fact, new crops and new rotations were not immediately introduced after the enclosure: the pattern of rotation which had been the rule in about 1800[77] was still being used in 1820 by at least one large farmer in Etton: but still the amount of labour these crops demanded was unlikely to have been less in 1820 than earlier. Furthermore, in Helpston an area of heath (of indeterminate size) was brought into cultivation after the enclosure; and, clearly enough, as the cultivated area of a parish increased, so did the demand for labour.

It is now very generally argued, of course, that the biggest single factor in the increasing poverty of the agricultural labourer in the early nineteenth century was the rise in the rural population, which in Helpston, as we have seen, was considerable; and it is likely that in many parishes, even where the demand for labour was increasing, it was not increasing as fast as the population. This does not seem to have been the case with Helpston, however, which as we have seen received a considerable influx of population from outside between 1811 and 1831, and seems to have been able to support this influx after a fashion. It seems unlikely, then, that in Helpston the enclosure 'reduced the chance of near and permanent work'. The evidence, indeed, points the other way, and suggests that had it not been for the enclosure, the demand for labour would have diminished considerably, and the problem of poverty would have been that much more severe. The enclosure, as we have seen, though conceived at a time of great agricultural prosperity, was carried into execution during an agricultural depression. But the actual work of enclosing – the making of new roads, the planting of hedges – could not be put off until better days; and in this way the enclosure must to some extent have protected the labourer of Helpston from the effects of the depression, in that it enabled him to tap his employer's capital for his wages, instead of waiting for them to come out of his employer's falling profits.

Finally, however, there is quite simply not enough evidence to allow us to say for sure that, in its economic effects at least, the enclosure of Helpston was not as disastrous to the agricultural labourer as the traditional view of enclosure would suggest. This is so not only because the figures for poor-relief are so difficult to interpret, but also because, although we are probably safe in assuming that employment was more available in Helpston after the enclosure than usually it was elsewhere, we still cannot measure the effect of the loss suffered by the agricultural labourers of traditional ways of supplementing their wages. The right to collect fuel, the right to gleanings,[78] must have been extinguished at the enclosure, and it is possible too that there were villagers who before the enclosure had kept cows, but at the enclosure had been unable to persuade the commissioners of their right to do so; we must remember too that the poor received no allotments of land in the Award. Such evidence as there is suggests that in strictly economic terms the poor were better off after enclosure; but the unmeasurable factors – the loss of customary rights of common, and the others – could conceivably have been important enough to counteract this apparent improvement.

Notes

1. *The Idea of Landscape in the eighteenth century*

1 The word appears in line 70 of 'L'Allegro', namely:
Streit mine eye hath caught new pleasures
Whilst the Lantskip round it measures.
2 *Elements of Criticism, the sixth edition with the author's last corrections and additions* (Edinburgh, 1785), vol. I, p. 332.
3 For example by Elizabeth Wheeler Manwaring, *Italian Landscape in Eighteenth-Century England* (New York, 1925; London, 1965); see also Christopher Hussey, *The Picturesque* (London, 1927); Edward Malins, *English Landscaping and Literature 1660–1840* (London, 1966).
4 *Boswelliana*, ed. Rogers (London, 1876), p. 239.
5 Joseph Addison, *Remarks on Several Parts of Italy* (London, 1705).
6 See Deborah Howard, 'Some eighteenth-century English followers of Claude', *Burlington Magazine*, December 1969, p. 727.
7 *Ibid.*, p. 728.
8 For example, Jean Baptiste Claude Chatelain, Richard Earlom, George Knapton, Arthur Pond, Francis Vivares, John Wood, William Woollett.
9 See, for example, Susanna Harvey Keir, *The History of Miss Greville* (London, 1787) (referred to above, p. 43); Charlotte Smith, *Emmeline, The Orphan of the Castle* (London, 1788), and other novels; Mrs Radcliffe, *The Italian* (London, 1797), and other novels; and of course Jane Austen, *Sense and Sensibility* (London, 1811) in particular. For a fuller list, see Manwaring, *Italian Landscape*, ch. 8.
10 From a fragment published in C. P. Barbier, *William Gilpin* (Oxford, 1963), p. 177.
11 *Essays on the Picturesque* (London and Hereford, 1794–8), vol. I, p. 9 n.
12 See Manwaring, *Italian Landscape*, pp. 38–9.
13 Howard, 'Some eighteenth-century English followers of Claude', p. 727.
14 John Hayes, *Richard Wilson* (London, 1966), p. 3.
15 Introduction to *The Art of Claude Lorrain* (catalogue of an exhibition at the Hayward Gallery, London, 1969), p. 7.
16 *Ibid.*
17 'Enchanted Castles', *Sunday Times Magazine*, 9 November 1969, p. 31.
18 From a note on an earlier draft of this chapter, quoted by permission of Mr Clark.
19 *Landscape into Art* (London, 1949), p. 63.
20 Quoted by Hayes, *Richard Wilson*, pp. 5–6.

21   *Aristotle's Treatise on Poetry* (1789), Dissertation I, 'On poetry considered as an imitative art', reprinted in *Eighteenth-Century Critical Essays*, ed. Elledge (New York, 1961), vol. II, p. 1001.

22   This was the first (London) publication of 'Autumn', and of the concluding 'Hymn'. A version of 'Winter' had appeared in 1726; 'Summer' first appeared in 1727, and 'Spring' in the following year.

23   In *Miscellaneous Poems and Translations*, ed. Richard Savage (London, 1726). The final version of the poem appeared in *Miscellaneous Poems*, ed. Lewis (London, 1726).

24   'Some eighteenth-century English followers of Claude', p. 726.

25   This revised version was prepared largely in 1743, with the help of George, Lord Lyttelton.

26   London, 1964.

27   *Essays on the Picturesque*, vol. I, p. 121.

28   'On poetry considered as an imitative art', p. 1001.

29   London, 1757.

30   Quoted by Manwaring, *Italian Landscape*, p. 101.

31   All quotations from *The Seasons* taken from the Oxford Standard Authors edition, ed. Robertson (Oxford, 1908).

32   *Art of Discrimination*, p. 219.

33   *Ibid.*, p. 217.

34   *Ibid.*, p. 218.

35   See lines 71–80.

36   Manwaring, *Italian Landscape*, p. 104; quoted by Cohen, *Art of Discrimination*, p. 236.

37   Cohen, *ibid.*

38   *Aspects of Eighteenth-Century Nature Poetry* (Oxford, 1935).

39   *Ibid.*, p. 17; quoted by Cohen, *Art of Discrimination*, p. 238.

40   Cohen, *ibid.*

41   *The Guardian*, no. 57 (22 May 1753); quoted by D. Jones, 'Common trends in landscape painting and nature poetry in the eighteenth century', unpublished M.A. dissertation, Aberystwyth, 1954, ch. 2.

42   Cohen, *Art of Discrimination*, p. 247.

43   *Critical Essays* (London, 1785), pp. 320–1.

44   This suggestion I have adapted from Deane, *Aspects of Eighteenth-Century Nature Poetry*, p. 102; but see next note.

45   Deane (*ibid.*, pp. 105–6) offers an interesting if rather confused account of this passage. He takes the singular nouns at the start of the passage, as did Miller, to stand for 'an innumerable quantity' of objects, and compares the 'crowded profusion of the foreground' with the 'indistinctness of the horizon', just 'a feature here and there' represented by plurals. He also explains the lack of epithets in the line 'And snatched', etc., by saying that 'the rapidity of the glance' – and not, apparently, the profusion of objects – 'leaves no room' for them. It is hard, however, to see why the foreground should be more crowded with objects than the distance (unless we accept the sort of naturalistic explanation that appeals to Cohen, and say that at Hagley it actually *is* more crowded); and it is hard, too, to see why, if it does appear so, the profusion of

objects should be represented by singular nouns, while 'a feature here and there' on the horizon is represented by plurals. Deane is anxious to put the maxim, *ut pictura poesis*, 'on a new footing', somewhere between Miss Manwaring's over-eager identification of the techniques of landscape-painting with those of poetry, and Lessing's dictum that 'to enumerate one by one to the reader, in order to afford him an idea of the whole, several parts of things, which, if they are to produce a whole I must necessarily in nature take in at one glance, is an encroachment by the poet on the sphere of the painter' (quoted by Deane, p. 67). I think (as does Cohen, *Art of Discrimination*, p. 240) that Deane fails to make good his claim to have discovered 'methods of composition...purely poetic in substance and execution'. This analysis, at any rate, rests on some strange assumptions; and even Deane's remark about Thomson's epithets, which are seen as distinguishing not the areas of a composition but, simply, the different objects in the view, does not serve to establish the passage (by this account) as a composition, as more than a mere enumeration.

46 Richard Jago, *Edge-Hill; or, the Rural Prospect, Delineated and Moraliz'd* (London, 1767).
47 *Ibid.*, line 37.
48 Hussey, *The Picturesque*, p. 107.
49 Book v, line 741.
50 See for example *Modern Painters*, vol. III (London, 1856), ch. IX, p. 16.
51 In an article on Young, published in *Mercure de France*, 5 germinal an X (26 March 1802), Chateaubriand cited the line from Thomson, 'Pleas'd have I wanderd thro your rough domain', which he translated thus: 'Combien de fois n'ai-je point erré avec ravissement dans les régions des tempêtes.'
52 See lines 57–70.
53 John Cunningham, *Poems Chiefly Pastoral* (Newcastle, 1766), p. 52.
54 Lines 518–19.
55 The translation quoted is by Dorothy Halton, and appeared in *Northamptonshire Past and Present*, I (1951), 35–41. The original Latin version has, I believe, never been printed, and is kept in the parish chest at Great Addington.
56 *Ibid.*, p. 36.
57 *Ibid.*
58 *Village Scenes, The Progress of Agriculture, and Other Poems* (London, 1804), line 272.
59 P. 37. Later, however (p. 40), Hussey appears to contradict himself, and says, 'Dyer had very little sense of form, or of composition and unity.'
60 *Observations on the River Wye...Relative Chiefly to Picturesque Beauty* (London, 1782), section VIII.
61 *Critical Essays*, p. 112.
62 *The Ruins of Rome: a Poem* (London, 1740).
63 Coleridge to Sotheby, 10 September 1802, *Letters*, ed. Griggs (Oxford, 1956–9), vol. II, p. 864.
64 In *Studies in Romanticism*, IV (1964–5), 20.

65 Gilpin's phrase: see for example his letter to Mason, 12 February 1784, published in Barbier, *William Gilpin*, p. 72.
66 *The Tempest*, act II, scene i, line 163.
67 'The Garden', line 40, in *Poems and Letters of Andrew Marvell*, ed. Margoliouth (Oxford, 1952), vol. I, pp. 48–50.
68 First published in *Tonson's Miscellanies* (London, 1709).
69 Lyttelton, *The Progress of Love. In four eclogues* (London, 1732).
70 *The Natural History and Antiquities of Selborne* (London, 1789).
71 First published in the edition of J. W. White (= J. White ?) (London, 1813).
72 *Amwell, A Descriptive Poem* (London, 1776).
73 Ann Arbor, 1949.
74 *History of Miss Greville*, vol. I, p. 111.
75 Ellis Waterhouse, *Gainsborough* (London, 1958), p. 16.
76 See, for example, Derek Clifford, *A History of Garden Design* (London, 1962), p. 128; Hussey, *The Picturesque*, p. 61.
77 *Anecdotes of Painting in England...to which is added The History of the Modern Taste in Gardening* (London, 1771), vol. IV, pp. 137–8.
78 William Chambers, *Designs of Chinese Buildings...* (London, 1757).
79 Thomas Gray, *Correspondence*, eds. Toynbee and Whibley (Oxford, 1935), vol. II, p. 814.
80 'Picturesque Farming', a series of four articles in *Annals of Agriculture* (ed. Arthur Young (46 vols., London, 1784–1815), VI–IX. This quotation is from VI, 177.
81 Walpole, *Anecdotes of Painting*, vol. IV, p. 138.
82 *Ibid.*
83 See Manwaring, *Italian Landscape*, p. 131.
84 Joseph Spence, *Observations, Anecdotes, and Characters...*, ed. Osborn (Oxford, 1966), p. 252.
85 National Gallery, London.
86 Quoted by Manwaring, *Italian Landscape*, p. 140; and by Hussey, *The Picturesque*, p. 138.
87 *Mrs Montagu, 'Queen of the Blues'*, ed. Blunt (London, 1924), vol. II, p. 123; quoted by Manwaring, *Italian Landscape*, p. 141; by Hussey, *The Picturesque*, p. 137.
88 *Memoirs of the Life and Correspondence of...Hannah More*, ed. W. Roberts (London, 1824), vol. II, p. 267; quoted by Clifford, *History of Garden Design*, p. 159.
89 By Hussey, for example, *The Picturesque*, p. 139.
90 Dorothy Stroud, *Capability Brown* (London, 1957), pp. 198–9.
91 *Ibid.*, p. 217.
92 'Epistle to Burlington', line 57.
93 Gilpin to Mason, 25 April 1772; Barbier, *William Gilpin*, p. 50.
94 *Observations on the Western Parts of England, Relative Chiefly to Picturesque Beauty* (London, 1798), p. 107.
95 'The immensity of nature is beyond human comprehension. She works on a vast scale; and, no doubt, harmoniously, if her schemes could be comprehended...' (*Observations on the River Wye...*, p. 16; quoted by Barbier, *William Gilpin*, p. 103).

96 Gilpin, *Remarks on Forest Scenery* (London, 1791), vol. II, p. 274.
97 For an account of this controversy, see Barbier, *William Gilpin*, ch. 6.
98 Gilpin to Mason, 12 February 1784; *ibid.*, p. 72.
99 This first tour originally came out in the *Poetical Magazine*; it was followed in 1820 by *The Second Tour of Dr Syntax in Search of Consolation*, and in 1821 by *The Third Tour of Dr Syntax in Search of a Wife*.
100 *The Letters of Thomas Gainsborough*, ed. Woodall (London, 1963), p. 91.
101 *Walks in a Forest*, 9th edition, with the author's final revisions (London, 1814).
102 *A Philosophical Enquiry into the Origin of our Ideas of the Sublime and the Beautiful* (London, 1757).
103 For the best discussions of Gilpin's theory, see Barbier, *William Gilpin*, ch. 8; W. J. Hipple, *The Beautiful, the Sublime, and the Picturesque in Eighteenth-Century British Aesthetic Theory* (Carbondale, 1957); Samuel H. Monk, *The Sublime* (New York (M.L.A.), 1935), esp. chs. 7, 8; and J. R. Watson, *Picturesque Landscape and English Romantic Poetry* (London, 1970), ch. 1.
104 In a postscript to the second edition of his poem *The Landscape* (London, 1795); and in *An Analytical Inquiry into the Principles of Taste* (London, 1805).
105 William Hazlitt, 'On the Picturesque and the Ideal', *Table Talk*, Essay XXXII, in *Works*, ed. Howe (London, 1930–4), vol. VIII, p. 317.
106 *Ibid.*, pp. 320, 321.
107 *The Deserted Village* (London, 1770), line 282.
108 *Anecdotes of Painting*, vol. IV, p. 115.
109 The five Uvedale Price quotations are from *Essays on the Picturesque*, vol. II, pp. 428, 400, 403, 403 and 400 respectively.
110 *Columella; or, The Distressed Anchoret* (London, 1779).
111 Quoted by Manwaring, *Italian Landscape*, p. 209; by Hussey, *The Picturesque*, p. 131.
112 'Epistle to Burlington', line 59.
113 *Planting and Rural Ornament* (London, 1796), vol. I, p. 270.
114 *Ibid.*, p. 271.
115 William Mason, *The English Garden* (London, 1772), book I, lines 74–7; quoted by Marshall, *Planting and Rural Ornament*, vol. I, p. 271.
116 Quoted by Barbier, *William Gilpin*, p. 49.
117 Gilpin to Mitford, 3 July 1770; Barbier, *William Gilpin*, p. 50.
118. *The Prelude* (1805 version), book XI, line 163.

2. *The landscape of agricultural improvement*

1 The *General Views* were reports on the agricultural practice of the various counties in England, Wales and Scotland. The first series appeared mainly in 1794, and each report was printed with wide margins, so that local farmers could write their comments on it and return it to the Board of Agriculture. The idea was that the substance of the comments thus

elicited could be included in the series of revised and enlarged *General Views*, which appeared between 1805 and 1817.

2 'The old Board of Agriculture', *English Historical Review*, vol. LXXIV (1959), 50–1.

3 *Ibid.*, p. 43.

4 See G. E. Mingay, *English Landed Society in the Eighteenth Century* (London, 1963), especially ch. 7, from which much of the material in this paragraph and the next is derived.

5 Quoted by Mingay, *ibid.*, p. 166.

6 *Ibid.*

7 *Ibid.*

8 *Annals of Agriculture*, ed. Arthur Young, 46 vols., (London, 1784–1815).

9 *A General View of the Agriculture of the County of Lincoln* (London, 1794).

10 *A Review of the Reports to the Board of Agriculture on the Several Counties of England*, vol. III (*Eastern Department*) (York, 1811), p. 11.

11 'Arthur Young and the English landed interest, 1784–1813', Ph.D. thesis, London University, 1959.

12 *Ibid.*, ch. 1. I am indebted to this work for the material in this paragraph and the following.

13 See W. H. R. Curtler, *The Enclosure and Re-distribution of Our Land* (Oxford, 1920), ch. 16.

14 Mitchison, 'The old Board of Agriculture', p. 49.

15 *Ibid.*

16 See G. E. Mingay, 'The eighteenth-century land steward', *Land, Labour, and Population in the Industrial Revolution*, eds. E. L. Jones and Mingay (London, 1967).

17 William Custance, for example, one of the commissioners acting in the enclosure of Clare's village, Helpston, operated from an office in Great Russell Street, London, but acted as a surveyor and valuer chiefly in Cambridgeshire and other East Midland counties of England (Evidence of Custance, 4 April 1821, in the *Minutes of Evidence* to the Select Committee of the House of Commons on Agricultural Distress, 1821).

18 Many professional men found enough employment as enclosure-commissioners to allow them to come to regard themselves as professionals in that field. See for example Stone, *A General View of...the County of Lincoln*, p. 84; this remark quoted of a Mr Elmhirst: 'I acted as a commissioner a great many years and was at one time concerned in nine different enclosures.'

19 The enclosure of Helpston and five other parishes in the old Soke of Peterborough was not completed until eleven years after the Enclosure Act was passed (1809–20); the enclosure of Charnwood Forest, in Leicestershire, took twenty-one years to complete (1808–29).

20 M. W. Beresford, in his essay 'The commissioners of enclosure' (*Economic History Review*, XVI (1946), reprinted in *Essays in Agrarian History*, ed. Minchinton (Newton Abbot, 1968), vol. II, pp. 89–102), quotes the examples of George Maxwell, who between 1773–1800 had been over 100 times a commissioner, and who on several occasions worked with Edward Hare, a commissioner in the Helpston enclosure; of William Custance

(see above, note 17), also involved in the enclosure of Helpston, who attended 443 meetings of commissioners in 22 years; and of Rev. William Homer, who is 'known to have been a commissioner in all the Midland Counties'. 'This is the author', writes Beresford, 'called "Horner" by E. C. K. Gonner, *Common Land and Inclosure*, 1912'; and on the subject of incorrect references, it was not of course 'Elmhirst', as Beresford says it was, who wrote *A General View of...the County of Lincoln* (see above, note 9); the author was Thomas Stone, who on page 84 of that work quotes a remark made by a Mr Elmhirst (see above, note 18), which is reproduced in Curtler (see above, note 13), ch. 14. The impression given by Beresford's article is that a large number of the enclosure-commissioners working at least in the Midland counties around 1800 were professionals who derived a considerable proportion of their income from supervising enclosures.

21 *A General View of the Agriculture of the County of Oxford* (London, 1809), p. 269.
22 *A Review*, vol. IV (*Midland Department*) (York, 1815), p. 467.
23 In *The Poems of John Langhorne* (London, 1822).
24 See line 42: 'And Peace and Plenty tell, a STUART reigns'.
25 See, for example, *Windsor Forest*, lines 26–42, and 'Epistle to Burlington', lines 173–6, 185–90.
26 See, for example, Joseph Warton, *An Essay on the Genius and Writings of Pope*, 4th edition, corrected (London, 1782), esp. section II.
27 James Donaldson, *A General View of the Agriculture of the County of Northampton* (London, 1794), pp. 5–6.
28 In 1712.
29 *Rural Rides* (London, 1830). Quotations in this chapter are taken from the Everyman Edition, ed. Briggs (London, 1957). This quotation is from vol. I of that edition, p. 80.
30 *Ibid.*
31 *A Tour in Ireland: with General Observations on the Present State of that Kingdom: made in the years 1776, 1777, and 1778, and brought down to the end of 1779* (London, 1780), p. 185.
32 Tyley, 'Inclosure of Open Fields in Northamptonshire', p. 36.
33 *Tours in France During the Years 1787, 1788, and 1789*, ed. Maxwell (Cambridge, 1929), p. 15.
34 *A General View of the Agriculture of the County of Bedford* (London, 1808).
35 *Village Scenes*, lines 271–4.
36 *A General View of the Agriculture of the County of Northampton* (London, 1809).
37 *Ibid.*, p. 8.
38 *A General View of The Agriculture of the County of Worcestershire* (London, 1794).
39 *Ibid.*, p. 7.
40 *Ibid.*, pp. 7–8.
41 In *Annals of Agriculture*, VI–IX.
42 *Ibid.*, IX, 8.
43 Young, *A Tour in Ireland*, p. 53.

44 *Rural Rides*, vol. I, p. 152.
45 *Planting and Rural Ornament*, vol. I, *passim*.
46 *The Picturesque*, p. 140.
47 *The Landscape, A Didactic Poem, in three books* (London, 1794), lines 180–1.
48 *Observations on Several Parts of England*, vol. I, pp. 35–6.
49 Barbier, *William Gilpin*, p. 112.
50 *Ibid.*
51 *Essay on the Nature and Principles of Taste*, 6th edition (Edinburgh, 1825), vol. I, p. 121.
52 *A General View of the Agriculture of the County of Somerset* (London, 1794), p. 83.
53 *A General View of the Agriculture of the County of Leicester* (London, 1809), p. 171.
54 Clark, *A General View of the Agriculture of the County of Hereford* (London, 1794).
55 *An Answer to Mr Shaw's Inquiry into the Authenticity of the Poems Ascribed to Ossian* (London, 1781).
56 *A General View of...Hereford*, p. 8.
57 *Ibid.*
58 *Ibid.*
59 *Ibid.*, p. 9.
60 *A Review*, vol. II (*Western Department*) (York, 1808), p. 262.
61 *A General View...of Hereford*, p. 9.
62 *Ibid.*, pp. 10–11.
63 *Ibid.*, pp. 9–10.
64 Young, *A Six Months Tour through the North of England* (London, 1770).
65 *A Tour in Ireland*, p. 91.
66 *Ibid.*, p. 92.
67 Vol. II, p. 200.
68 *Ibid.*
69 *Ibid.*, pp. 200–1.
70 *Annals*, VI, 176.
71 *Ibid.*, p. 182.
72 *Ibid.*, VII, 25–6.
73 *Ibid.*, VI, 177 ff.
74 *Ibid.*, VII, 28.
75 See G. A. Cranfield, *The Provincial Newspaper* (Oxford, 1960), esp. ch. 9; and R. M. Wiles, *Freshest Advices* (Ohio, 1965), esp. ch. 4.
76 Quoted by Wiles, *ibid.*, pp. 169–70.
77 Quoted by Cranfield, *Provincial Newspaper*, p. 197.
78 See Ernle (R. E. Prothero), *English Farming Past and Present* (London, 1912), p. 284.
79 These two Acts reinforced the previous legislation on the liability of parishes to repair roads running through them, transferred the task of appointing road-surveyors to the Justices of the Peace, authorised the levy of a rate (maximum 6*d.* in the £) for the provision of road materials, and made a number of other small changes in highway legislation.

John Scott of Amwell, incidentally, the poet whose work we encountered several times in the first chapter, was also the author of *Digests of the General Highway and Turnpike Laws* (London, 1778).

80　See Ernle, *English Farming*, p. 284; and John Copeland, *Roads and their Traffic, 1750–1850* (Newton Abbot, 1968), pp. 109–14.

81　*A General View of the Agriculture of the County of Buckingham* (London, 1810).

82　*Ibid.*, pp. 339–40.

83　*A General View of...Leicester*, p. 311.

84　Tyley 'Inclosure of Open Fields in Northamptonshire', p. 36.

85　*Northern Tour*, vol. IV, p. 573.

86　*A General View of...Oxford*, p. 324.

87　Rev. A. Young, *A General View of the Agriculture of the County of Sussex* (London, 1808), p. 417. This is the son of the famous Arthur Young.

88　*Ibid.*, p. 419.

89　*Ibid.*

90　*Tours in France*, p. 79.

91　*Ibid.*, p. 49.

92　*A General View of...Buckingham*, pp. 342–3.

93　*A Review*, vol. IV (*Midland Department*), p. 194.

94　*Ibid.*, vol. I (*Northern Department*) (York, 1808), pp. 5–9.

95　See, for example, Marshall's remarks (*Midland Department*, p. 60) on Thomas Brown's *General View of the Agriculture of the County of Derby* (London, 1794).

96　Marshall, *A Review*, vol. I (*Northern Department*), p. xl.

97　*Ibid.*

98　*Ibid.*, p. xxxix.

99　*Tours in France*, p. 50.

100　*Ibid.*, p. 51.

101　*Ibid.*, p. 79.

102　Abraham and William Driver, *A General View of the Agriculture of the County of Hampshire* (London, 1794), p. 10.

103　For a fuller description of the process of enclosure, see W. E. Tate, *The English Village Community and the Enclosure Movements* (London, 1967), chs. 9, 10.

3. The sense of place in the poetry of John Clare

1　*Sketches in the Life of John Clare, Written by Himself*, ed. Edmund Blunden (London, 1931), p. 45.

2　Quoted in J. W. and Anne Tibble, *John Clare, His Life and Poetry* (London, 1956), p. 1.

3　A 'land', however, is not to be confused with a 'strip'; a land is a long ridge of ploughed land; a strip of arable land in an open field may consist of one land, or of several lying together and all owned by the same man. For a full discussion of 'lands', see C. S. and C. S. Orwin, *The Open Fields* (Oxford, 1938).

4 A ridge was made by ploughing a land first down its centre-length, and turning then in an ever-widening arc at the ends of the lands, and throwing the mould of ploughed soil always toward the centre of the land (see Orwins, *ibid.*). An understanding of this 'ridge-and-furrow' technique of ploughing will elucidate a number of passages of English pastoral poetry, as, for example, these lines from Thomson and from Bloomfield:

> Meanwhile incumbent o'er the shining share
> The master leans, removes th'obstructing clay,
> *Winds* the whole work, and sidelong lays the glebe.
>
> (*The Seasons*, 'Spring', lines 41–3; my italics)

> But, unassisted through each toilsome day,
> With smiling brow the Plowman cleaves his way,
> Draws his fresh parallels, and *wid'ning still*,
> Treads slow the heavy dale, or climbs the hill.
>
> (*The Farmer's Boy*, 'Spring', lines 71–4; my italics)

5 Quoted in Marc Bloch, *French Rural History*, trans. Sondheimer (London, 1966), p. 38. There are remarkable descriptions of the open-field landscape of Alsace–Lorraine in a number of works by Barrès, notably *Amori et Dolori Sacrum* (Paris, 1903), *La Colline Inspirée* (Paris, 1913), and *Colette Baudoche* (Paris, 1919).

6 *La Formation du paysage rural français* (Tours, 1934), p. 3.

7 Map 1 is based on a number of sources: in particular on Eyre's map of Northamptonshire (1779); on a 'map of the Lordship of Marham with other lands adjoining thereto in Glinton, Etton cum Woodcroft, and Helpston …belonging chiefly to the…Earl Fitzwilliam, 1772', by Edward Hare, later one of the commissioners for the enclosure of Helpston (Northamptonshire Record Office, Map 1072); and on aerial photographs taken by Dr J. K. St Joseph of Selwyn College, Cambridge. Furlong names and other local place-names of pre-enclosure Helpston can be supplied from Clare's own writings, particularly the *Journal, 1824–5*, published in *The Prose of John Clare*, eds. J. W. and Anne Tibble (London, 1951) (henceforth referred to as *Prose*); from Northamptonshire Record Office (henceforth referred to as N.R.O.), Fitzwilliam (Milton) Collection, Misc. vol. 89 – a terrier of Earl Fitzwilliam's lands in Helpston, completed at approximately the same time as Hare's map referred to above; and from the terrier and valuation of the glebe-land in Helpston, made in 1797 and kept at Christ's College, Cambridge. To some slight extent the map is conjectural only: the land-drainage effected at the enclosure has made it difficult for the precise course of the streams at the north of the parish to be determined, and for the same reason the area of meadow to the east of the parish, referred to for example in Fitzwilliam (Milton) Misc. vol. 89, and known as 'Rotten Moor' and 'Dead Moor', cannot precisely be located.

8 According to Hare's map, referred to above, the entire area of the heath was fenced by the Fitzwilliams: Hare represents these fences, however, by dotted lines, and these might indicate open-field closes, open to be grazed

by the cattle of the parish when the rest of the field was so open. Eyre's map, which I have followed in mine, shows the whole area south of the road from Ufford to Peterborough as Helpston Heath, apparently unfenced. This seems the most likely – it is clear from numerous passages in Clare's writing that there was an area of unfenced heath in Helpston before the enclosure.

9   Dotted lines on Eyre's map; not marked on Hare's.

10 *La Formation du paysage rural*, p. 40.

11 Namely Hare's map, see above, note 7.

12 Tyley, 'Inclosure of Open Fields in Northamptonshire.'

13 Lizerand, *Le Régime rural de l'ancienne France* (Paris, 1942), p. 108.

14 *Ibid.* I should apologise, perhaps, for making such frequent use of French historians to describe a system of farming which was as native to England as it was to France. The landscape of open field was, however, in France, a good deal purer, because a good deal more stagnant, than it was in England – as Lizerand's remark about the eye there being unobstructed by trees suggests. It is either for this reason, or because all structures are so much easier to grasp *as* structures in France, that French historians are so much more helpful, in the accounts they give of the open-field landscape, than are historians in England; who have excelled in noting rather the exceptions to the rule than the rule itself, as perhaps also English farmers in the seventeenth and eighteenth centuries were more concerned to adapt the system to the demands of an expanding agriculture than to preserve it in its original, feudal form. In any case, that the system did survive in a much purer form in France than in England does not mean that the passages I have cited, from Dion and Lizerand, cannot properly be applied to the open-field landscape, and the open-field system, as they existed in England.

15 *Appropriation and Inclosure of Commonable Lands* (London, 1801), p. 6. Pages 1–12 of this work contain a remarkably good and sympathetic description of 'the origin of commonable and intermixed lands'.

16 *French Rural History*, p. 38.

17 Public Record Office HO 67/19; the returns for the diocese of Peterborough (which includes Helpston) are to be looked for in the bundle marked 'Pembroke'.

18 These are to be found in the MS volume kept at the house of Mr Daniel Crowson, Parish Clerk of Helpston, to whom I am most grateful for having brought them to my attention and for having, in some cases, transcribed them for me.

19 Fitzwilliam (Milton) Misc. vol. 89 (see above, note 7); see letter attached to that volume by Henry Cole, agent to Earl Fitzwilliam, addressed to the commissioners. The enclosure-claims for Helpston are kept at the N.R.O., Delapre Abbey, Northampton.

20 According to the enclosure-award, which is kept at Huntingdon and Peterborough County Record Office, the area of Helpston before the enclosure was 1,448 acres, of which 302 acres were already enclosed, leaving 1,146 acres of mostly arable land, with some meadow-land and common. According to the acreage returns (see above, note 17), some

780 acres of the parish were sown in 1801 with roughly equal areas of wheat, barley, and beans, although it would appear that some oats were sown, probably in the barley-field, and there were also some turnips. Even if we assume that all the old enclosures were permanent pastures (and woodland), we still have 366 acres of the parish to account for – an area which seems very much too large to have been taken up with meadow-land and commons. It seems possible, therefore, that there was a fourth field of some 200+ acres lying fallow, a small area of which had been taken in for turnips: the bye-laws of the Manor of Helpston, drawn up in 1799 (see above, note 18), provide for the sowing of clover, under certain conditions, on the 'fallows field', and the bye-laws of 1808 provide also for the sowing of turnips on the fallow.

It is perhaps more likely, however, that an improved three-field system – winter corn, spring corn, and beans – was being used, in spite of the evidence to the contrary, as this was certainly more usual in the area at the time. This was the system – with beans sown as a 'fallow crop' – that Gilbert Slater found at the end of the nineteenth century, on the open fields of Castor and Ailesworth, the neighbouring parish to Helpston to the south (see Slater, *The English Peasantry and the Enclosure of Common Fields* (London, 1907), pp. 14 ff).

21 There is frequent reference, for example, in Fitzwilliam (Milton) Misc. vol. 89, to 'Huskey Close', in Heath Field, which was not, however, marked as old-enclosure by the commissioners on the Award map (see below, note 28).

22 See *The Midland Peasant* (London, 1957), esp. ch. IV; see also Hoskins, *Provincial England* (London, 1963), ch. VIII, 'The Leicestershire Farmer in the seventeenth century'.

23 See above, note 20.

24 49 Geo. III, *Cap.* 152.

25 See above, note 20; see also above, p. 221, note 19.

26 *Cambridge Chronicle*, 16 May 1811, 8 February 1812, 6 August 1813.

27 See above, note 18.

28 Map 2 is based on the Award map, N.R.O. map 1087. For a discussion of the landscape of parliamentary enclosure, see W. G. Hoskins, *The Making of the English Landscape* (London, 1955), ch. VI.

29 49 Geo. III, *cap.* 152, para. XVI.

30 The course of Green Dyke can be traced on the aerial photographs referred to above, note 7.

31 From Alexander Watford's valuation (29 October 1819) of the glebe at Helpston, kept at Christ's College, Cambridge.

32 *The Poems of John Clare*, ed. J. W. Tibble (London, 1935; henceforth referred to as *Poems*), vol. I, p. 3. Where possible, all poems are quoted from the more accurate and unpunctuated texts of Eric Robinson and Geoffrey Summerfield: *The Later Poems of John Clare* (Manchester, 1964), *The Shepherd's Calendar* (London, 1964), *Selected Poems and Prose of John Clare* (London, 1967; henceforth referred to as *Selected Poems*). Poems not published in the three last-named editions are quoted in Tibble's text, except where noted.

33 *Poems Descriptive of Rural Life and Scenery* (London, 1820).
34 *Poems*, vol. I, p. 35.
35 *The Village Minstrel* (London, 1821).
36 *Poems*, vol. I, p. 70.
37 The 'Sonnet' first published in 1775; the 'Ode' in 1747.
38 'Helpstone Green', lines 3, 5.
39 *Poems*, vol. I, p. 238.
40 *Selected Poems*, p. xvii.
41 *Ibid.*, pp. xvi–xvii.
42 By 1820, when Clare's first volume was published, his reading in English poetry was by no means inconsiderable: he had read in Thomson, Cowper, Goldsmith, Bloomfield, Chatterton, Mallet, Cunningham, Parnell, Milton, Cowley, and Carew, and was familiar with Walton's *Compleat Angler* (see J. W. and Anne Tibble, *John Clare* (London, 1932), pp. 39, 42, 55–6, 88).

Clare claimed to have written 'Helpstone' in 1809, when he was sixteen; and when a certain 'H.B.' wrote to him from London (*The Letters of John Clare*, eds. J. W. and Anne Tibble (London, 1951, p. 335), and pointed out that this claim was contradicted by one of the couplets in the poem –

Dear, native spot! which length of time endears,
The sweet retreat of twenty lingering years

(lines 35–6)
– Clare wrote to his publisher Taylor complaining of this 'd——d impertinent coxcomb of your fine city' (*Letters*, p. 336), and suggesting that H.B. was probably no better than he should be, 'a shoemaker or perhaps a rhyming shoe black' (*Letters*, p. 61). Nevertheless, although the poem may have been begun by 1809, it was certainly still being added to in 1813, when Clare was twenty, and before when the effects of enclosure on the landscape of Helpston, which Clare describes in the poem, had not taken place. If in fact the poem was begun earlier, this may explain the confusion in the poem's theme: the poem began in one convention, but after the enclosure was moved into the other.
43 'The Lamentations of Round Oak Waters', line 1.
44 *Ibid.*, lines 55–6.
45 *Selected Poems*, p. 55.
46 *Poems*, vol. I, p. 420.
47 The *Journal, 1824–5*, published in *Prose*; this passage is on pages 109–10.
48 *Selected Poems*, p. 79.
49 London, 1771–4.
50 *Letters*, p. 48.
51 *John Clare, His Life and Poetry*, p. 84.
52 *Ibid.*
53 Published in *Prose*, pp. 163–94.
54 *Ibid.*, pp. 261–91.
55 *Ibid.*, pp. 11–100.
56 *Ibid.*, p. 13.
57 *Ibid.*

58   London, 1824.
59   *Ibid.*, vol. I, p. 85.
60   *Prose*, p. 13.
61   *Ibid.*, p. 20.
62   *Ibid.*, p. 28.
63   *Ibid.*
64   *Ibid.*, p. 23.
65   *Poems*, vol. I, p. 31, line 20.
66   *Letters*, p. 132.
67   *Selected Poems*, p. 69.
68   *Ibid.*, p. 139.
69   *The Letters of Charles Lamb*, Everyman Edition (London, 1909), vol. II, p. 22.
70   Quoted in Tibbles, *John Clare*, p. 174.
71   London, 1827.
72   *John Clare*, p. 293.
73   *Review of English Studies*, new series, XIV, 56 (November 1963), 359–69.
74   *Ibid.*, pp. 367–8.
75   Edmund Blunden, *Keats's Publisher* (London, 1936), p. 107.
76   *Letters*, p. 67.
77   *Ibid.*, p. 25.
78   *Poems*, vol. I, p. 25.
79   Quoted in *John Clare*, p. 124.
80   *New Statesman*, 19 June 1964.
81   'Autumn', *The Later Poems of John Clare*, p. 187, lines 7–8.
82   *New Statesman*, 19 June 1964, p. 964.
83   *Prose*, p. 52.
84   *Purity of Diction in English Verse* (London, 1952), p. 85.
85   *Letters*, p. 133.
86   *New Monthly Magazine*, March 1820, p. 328.
87   Blunden, *Keats's Publisher*, p. 108.
88   Quoted in *Selected Poems*, p. xxvi.
89   *Poems*, vol. I, p. 190.
90   *John Clare*, p. 135.
91   *Ibid.*, pp. 156–7.
92   Quoted in *Selected Poems*, p. xxvi.
93   *Selected Poems*, p. 109.
94   *John Clare and Other Studies* (London, 1950), p. 20.
95   *Ibid.*, pp. 19–20.
96   *New Statesman*, 19 June 1964, p. 964.
97   London, 1800.
98   'Summer', line 356.
99   'Summer', lines 171–6.
100 'The Harvest Morning', *Selected Poems*, p. 7, line 65.
101 *Selected Poems*, p. 7.
102 *Poems*, vol. I, p. 116.
103 *Ibid.*, p. 137.
104 *Prose*, p. 25.

105 *Ibid.*
106 Peterborough MS 19, p. 9, lines 1–5.
107 *Poems,* vol. I, p. 163.
108 *Poems,* vol. I, p. 31.
109 Line 56.
110 *Poems,* vol. I, p. 65.
111 *Selected Poems,* p. 169.
112 'Essay on landscape', *Prose,* pp. 211–15.
113 *Ibid.,* p. 211.
114 *Ibid.*
115 *Ibid.,* p. 212.
116 *Ibid.,* p. 214.
117 Quoted in *John Clare, His Life and Poetry,* p. 77.
118 *Remains,* vol. I, p. 112.
119 *Works,* ed. Howe, vol. IX, p. 243.
120 London, 1811.
121 *Poems,* vol. I, p. 253.
122 *Prose,* p. 212.
123 *Poems,* vol. II, p. 121.
124 *Selected Poems,* p. 151.
125 *Ibid.,* p. 154.
126 *Selected Poems,* p. 112.
127 *Selected Poems,* p. 138.
128 London, 1955, ch. II.
129 London, 1835.
130 *Blackwood's,* August 1835, p. 233.
131 Quoted in *Selected Poems,* p. xxii.
132 Quoted in *John Clare,* p. 155.
133 *John Clare and Other Studies,* p. 19.
134 *Selected Poems,* p. 159.
135 *Ibid.,* p. 77.
136 See *John Clare,* p. 357.
137 Peterborough MS 75, p. 51 a.
138 *Selected Poems,* p. 134.
139 *Ibid.,* p. 145.
140 *John Clare and Other Studies,* p. 14.
141 *John Clare, His Life and Poetry,* p. 153.
142 *The Shepherd's Calendar,* eds. Robinson and Summerfield, p. 131, line 13.
143 See for example 'March', 'June', and 'July', in *Les Très riches heures du duc de Berry;* 'September', in the early sixteenth-century Flemish Calendar, Brit. Mus. Add. MS 24098, f, 26 b.
144 *L'Encyclopédie,* Planches, vol. I (Paris, 1762).
145 *Letters,* p. 257.
146 *Ibid.,* p. 258.
147 *Selected Poems,* p. 174.
148 *Ibid.,* p. 176.
149 'The Flitting', lines 89–90.
150 *Ibid.,* line 91.

151   *Selected Poems*, p. 182.

152   Quoted in *John Clare*, p. 89.

153   *Poems*, vol. II, p. 339.

154   *Ibid.*, p. 367.

155   *Ibid.*, p. 339.

156   *Ibid.*, p. 369.

157   *Ibid.*, p. 371.

158   See especially Geoffrey Grigson's introduction to his edition, *The Poems of John Clare's Madness* (London, 1949).

159   *Prose*, p. 239.

160   *Ibid.*, p. 239.

161   'Tintern Abbey', line 49.

162   In *From Sensibility to Romanticism, Essays Presented to Frederick A. Pottle*, eds. Hilles and Bloom (New York, 1965).

163   London, 1891, ch. II.

164   *Selected Poems*, p. 100.

165   Ch. XVI.

166   London, 1887, ch. I.

167   *Longman's Magazine*, July 1883, pp. 252–69; reprinted in *Thomas Hardy, Personal Writings*, ed. Orel (London, 1967), pp. 168–91.

168   *Ibid.* (Orel edition), p. 180.

169   *Ibid.*, p. 80.

170   London, 1874, ch. VI.

Appendix: John Clare and the enclosure of Helpston

1   London, 1911.

2   *John Clare, His Life and Poetry*, p. 25.

3   *Unprofessional Essays* (London, 1956), p. 89.

4   *Selected Poems* (see above, p. 227, note 32), p. xvi.

5   See *The Wheelwright's Shop* (Cambridge, 1923).

6   Peterborough MS 75. *The Parish* has never been printed in full; the best version is to be found in *John Clare, Selected Poems*, ed. Feinstein (London, 1968).

7   *Selected Poems*, p. xv.

8   *Selected Poems of John Clare*, ed. Reeves (London, 1954).

9   *Ibid.*, p. xviii.

10   *Unprofessional Essays*, p. 101.

    Agrarian Age (New Haven, 1950), p. 47.

    ohn Clare, p. 65.

    l.

    bove, p. 226, note 20.

    Clare, His Life and Poetry, p. 26.

    monds, *Village Labourer*, p. 100.

19 J. D. Chambers and G. E. Mingay, *The Agricultural Revolution, 1750–1780* (London, 1966), ch. IV.

20 Mingay, 'The size of farms in the eighteenth century', *Economic History Review* (2nd series, XIV (1961–2), 483). Mingay repeats the phrase, or nearly – 'the weeding-out of inefficient small men' – in *Enclosure and the Small Farmer in the Age of the Industrial Revolution* (London, 1968), p. 30.

21 *Times Literary Supplement*, 16 February 1967, p. 117.

22 *The Making of the English Working Class* (London, 1965), p. 213.

23 *Economic History Review*, I (1927), 87–113.

24 *Ibid.*, p. 95.

25 Quoted in *John Clare's Selected Poems*, eds. J. W. and Anne Tibble, Everyman Edition (London, 1965), p. 140.

26 *John Clare*, p. 329.

27 Peterborough MS 75.

28 *Poems*, vol. II, p. 18.

29 *The Parish*, line 1,763.

30 *Ibid.*, line 1,539.

31 *Ibid.*, lines 1,534 ff.

32 'whats he know of the distresses of the poor musing over a snug coal fire in his parsonage box – if I had an enemy I coud wish to torture I woud not wish him hung nor yet at the devil my worst wish shoud be a weeks confinement in some vicarage to hear an old parson & his lecture on the wants & wickedness of the poor' (*Letters*, p. 75).

33 *John Clare's Selected Poems*, p. 140.

34 Raymond Williams, 'Literature and rural society', *The Listener*, 16 November 1967, p. 631.

35 George Crabbe, *The Village* (London, 1783).

36 See above, note 34.

37 See Williams's discussion of Cobbett in *Culture and Society* (London, 1958), ch. I.

38 See for example, *The Splendid Village* (London, 1833–5); Elliott, who is remembered nowadays only for his *Corn Law Rhymes*, is far more worth remembering on account of *The Splendid Village* and *The Village Patriarch* (London, 1829).

39 'Literature and rural society', pp. 630, 631.

40 *Political Register*, 14 April 1821; quoted in *Culture and Society*, p. 15.

41 *Selected Poems*, p. 169.

42 See 'The revolution in low life', published in *Lloyd's Evening Post*, 14–16 June 1762; reprinted in *Collected Works*, ed. Friedman (Oxford, 1966), vol. III, pp. 195–8.

43 The loss of freedom Clare is writing about in 'The Fallen Elm' is a direct result of the enclosure of the commons; labourers without even unofficial (so to speak) rights of common were usually able to collect firewood on heath-land, as they were in Helpston, and the loss of the commons often made the labourer completely dependent on the money-wages he recei from his employer. It is worth recalling here that one important motiv enclose was often, precisely, to deprive the labourer of his right of ac

to commons, to make him more dependent on his wages, and thus to create a surplus of labour and keep wages low. This was a motive behind various suggestions to enclose the enormous and productive commons at Chailley, in Sussex, which it was said allowed the local population to live in idleness (E. C. K. Gonner, *Common Land and Inclosure* (London, 1912), p. 361 n.); and E. P. Thompson quotes a remark by Lord Winchilsea, writing in 1796, that in the Midland counties landowners often enclosed because 'they rather wish to have the labourers more dependent upon them' (*Making of the English Working Class*, p. 217).

44 For a discussion of how much an enclosure by Act of Parliament might cost, see W. E. Tate's optimistic article, 'The cost of parliamentary enclosure', *Economic History Review* (2nd series), v (1952–3), 258–65. Tate bases his conclusions on data from late eighteenth-century enclosures in Oxfordshire; for a less optimistic view, see J. M. Martin, 'The cost of parliamentary enclosure in Warwickshire', *University of Birmingham Historical Journal*, IX (1964), 146 ff.

45 Kept at the N.R.O., Delapre Abbey, Northampton.

46 G. E. Mingay, 'The land tax assessments and the small landowner', *Economic History Review* (2nd series), XVII (1964–5), 381–8.

47 *Ibid.*, p. 385.

48 *Ibid.*, p. 388.

49 *Letters*, p. 129.

50 Kept at Delapre Abbey.

51 Ch. IV.

52 See above, p. 226, note 20.

53 F. M. L. Thompson, *English Landed Society in the Nineteenth Century* (London, 1963), p. 223.

54 See valuations of glebe at Helpston, kept at Christ's College, Cambridge.

55 P. 228.

56 See above, note 54.

57 *The Agricultural Revolution*, p. 129.

58 M. Compton and G. E. Fussell, 'Agricultural adjustments after the Napoleonic Wars', *Economic History*, III, 14 (February 1939), 201.

59 N.R.O. Fitzwilliam (Milton), Misc. vol. 527.

60 Figures for expenditure on poor-relief for 1816 to 1821, in Helpston and the other parishes involved in the 1809 enclosure, are to be found in *Parliamentary Papers 1822*, vol. v, p. 678; the corresponding figures for 1827 (see Table B, above, p. 211), are in *Parliamentary Papers 1830–1831*, vol. XI, p. 366.

61 The returns for Helpston, Etton, etc., are to be found in the census *Abstracts*, 1801 (p. 252), 1811 (p. 230), 1821 (p. 229), 1831 (p. 186, pp. 184–9).

62 Kept in the parish chest at St Botolph's, Helpston.

63 See *Prose*, p. 26; *Sketches*, p. 60.

64 *Prose*, p. 32.

65 *John Clare, His Life and Poetry*, p. 26.

66 *John Clare*, p. 67.

67 *Prose*, p. 47.

68 *Ibid.*, p. 34.

69 *John Clare, His Life and Poetry*, p. 31.
70 *Ibid.*, p. 42.
71 *Sketches*, p. 74.
72 *Prose*, p. 67.
73 *Ibid.*, p. 55.
74 See N.R.O. Fitzwilliam (Milton) Misc. vols. 106, 107. These are labour-accounts for the period around 1820, from which it appears that the standard weekly wage in 1820 in Helpston was 6s.
75 Clare's name is to be found in the account books mentioned in the previous note.
76 *John Clare*, p. 145.
77 See above, p. 226, note 20.
78 One such traditional way of supplementing money-wages, however, probably survived the enclosure: Viscount Milton, heir to the Fitzwilliam title, writing in 1824 to the Master of Christ's College, Cambridge (where his letter is kept), complained of the 'immorality and lawlessness of the population' of Helpston, which he explained as in part caused by the lack of any 'resident clergyman'. He was referring, no doubt, to poaching: the extensive woods within the parish belonged exclusively to the Fitzwilliams, and were not, of course, cut down at the enclosure.

Bibliography

This is a list of works cited in the text and notes of this book. It is not a complete list of works consulted, and it does not include references to primary historical sources, which will be found among the notes to the prologue to Chapter 3, and in the notes to the appendix.

Addison, Joseph. *Remarks on Several Parts of Italy.* London, 1705.

Alison, Archibald. *Essay on the Nature and Principles of Taste,* 6th edition. Edinburgh, 1825.

Arthos, John. *The Language of Natural Description....* Ann Arbor, 1949.

Austen, Jane. *Sense and Sensibility.* London, 1811.

Barbier, C. P. *William Gilpin.* Oxford, 1963.

Barrès, Maurice. *Amori et Dolori Sacrum.* Paris, 1903.

La Colline inspirée. Paris, 1913.

Colette Baudoche. Paris, 1919.

Batchelor, Thomas. *Village Scenes, The Progress of Agriculture....* London, 1804.

A General View of the Agriculture of the County of Bedford. London, 1808.

Beattie, James. *The Minstrel.* London 1771–4.

Beresford, M. W. 'The commissioners of enclosure.' *Economic History Review,* xvi (1946). Reprinted in *Essays in Agrarian History,* ed. Minchinton. Newton Abbot, 1968.

Billingsley, John. *A General View of...Somerset.* London, 1794.

Bloch, Marc. *French Rural History,* trans. Sondheimer. London, 1966.

Bloomfield, Robert. *The Farmer's Boy.* London, 1800.

The Banks of Wye. London, 1811.

The Remains of Robert Bloomfield. London, 1824.

Blunden, Edmund. *Keats's Publisher.* London, 1936.

Boswell, James. *Boswelliana,* ed. Rogers. London, 1876.

Brown, Thomas. *A General View of...Derby.* London, 1794.

Burke, Edmund. *A Philosophical Enquiry into...the Sublime and the Beautiful.* London, 1757.

Chambers, J. D. and Mingay, G. E. *The Agricultural Revolution 1750–1780.* London, 1966.

Chambers, William. *Designs of Chinese Buildings....* London, 1757.

Chateaubriand, F.-R. de. 'Edward Young,' *Mercure de France,* 26 March 1802.

Clare, John. *Poems Descriptive of Rural Life and Scenery.* London, 1820.

The Village Minstrel, and Other Poems. London, 1821.

The Shepherd's Calendar.... London, 1827.

The Rural Muse. London, 1835.

The Poems of John Clare, ed. J. W. Tibble. London, 1935.

The Poems of John Clare's Madness, ed. Geoffrey Grigson. London, 1949.

Selected Poems of John Clare, ed. James Reeves. London, 1954.

The Later Poems of John Clare, eds. Eric Robinson and Geoffrey Summerfield. Manchester, 1964.

The Shepherd's Calendar, eds. Robinson and Summerfield. London, 1964.

John Clare's Selected Poems, eds. J. W. and Anne Tibble. London, 1965.

Selected Poems and Prose of John Clare, eds. Robinson and Summerfield. London, 1967.

John Clare, Selected Poems, ed. Elaine Feinstein. London, 1968.

The Parish. Peterborough Museum MS 75.

Sketches in the Life of John Clare, Written by Himself, ed. Edmund Blunden. London, 1931.

The Letters of John Clare, eds. J. W. and Anne Tibble. London, 1951.

The Prose of John Clare, eds. J. W. and Anne Tibble. London, 1951.

Clark, John. *The Poems Ascribed to Ossian.* London, 1781.

A General View of...Hereford. London, 1794.

Clark, Kenneth. *Landscape into Art.* London, 1949.

Clifford, Derek. *A History of Garden Design.* London, 1962.

Cobbett, William. *Political Register,* London, 14 April 1821.

Rural Rides. London, 1830.

Cohen, Ralph. *The Art of Discrimination.* London, 1964.

Coleridge, S. T. *Letters,* ed. Griggs. Oxford, 1956–9.

Combe, William. *Dr Syntax in Search of the Picturesque.* London, 1809.

Compton, M. and Fussell, G. E. 'Agricultural adjustments after the Napoleonic Wars.' *Economic History,* III, 14 (February, 1939).

Copeland, John. *Roads and their Traffic, 1750–1850.* Newton Abbot, 1968.

Cowper, William. *The Task.* London, 1785.

'Yardley Oak', in *Poems,* ed. Milford. Oxford, 1905.

Crabbe, George. *The Village.* London, 1783.

Cranfield, G. A. *The Provincial Newspaper.* Oxford, 1960.

Cunningham, John. *Poems Chiefly Pastoral.* Newcastle, 1766.

Curtler, W. H. R. *The Enclosure and Re-distribution of our Land.* Oxford, 1920.

Davie, Donald. *Purity of Diction in English Verse.* London, 1952.

Articulate Energy. London, 1955.

'John Clare.' *New Statesman,* 19 June 1964.

Davies, E. 'The small landowner in the light of the land tax assessments.' *Economic History Review,* I (1927).

Deane, C. V. *Aspects of Eighteenth-Century Nature Poetry.* Oxford, 1935.

Dion, Roger. *La Formation du paysage rural français.* Tours, 1934.

Donaldson, James. *A General View of...Northampton.* London, 1794.

Driver, Abraham and William. *A General View of...Hampshire.* London, 1794.

Dyer, John. 'Grongar Hill.' London, 1726.

The Ruins of Rome. London, 1740.

The Fleece. London, 1757.

Elliott, Ebenezer. *The Village Patriarch.* London, 1829.

BIBLIOGRAPHY

The Splendid Village. London, 1833–5.

Ernle, Lord (R. E. Prothero). *English Farming Past and Present.* London, 1912.

Fussell, G. E. *See under* Compton, M.

Gainsborough, Thomas. *The Letters of Thomas Gainsborough,* ed. Woodall. London, 1963.

Gilpin, William. *Observations on the River Wye....* London, 1782.

Remarks on Forest Scenery. London, 1791.

Observations on the Western Parts of England.... London, 1798.

Observations on Several Parts of England.... Third edition, London, 1808.

Gisborne, Thomas. *Walks in a Forest.* 9th edition. London, 1814.

Goldsmith, Oliver. 'The revolution in low life', in *Collected Works,* ed. Friedman. Oxford, 1966.

The Deserted Village. London, 1770.

Gonner, E. C. K. *Common Land and Inclosure.* London, 1912.

Graves, Richard. *Columella; or, The Distressed Anchoret.* London, 1779.

Gray, Thomas. *Complete Poems,* eds. Starr and Hendrickson. Oxford, 1966.

Correspondence, eds. Toynbee and Whibley. Oxford, 1935.

Hammond, J. L. and Barbara. *The Village Labourer.* London, 1911.

Hardy, Thomas. *Far From the Madding Crowd.* London, 1874.

The Woodlanders. London, 1887.

Tess of the D'Urbervilles. London, 1891.

'The Dorsetshire labourer', in *Thomas Hardy, Personal Writings,* ed. Orel. London, 1967.

Hartman, Geoffrey. 'Wordsworth, inscriptions, and Romantic nature poetry', in *From Sensibility to Romanticism, Essays Presented to Frederick A. Pottle,* eds. Hilles and Bloom. New York, 1965.

Hayes, John. *Richard Wilson.* London, 1966.

Hazlitt, William. 'On the picturesque and the ideal', in *Works,* ed. Howe. London, 1930–4, vol. VIII.

'Critical list of Authors'. *Works,* vol. IX.

Hipple, W. J. *The Beautiful, the Sublime, and the Picturesque,....* Carbondale, 1957.

Hoskins, W. G. *The Making of the English Landscape.* London, 1955.

The Midland Peasant. London, 1957.

Provincial England, London, 1963.

Howard, Deborah. 'Some eighteenth-century English followers of Claude.' *Burlington Magazine,* December 1969.

Hussey, Christopher. *The Picturesque.* London, 1927.

Jago, Richard. *Edge-hill....* London, 1767.

Jones, D. 'Common trends in landscape painting and nature poetry in the eighteenth century.' Unpublished M.A. dissertation, Aberystwyth, 1954.

Kames, Lord. *Elements of Criticism,* 6th edition. Edinburgh, 1785.

Keir, Susanna Harvey. *The History of Miss Greville.* London, 1787.

Kitson, Michael. *The Art of Claude Lorrain.* London, 1969.

'Enchanted castles.' *Sunday Times Magazine,* 9 November 1969.

Knight, Richard Payne. *The Landscape,* 2nd edition. London, 1795.

An Analytical Inquiry into the Principles of Taste. London, 1805.

Lamb, Charles. *Letters.* Everyman Edition, London, 1909.

Langhorne, John. *Poems*. London, 1822.

Lizerand, Georges. *Le Régime rural de l'ancienne France*. Parıs, 1942.

Lyttelton, Lord. *The Progress of Love*. London, 1732.

MacLean, Kenneth. *Agrarian Age*. New Haven, 1950.

Malins, Edward. *English Landscaping and Literature 1660–1840*. London, 1966.

Manwaring, Elizabeth Wheeler. *Italian Landscape in Eighteenth-Century England*. New York, 1925; London, 1965.

Marshall, J. D. *The Old Poor Law 1795–1834*. London, 1968.

Marshall, William. *Planting and Rural Ornament*. London, 1796.

Appropriation and Inclosure of Commonable Lands. London, 1801.

A Review of the...Northern Department. York, 1808.

A Review of the...Western Department. York. 1808.

A Review of the...Eastern Department. York, 1811.

A Review of the...Midland Department. York, 1815.

Martin, J. M. 'The cost of parliamentary enclosure in Warwickshire'. *University of Birmingham Historical Journal*, IX (1964).

Marvell, Andrew. *Poems and Letters*, ed. Margoliouth. Oxford, 1952.

Mason, William. *The English Garden*. London, 1772.

Miller, Hugh. *First Impressions of England....* London, 1845.

Milton, John. *Poetical Works*, ed. Darbishire. Oxford, 1952.

Mingay, G. E. 'The size of farms in the eighteenth century.' *Economic History Review* (2nd series), XIV (1961–2).

English Landed Society in the Eighteenth Century. London, 1963.

'The land tax assessments and the small landowner.' *Economic History Review* (2nd series), XVII (1964–5).

'The eighteenth-century land steward.' *Land, Labour, and Population...*, eds. E. L. Jones and Mingay. London, 1967.

Enclosure and the Small Farmer.... London, 1968.

See also under Chambers, J. D.

Mitchison, Rosalind. 'The old Board of Agriculture.' *English Historical Review*, LXXIV (1959).

Monk, Samuel H. *The Sublime*. New York, 1935.

Montagu, Elizabeth. *Mrs. Montagu, 'Queen of the Blues'*, ed. Blunt. London, 1924.

More, Hannah. *Memoirs*, ed. Roberts. London, 1824.

Morton, John. *The Natural History of Northamptonshire*. London, 1712.

Munday, F. N. C. *Needwood Forest*. Lichfield, 1776.

Murry, J. Middleton. *John Clare and Other Studies*. London, 1950.

Unprofessional Essays. London, 1956.

Orwin, C. S. and C. S. *The Open Fields*. Oxford, 1938.

Pitt, William. *A General View of...Leicester*. London, 1809.

A General View of...Northampton. London, 1809.

Pomeroy, W. T. *A General View of...Worcester*. London, 1794.

Pope, Alexander. *Poems*, ed. Butt. London, 1963.

Price, Sir Uvedale. *Essays on the Picturesque*. London and Hereford, 1794–8.

Priest, Rev. St John. *A General View of...Buckingham*. London, 1810.

Radcliffe, Mrs. *The Italian*. London, 1797.

Robinson, Eric and Summerfield, Geoffrey. 'John Taylor's editing of Clare's

BIBLIOGRAPHY

Shepherd's Calendar.' Review of English Studies (New Series), XIV, **56** (November 1963).

Ruggles, Thomas. 'Picturesque farming.' *Annals of Agriculture*, VI–IX.

Ruskin, John. *Modern Painters*, vol. III. London, 1856.

Scott, John. *Amwell, A Descriptive Poem.* London, 1776.

Digests of the General Highway and Turnpike Laws. London, 1778.

Critical Essays. London, 1785.

Slater, Gilbert. *The English Peasantry and the Enclosure of Common Fields.* London, 1907.

Smith, Charlotte. *Emmeline, The Orphan of the Castle.* London, 1788.

Spence, Joseph. *Observations, Anecdotes, and Characters...*, ed. Osborn. Oxford, 1966.

Stone, Thomas. *A General View of...Lincoln.* London, 1794.

Stroud, Dorothy. *Capability Brown.* London, 1957.

Sturt, George. *The Wheelwright's Shop.* Cambridge, 1923.

Summerfield, Geoffrey. *See under* Robinson, Eric.

Tate, W. E. 'The cost of parliamentary enclosure.' *Economic History Review* (2nd series), V (1952–3).

The English Village Community and the Enclosure Movements. London, 1967.

Thompson, E. P. *The Making of the English Working Class.* London, 1965.

Thompson, F. M. L. *English Landed Society in the Nineteenth Century.* London, 1963.

Thomson, James. *The Seasons.* London, 1730; revised ed., 1744.

Poetical Works, ed. Robertson. Oxford, 1908.

Tibble, J. W. *and* Anne. *John Clare.* London, 1932.

John Clare, His Life and Poetry. London, 1956.

Twining, Thomas. *Aristotle's Treatise on Poetry* (1789), Dissertation I. Reprinted in *Eighteenth-Century Critical Essays*, ed. Elledge. New York, 1961.

Tyley, Rev. James. 'Inclosure of open fields in Northamptonshire', trans. Halton. *Northamptonshire Past and Present*, I (1951).

Veliz, Claudio. 'Arthur Young and the English Landed Interest, 1784–1813.' Unpublished Ph.D. thesis, London University, 1959.

Walpole, Horace. *Anecdotes of Painting in England...to which is added The History of the Modern Taste in Gardening.* London, 1771.

Warton, Joseph. *An Essay on the Genius and Writings of Pope.* Fourth edition, London, 1782.

Warton, Thomas. *The Guardian* 57, 22 May 1753.

Wasserman, Earl. 'The English romantics: the grounds of knowledge.' *Studies in Romanticism*, IV (1964–5).

Waterhouse, Ellis. *Gainsborough.* London, 1958.

Watson, J. R. *Picturesque Landscape and English Romantic Poetry.* London, 1970.

White, Gilbert. *The Natural History and Antiquities of Selborne*, ed. J. W. White. London, 1813.

Wiles, R. M. *Freshest Advices.* Ohio, 1965.

Williams, Raymond. *Culture and Society.* London, 1958.

'Literature and rural society.' *The Listener*, 16 November 1967.

Wilson, John. Review of Clare's *Rural Muse* in *Blackwood's*, August 1835.

Wordsworth, William. *The Prelude,* text of 1805, ed. de Selincourt. London, 1960.

Poetical Works, eds. de Selincourt and Darbishire. Oxford, 1940–54.

Young, Arthur. *A Six Months Tour through the North of England.* London, 1770.

A Tour in Ireland.... London, 1780.

A General View of...Oxford. London, 1809.

Tours in France..., ed. Maxwell. Cambridge, 1929.

Young, Rev. A. *A General View of...Sussex.* London, 1808.

Index